PIMLICO

639

THE REBEL RAIDERS

James Tertius deKay is also the author of *Monitor: The Story of the Legendary Civil War Ironclad and the Man Whose Invention Changed the Course of History* (also published in Pimlico) and *Chronicles of the Frigate Macedonian*. He lives in Pawcatuck, Connecticut.

THE REBEL RAIDERS

The Astonishing History of
the Confederacy's Secret Navy

————————

JAMES TERTIUS deKAY

PIMLICO

Published by Pimlico 2004

2 4 6 8 10 9 7 5 3 1

Copyright © James Tertius deKay 2003

First published in the United States by The Ballantine Publishing Group
in 2003, a division of Random House, Inc., New York, and simultaneously
in Canada by Random House of Canada Limited, Toronto.
First published in Great Britain by Pimlico in 2004

Pimlico
Random House, 20 Vauxhall Bridge Road,
London SW1V 2SA

Random House Australia (Pty) Limited
20 Alfred Street, Milsons Point, Sydney,
New South Wales 2061, Australia

Random House New Zealand Limited
18 Poland Road, Glenfield,
Auckland 10, New Zealand

Random House South Africa (Pty) Limited
Endulini, 5A Jubilee Road, Parktown 2193, South Africa

Random House UK Limited Reg. No. 954009

A CIP catalogue record for this book is available from the British Library

ISBN 0-7126-6490-4

Papers used by Random House UK Limited are natural, recyclable
products made from wood grown in sustainable forests. The manufacturing
processes conform to the environmental regulations of the country of origin

Printed and bound in Great Britain by Clays Ltd, St Ives PLC

FOR
OLIVER PURVES

The English Government, at the bottom of its heart, desires the separation of North America into two republics. . . . Then England . . . would have nothing to fear from either; for she would dominate them.

Baron de Brunow, Russian minister to England, to Prince Gortchakov, Russian foreign secretary, January 1, 1861

Contents

James Dunwoody Bulloch, the Confederate Navy's chief agent in Europe, who was responsible for the deployment of the Alabama, *the* Florida, *and the* Shenandoah, *as well as the construction of the Laird rams and many other ironclads and blockade–runners.*

I

—————

Bulloch

ONE

Montgomery

Throughout the early spring of 1861, the sleepy little city of Montgomery, Alabama, found itself caught up in a state of jubilant uproar and patriotic euphoria. Ever since February, when it was proclaimed provisional capital of the Confederate States of America, trainloads of strangers had been pouring into town from all across the South—patriots and adventurers, visionaries and opportunists—crowding the city's streets and monopolizing its facilities, eagerly clamoring to participate in the creation of a huge new nation the size of western Europe.

In April, the level of excitement in Montgomery ratcheted up to new heights when news of the bombardment of Fort Sumter came clattering over the telegraph from Charleston. Overnight, a new martial spirit gripped the city, and a heady sense of participating in the unfolding of great events was everywhere apparent. The fledgling Confederate government, suddenly faced with the need to put itself on a war footing, quickly ran out of office space and was forced to take rooms in the Exchange Hotel.

Despite the sense of urgency generated by the news of war, President Jefferson Davis maintained a serene equanimity. For months he and other Southern leaders had hoped that the secession of the Southern states might be managed peacefully, but now that war had come, he remained optimistic. He was convinced that the war would all be over in a matter of weeks. It could not last much longer than that. Neither side was prepared for a more extended conflict, and it was bound to sputter to an inconclusive end as soon as the hotheads in Washington came to understand the futility of trying to force the seceded states back into the Union against their will.

Besides, the Europeans would not allow a long war. Both Great Britain and France maintained huge textile industries, which were totally dependent on regular supplies of raw cotton from the South. If those supplies were stopped by the blockade that President Abraham Lincoln had just announced, thousands of European textile mills would have to close, millions of factory hands would be thrown out of work, and there would be riots in the streets of Manchester and Lyons. Davis was confident that before that could happen, the British and French navies would steam across the Atlantic, force open the blockade, and give Mr. Lincoln a choice: He could either sue for peace or find himself battling not just the South but the great powers of Europe as well.

Davis was convinced that the key to victory was cotton, and for months he had been encouraging cotton growers to hold their harvest off the market in order to increase pressure on Europe. The less raw cotton the mills had in inventory, the faster their governments would act to ensure the supply. It was just another precautionary step on his part to guarantee a short war.

Most of the members of Jefferson Davis's cabinet shared his optimism, but since there was no guarantee that the Yankees would behave in a reasonable manner, they continued to labor diligently to meet the Northern threat. It was always possible, after all, that the war might drag on for as long as a year.

During those first hectic weeks of the war, the cabinet officer under the most immediate pressure was probably Stephen R. Mallory, the newly appointed secretary of the navy. It was his responsibility to organize a response to the blockade the Yankees were already putting in place, and that was not going to be easy. The South had virtually nothing in the way of a navy with which to fight back. The entire Confederate fleet consisted of a sorry collection of four small revenue cutters, three leaky slavers, and a handful of smaller boats inherited from the seceded states, and there was no chance of improving the situation in the immediate future. It takes time and money to build proper warships, and Mallory had little of either.

With his round, open face and vaguely distracted appearance, the forty-nine-year-old Mallory bore a striking resemblance to Mr. Pickwick. The similarity was enhanced by his penchant for swallowtail coats and his fondness for good company and a liberally fortified punch bowl. But Mallory was no Dickensian innocent. Behind his genial manner lay a sharp and imaginative intellect. He was a highly skilled admiralty lawyer and a practiced politician. He was also the only member of the Confederate executive who had any real grasp of war at sea or understanding of the true power of navies.

Mallory was something of an outsider. Many of the politicians in Montgomery had opposed his nomination for secretary of the navy. Some distrusted him because he had originally cautioned against secession, while others were suspicious of him because he owned no slaves. It did not help that he was also a Roman Catholic, which made him something of a curiosity in a society that was predominantly Episcopalian and Presbyterian. In the end, he had been selected because Jefferson Davis felt he needed someone from Florida in his cabinet.

In the years before the war, Mallory had served in the United States Senate, where, as chairman of the Committee on Naval Affairs, he made it his business to learn everything he could about the revolutionary developments in steam power, shell guns, and armor plate that were rapidly transforming the navies of the world. In time he would put that knowledge to good use. Under his leadership the Confederate Navy would establish an impressive record for innovation. But any plans he might have to create a modern fleet for the South still lay far in the future. His immediate problem was to find some way to deal with the Yankee blockade.

It was a formidable challenge. The proposed blockade was to be a colossal enterprise, an immense cordon of U.S. Navy warships that would eventually stretch 3,500 miles from Chesapeake Bay to the Mexican border at Matamoros. Mallory knew that the Yankees did not as yet have the ships to mount such a seaborne offensive, but he had no doubt they would build the necessary vessels soon enough, and when they did, it would be up to him to find a way to counter the threat. If he failed, the Federal fleet would eventually strangle the South, choking off access to the European military supplies the Confederacy needed to fight the war, as well as the outward flow of cotton bales required to pay for them.

Undoubtedly, had it been within his power, Mallory would have chosen to smash the blockade with a squadron of modern ironclad steamers, each one armed with powerful rifled guns, firing the new explosive shells. Such an invincible fleet could reduce the Yankees' wooden warships to kindling, and open the South's ports to the world.

But Mallory knew that the immediate prospect for such a force was little more than a pipe dream. The South, for all its fine harbors and broad rivers, had never developed a maritime infrastructure. It was an agricultural society, dependent almost entirely on slave labor, with neither the shipyards nor the skilled workforce needed to build the warships it now so desperately needed. Before Mallory could build them, he would have to create the necessary ironworks, foundries, and rolling mills and either import or train the shipwrights, mechanics, and engineers needed to operate them, all of which was going to take much time and energy.

Meanwhile, he needed some sort of stopgap measure that would at least make things difficult for the Yankees. Toward that end, he developed a secondary strategy, a simpler and cheaper scheme that he could put into operation much more quickly. He would build or buy a handful of inexpensive wooden ships, each one lightly armed with a few guns, and send them out to sea, not to wage war against the powerful blockading squadrons of the U.S. Navy but against a far larger and more vulnerable Yankee fleet—the huge armada of American commercial vessels that plied the trade routes of the world. These ships represented one of the North's most valuable economic assets. Unarmed Yankee merchant vessels would make easy targets for his commerce raiders, and Mallory calculated it would take only a few such cruisers to create so much havoc that the Union Navy would be forced to withdraw large numbers of its own vessels from the blockade in order to hunt down the gunships, thereby opening up the vital trade routes to Europe.

Mallory hoped to create the raiders simply by purchasing ordinary merchant ships and arming them. He had originally expected to find the ships he needed in Southern ports, but when he sent out inquiries, he quickly discovered there were almost no commercial vessels to be had in the Confederacy. His search turned up only one likely candidate, a Gulf Coast packet steamer named the *Habana,* which was laid up in New Orleans. Mallory sent one of his senior officers, Commander Raphael Semmes, to investigate, and Semmes had reported back by telegraph, expressing cautious optimism. With Mallory's approval he purchased the little steamer, which he rechristened the CSS *Sumter,* and had started the process of reinforcing and arming her. The *Sumter* would be a beginning, Mallory hoped, but neither he nor Semmes considered her anything more than a temporary expedient.

It was evident to Mallory that if he wanted cruisers, he was going to have to look outside the Confederacy. For various reasons he decided to try Great Britain. If he could not find what he wanted in England, there were any number of superior shipyards there, and he could always arrange to have his gunships built to order.

The trick was going to be finding the right man to send across the Atlantic. Obviously Mallory needed someone who knew his way around shipbuilding facilities and who understood naval construction, steam engines, and modern armament. But equally important, Mallory needed someone he could trust, and trust implicitly. Whomever he sent to England would be operating on his own, thousands of miles from any supervision, making important decisions involving hundreds of thousands of dollars of government money, and working in a rough-and-ready marketplace notorious for its under-the-table kickbacks and other forms of financial chicanery. The opportunities for mischief were manifold.

Choosing the right man would be one of the most critical decisions Mallory would make as naval secretary, and undoubtedly he would have preferred to make his selection carefully, and only after due deliberation, but in the spring of 1861, there was no time for such luxuries. He had to act quickly. He would have to take whomever he could find, pack him off to England, and hope for the best.

As it turned out, the man he selected for the highly sensitive assignment of European purchasing agent for the Confederate Navy was a man he had never met and of whom he knew almost nothing. His name was James Bulloch, and Mallory picked him solely on the basis of a brief conversation with his fellow cabinet officer Judah P. Benjamin, the Confederate attorney general, who happened to be a mutual friend of both men.

———

James Dunwoody Bulloch, thirty-eight years old, came from a prominent Georgia family. He had served originally as an officer in the United States Navy. Later, he had resigned his commission to become a commercial sea captain operating out of New York, where he had made his home for many years. In a lifetime at sea, he had retained few ties to his native state, but his loyalty to his family and to the South had remained steadfast, and immediately on the outbreak of war, he had contacted his friend Judah Benjamin, offering his services to the Confederacy. Benjamin mentioned Bulloch to Mallory, who immediately expressed interest. Benjamin's sketchy description of his friend may have been short on details, but he made the point that Bulloch was an experienced naval officer with an intimate knowledge of commercial shipping. That, plus the fact that Benjamin vouched for him, was enough to convince Mallory that he had found the right man for the European assignment.

Another factor that undoubtedly influenced Mallory's choice was the almost casual nobility of Bulloch's act of patriotism. Hundreds of Southern-born U.S. Navy officers had resigned their commissions to "go South" and join the Confederacy. But how many men, he wondered, would have deliberately forsaken an important civilian career in New York to throw in their lot with the South? Bulloch's offer to serve was an eloquent gesture and persuaded Mallory that here was a man he could trust. At Mallory's urging, Benjamin immediately sent word to New York, instructing Bulloch to report to Montgomery as soon as possible. It was one of the last messages to make it through the lines before all official communications ceased between the warring sections.

———————

As soon as Bulloch received Benjamin's instructions, he took immediate steps to comply. He knew he would have to arrange his departure from New York with care. War fever was rampant, and federal agents, who were well aware of Bulloch's political leanings, were already rounding up suspected Confederate sympathizers. Working quietly, he settled his business affairs as swiftly and discreetly as possible before bidding a hasty farewell to those closest to him. "I mentioned to a few friends that I purposed going to Philadelphia, and possibly to Cincinnati," he would later write, "and in the early days of May, I started southward with light luggage, as if for a short journey." One of the few with whom he would have shared his secret was his beloved sister Martha, herself a loyal Georgian, who was the wife of the prominent New Yorker Theodore Roosevelt Sr. and mother of a sickly little boy, "Teedie," the future president. After a last hurried embrace of his wife, Harriet, Bulloch caught the railroad ferry to Hoboken and boarded a train for Philadelphia, where he spent the night. That evening, in parks and public squares, he saw "large bodies of men . . . drilling, and the streets were thronged with detachments of troops. Everywhere the din of bustle and preparation."

Proceeding to Pittsburgh the following morning, he pursued a deliberately circuitous route that took him first to Cincinnati, then across the Ohio, and finally into the still-uncommitted border states of Kentucky and Tennessee. From there the railroad took him into Alabama, and the Confederacy proper, and on to Montgomery, where he arrived late on Tuesday evening, May 7, 1861. The following morning he reported to his friend Judah Benjamin at the Exchange Hotel, and after a brief greeting, the attorney general escorted him down the hall to Mallory's office.

Bulloch's description of his hurried introduction to Mallory gives some suggestion of the sense of urgency that characterized the Confederate government in the first weeks of war.

"Mr. Secretary," Benjamin announced without ceremony, "here is Captain Bulloch."

"I am glad to see you," Mallory said, taking Bulloch's hand. Then, without so much as a pause, he continued, "I want you to go to Europe. When can you start?"

Bulloch, who had expected to be offered a commission and had hoped for a sea command, was startled by Mallory's totally unexpected announcement but did his best to hide his surprise. "I have no impedimenta," he replied evenly, "and can start as soon as you explain what I am to do."

His calm and assured response must have pleased Mallory. It indicated a man of unusual coolness and self-confidence, someone who could make complicated decisions easily and seemingly without effort.

Judah Benjamin excused himself, and Mallory waved his guest to a seat, pleased at last to have the opportunity to actually meet the man he had already determined would be his agent. The two men presented an interesting contrast—the weathered and sunburned ship's captain and the paler, more diffident politician and negotiator.

Bulloch's premature baldness made him look older than his thirty-eight years, and perhaps to compensate, he affected the flamboyant mustaches and muttonchops that were fashionable at the time. But Mallory was struck not so much by his visitor's appearance as by his demeanor. Bulloch had an air of authority, a gravitas, that was immediately apparent, and that inspired trust. He had an easy manner, and Mallory was quick to appreciate his ability to grasp subtle and complicated issues. As the interview progressed, he grew increasingly confident that he had selected the right man for the job.

They began by reviewing the threat posed by the blockade. Mallory sketched out in broad strokes his proposed response to it, briefly describing his long-range scheme for ironclads and then going into considerably more detail on his short-term plans for commerce raiders. Bulloch listened with interest, and then with growing respect, as he came to appreciate Mallory's sophisticated grasp of his subject. Clearly the secretary knew whereof he spoke. He was more than just a glib bureaucrat with a smattering of naval expertise.

Mallory described his difficulty in obtaining commerce raiders locally and explained why he was sending Bulloch to find them in Europe. He took pains not to monopolize the conversation and made it clear he wanted to know Bulloch's views, firing one question after another at his visitor. What kind of vessels did Bulloch think would make the best cruisers? How would he conduct his search for available ships? Did he think it likely he could find what they needed on the open market, or would it be necessary to build the commerce raiders to order? What might such vessels cost? What displacement seemed best? What draft? What sort of armament would be most effective? How many officers would the raiders require? What size crews? The two men fell easily into a freewheeling discussion as they sought to determine the combination of characteristics that would produce the fastest, most powerful, and most independent cruisers. They talked through lunch and on into the afternoon, and by evening the two men—now surrounded by ships' plans, tide tables, charts of ocean currents, and atlases—had finalized the preliminary plans for what would eventually prove to be the single most effective military initiative mounted by either side in the entire war.

That night Bulloch sat in his hotel room and outlined on paper, point by point, the substance of their discussion. The following morning, when he turned his notes over to Mallory, the secretary incorporated them into the official letter of instructions he was preparing for Bulloch, which he dictated to a clerk. The letter covered almost everything. One problem the two men had not satisfactorily resolved was where they planned to get the sailors to man the raiders. There would be no problem finding officers, Mallory assured Bulloch. The South had more than enough qualified men restlessly sitting at home, hoping for an assignment as soon as Mallory could come up with some ships. The problem was going to be locating sufficient able seamen, gunners, coal heavers, cooks, and other hands to work the ships. There were virtually no Southerners around with the right kind of experience. Mallory resolved the problem by adding, as a casual afterthought toward the end of his letter, "Crews of admirable seamen and firemen might be shipped, induced to come by the higher wages given in our Navy and hopes of promotion and prize money." Bulloch, in other words, was being asked not only to create a Confederate Navy in England but to find English sailors to serve in it as well.

While his clerk copied out the final instructions, Mallory spent the rest of the day going over housekeeping details with his newest agent. Bulloch was going to have to pay cash for whatever he bought in England, so the financial arrangements were a matter of vital importance. There were also the potential legal problems that needed to be discussed. Bulloch's mission might look straightforward enough when viewed from Montgomery, but what he was being asked to do was almost certainly against British law, and Mallory told Bulloch to familiarize himself with a parliamentary statute known as the Foreign Enlistment Act, which he thought would define the British government's rules concerning the sale of warships to belligerents.

Finally, there was the need for secrecy. Delicate discussions were already under way in London and Paris, where the representatives of President Davis were trying to negotiate diplomatic recognition of the Confederacy, and Bulloch would have to exercise great discretion to avoid upsetting them. Yankee agents would almost certainly be operating in England, and Mallory instructed Bulloch in the rudimentary techniques of espionage, what would today be called basic tradecraft, including the use of a cipher system for sending and receiving coded messages. Finally, at the close of the day, Mallory presented his new agent with some cash to cover his traveling expenses and wished him Godspeed.

While still in Mallory's office, Bulloch had seen reports from both the Atlantic and Gulf coasts indicating that the blockade was already well established off the South's major ports. Rather than risk capture at sea, he decided to cross to England by way of Canada. He left Montgomery by train that night, barely forty-eight hours after his arrival, retracing his route back through the border states. Before reaching the Ohio River, he committed to memory Mallory's entire letter of instructions—including all its complicated details, its names and addresses, and lists of war goods to be purchased on the navy's account—and then destroyed the letter and any other evidence that might link him to the Confederacy. Only then did he reenter the Union proper, which he managed without attracting notice, and caught the next train north. Portents of the war to come were everywhere. From his train window, he watched eager recruits drilling in almost every town through which he passed. On reaching Detroit, he crossed quietly into Canada, again without incident, and from there took the Grand Trunk Railway to Montreal, where he booked passage to England.

———————

As the Allan Line steamer *North America* made her way down the St. Lawrence toward the sea, Bulloch had ample time to ponder the task that lay ahead. By any measure it presented a formidable challenge. He was to single-handedly build a navy, in secret and from scratch, for an unrecognized government that had no credit and was so weak it could not even keep its own ports open. Even to someone as competent as James Bulloch, it might have seemed a daunting prospect.

Liverpool

J ames Bulloch arrived in Liverpool on June 4, 1861, almost a month after his departure from Montgomery. It was already late in the afternoon when his ship steamed up the river Mersey toward her berth, and Bulloch stood on deck with a telescope, surveying the nearly 5 miles of quays, docks, landing platforms, and dockyards that lined the harbor's waterfront. Everywhere he looked, he was gratified to see ships and shipbuilding facilities. The Mersey, a massive mile-wide estuary, swarmed with tugs, ferries, and river craft of every size and description. Tall ships from the far corners of the earth clustered along the wharves and floating docks.

Liverpool, in that summer of 1861, was a dynamic center of industry and trade, a thriving city of some 440,000 souls crowded onto the right bank of the river, while on the far side the equally busy community of Birkenhead mirrored the commercial vitality of one of the world's richest and busiest seaports.

Bulloch was heartened by what he saw. Liverpool, with its forests of derricks, cranes, and dry docks, looked like an ideal place to build a navy. The noisy, crowded confusion suggested he would be free to go about his business without attracting undue attention.

Soon after docking, Bulloch stepped ashore and experienced for the first time the busy disorder of the Liverpool waterfront. In his years at sea, he had spent a lot of time on waterfronts, but he had never encountered any seaport with quite the cosmopolitan dynamic of Liverpool. Still carrying the light luggage with which he had escaped from New York, he dodged the horsecarts and delivery vans and marveled to hear the local laborers and tradesmen cheerfully calling out to one another in a totally unintelligible dialect that seemed to have no connection to English.

Not everything he saw was unfamiliar. Mariners of every stripe, carousing and cursing in a score of tongues, stumbled in and out of the joss houses and pubs, throwing away their money with the manic abandon common to sailors the world over. Apparently he would have no trouble finding crews for his ships.

Enormous warehouses loomed over the narrow streets and crowded the water's edge, many built with two loading platforms—one facing the river; the other, the inshore railroad lines—so they could receive and disgorge their goods by land or sea. Most of the windowless buildings, Bulloch knew, were designed specifically for the cotton trade, some stacked to the rafters with bales of raw cotton, long-staple Sea Island and the cheaper short-staple upland, awaiting shipment inland to the mills of Yorkshire and Lancashire, there to be combed, spun, and woven into the textiles that made up half of England's export trade, while others were crammed with the finished products of those same mills—the myriad bolts of twill, calico, canvas, muslin, denim, ticking, and velveteen—ready to be shipped on board merchantmen and sent out to the marketplaces of the world.

Liverpool was the world's largest entrepôt for the cotton industry, and because of the importance of that commodity to the economy, the city had long maintained strong commercial and financial ties to the Southern states of America, where most of the world's supply was grown. The ties of trade had inevitably fostered a sympathy for Southern aspirations, and Bulloch was pleased to discover that almost every time he spoke to anyone, whether a porter or customs official or hack driver, his American accent, softened by his Southern heritage, invariably elicited a friendly response, followed, more often than not, by an ardent avowal of support for the Confederacy.

After a fortnight of enforced idleness at sea, Bulloch was eager to get to work, but by the time he booked himself into a hotel, most businesses had closed for the day, and it was too late to get started on his new assignment. It was not until early the next morning that he found his way to 10 Rumford Place and the countinghouse of Fraser, Trenholm & Company, the Charleston, South Carolina, cotton brokerage that was serving as the Confederacy's English bank. Fraser, Trenholm, with its close ties to the financial houses in the City of London, would continue to provide the credit behind the South's purchasing program throughout the war.

Bulloch wondered how he would be received. He carried no papers that could identify him as an agent of the Confederate government— he had destroyed all such evidence before making his dash north to Canada—and worried that he might be met with suspicion. But Fraser, Trenholm turned out to be an informal place. He quickly established his bona fides and was warmly welcomed by the resident partners, all young South Carolinians. The firm's managing partner, Charles K. Prioleau, also a South Carolinian, explained to Bulloch that for business reasons he had arranged to become a British subject but told his visitor that his new nationality was simply a legal formality, no more than a flag of convenience. His heart, he assured Bulloch, remained true to the South.

Bulloch described why he was in England and explained that he would soon need large amounts of money to carry out his assignment. Could he count on Fraser, Trenholm for financial support? Prioleau, who was eager to help, told Bulloch that no such funds had so far arrived but encouraged him to get started and promised to accept personal responsibility for any orders Bulloch wished to make until the money became available. It was an extremely generous offer, demonstrating great trust on Prioleau's part and involving real personal risk. Bulloch was both impressed and grateful.

Bulloch wasted no time. Having established a line of credit with

Prioleau in the morning, he caught an afternoon train to London and that evening introduced himself to William L. Yancey and Dudley Mann, the commissioners whom Jefferson Davis had sent over to represent the South in Great Britain. Using their office as his base, he spent the next few days in London, where he contacted ship brokers in different parts of England and quickly learned that no vessels suitable for his needs were presently on the market. He was going to have to build his commerce raiders from the ground up, which would make his job more complicated. He immediately began putting together the team of people he would need to create his little navy. He met with shipbuilders, naval architects, chandlers, weapons dealers, and other specialists and entered into informal understandings with a number of individuals and commercial representatives who would, in time, become important contributors to his operations. By the end of a week, he was back in Liverpool, having organized his own private military-industrial complex.

There was one final, crucial factor that required attention: he needed a good lawyer. Of all the numerous arrangements Bulloch initiated during that first, whirlwind week in England, none was to prove more important than those he made with a shrewd and highly imaginative Liverpool solicitor named F. S. Hull, the man he engaged to guide him through the intricacies of British law.

Almost certainly it was Prioleau who brought the two men together. By so doing, he performed a service of singular value to the Southern cause. The Englishman Hull was to become a pivotal figure in the history of the Confederate Navy. It was his ability to ferret out weaknesses in British law that made the construction of the commerce raiders possible. Without his discernment and cunning, it is quite likely the ships would never have come into being.

At their first meeting, Bulloch was able to take advantage of the confidentiality of their relationship and be completely open and frank with his lawyer. He explained precisely who he was, what government he worked for, and what it was he wanted to do. Could Hull advise him as to the legal ramifications? The solicitor promised to take the matter under advisement and, after consulting the relevant law, informed Bulloch that the principal stumbling block to building Confederate warships in England, as Mallory had predicted, was likely to be a law called the Foreign Enlistment Act. Enacted by Parliament in 1819 to protect the British government from getting caught up in foreign conflicts through the private activities of its nationals, the law set strict limits on the extent to which British subjects could involve themselves in such foreign adventures. As its title suggested, the act dealt first and foremost with the question of British nationals' serving in the armed' forces of foreign nations. It made it illegal for any foreign power to recruit military volunteers within Britain and decreed that any British national who enlisted in the armed forces of a foreign belligerent risked the loss of his government's protection.

The law covered many other eventualities. While British subjects were free to sell arms and other contraband to belligerents, Mr. Hull pointed out that there were restrictions, and in particular, he drew Bulloch's attention to section 7 of the act, which dealt with warships and made it illegal for any British subject to sell "any ship or vessel" to a foreign belligerent if the said ship was to be used with the "intent to cruise or commit hostilities against any . . . foreign state with which Britain was at peace." Since Bulloch proposed to build gunships specifically designed to commit hostilities against the United States, a country with which Britain was at peace, the act appeared to present an insurmountable obstacle to Bulloch's shipbuilding ambitions.

But Hull was not discouraged. When it came to the law, he pointed out cheerfully, matters were rarely black-and-white. It was one thing for Parliament to pass a law, but it was an entirely different matter to decide what Parliament meant by that law. As far as Hull was concerned, the most important fact about section 7 of the Foreign Enlistment Act was that in the forty-two years since its enactment, it had never once been tested in a court of law. No barristers had ever argued its merits. No judge had ever probed its meaning. No jury had ever weighed the interpretations of the court officials. This meant that there was no precedent to determine section 7's limitations. Therefore, Hull explained, while the wording of section 7 might appear to be clear and unambiguous, there was no one in Great Britain, from the law lords on down, who could state with any authority—beyond their own opinion—precisely what section 7 did or did not cover.

Since no legal precedent existed, Hull told Bulloch, he proposed to create one. He would draw up a hypothetical defense of the activities in which Bulloch planned to engage—mentioning no names—and submit it to two eminent English barristers for their consideration. For the plan to work, the barristers would have to be of the highest standing, men whose reputation at the bar was recognized throughout the legal profession. He would ask each barrister to submit his own opinion on Hull's brief, and if either one of them concurred with it, that would be enough to provide Bulloch with a useful legal precedent in support of his activities. If both barristers agreed with him, the prestige of their combined opinions would give Bulloch a very much stronger legal shield for his shipbuilding program.

Soliciting opinions from learned jurists on untested laws is a common enough practice within the legal profession. While such opinions are not likely to have the same authority as decisions reached in a court of law, they are a recognized alternative. What made Hull's initiative noteworthy was the brilliant way he framed his case, marshaling his arguments in such a way as to almost compel legal minds toward the predetermined verdict of his choice. The barristers to whom he submitted his case were not asked whether the law itself was being followed but to judge only the much subtler issue of whether Hull's interpretation of the law was appropriate.

The heart of Hull's legal argument lay in the distinction he made in defining the wording of the act. He argued that section 7 referred specifically to warships, which by itself appeared to be an unexceptional interpretation, but he then went on to argue that to be considered a warship, a vessel had to be equipped with guns. This, too, seemed at first an unexceptional definition, until one examined it closely, at which point, Hull argued, it was legal to sell any kind of ship to a belligerent, as long as the ship was not armed. Given such an interpretation, a British shipyard was free to build a warship for a belligerent foreign power, *so long as the ship's guns were not installed*, "because the offence is not the building but the equipping." Further, "any shipbuilder may build any ship in her Majesty's dominions, provided he does not equip her [with guns] within her Majesty's dominions." By this definition, Bulloch was free to buy warships in England so long as he did not mount guns in them until he was beyond the 3-mile limit, the marine league that defined the limits of Britain's sovereignty.

To anyone with even a passing familiarity with ships and shipbuilding, such a lawyerly interpretation of what constituted a warship would have been recognized as simpleminded. The design and construction of warships is inherently different from the design and construction of other kinds of ships, and to base the distinction solely on whether they were armed was nonsense, tantamount to arguing that a pianist was not a pianist unless he was actively engaged in playing a piano. To use a modern analogy, by Hull's definition an aircraft carrier could not be considered a ship of war unless it was carrying armed aircraft. Hull's interpretation might indeed fly in the face of reason, but Hull understood one overriding fact: that it was not reasonable people who interpreted laws, it was lawyers.

Hull proved to be right. Both of the barristers to whom he submitted his carefully worded hypothetical case fully endorsed his conclusions, thereby totally eviscerating the Foreign Enlistment Act and turning it on its head. Magically it was as if section 7 had never been written, much less enacted.

Hull was, of course, pleased with his triumph. His client was now free to build his ships. But he cautioned Bulloch that a certain discretion was still warranted. In spite of the broad freedom of action sanctioned by the opinion of the two barristers, Hull advised him that it would be prudent to keep quiet about the ultimate purpose of his ships and to withhold such information from any British national he might hire to build them.

Hull's successful brief was a masterstroke, and to maximize its effect, he made sure that the opinion was disseminated to as wide a circle of influential people as possible. As it happened, Hull's argument was a seed that fell on fertile soil. The people who actually ran Britain—the aristocrats, the financial and commercial leaders, the leading jurists, and the heads of both major political parties—were all, almost without exception, strongly in favor of the South in its war with the North. It was obvious to all of them that it was in Britain's interest to have America broken into two nations, and the ruling classes were quick to appreciate the fact that a clever solicitor in Liverpool had come up with a way to help the Confederacy by skirting an inconvenient act of Parliament. Within a remarkably brief time, most of Great Britain's movers and shakers had become familiar, at least in general terms, with Hull's bizarre interpretation of section 7 and were able to support with a straight face his whimsical and singularly simplistic interpretation of what constituted a warship. By a process of judicial osmosis, as it were, Hull's unchallenged definitions quickly came to be regarded as the law of the land.

Hull's legal legerdemain cleared the way for Bulloch to build his raiders, and by the end of June, he was ready to begin construction of his first ship. In the interests of speed and efficiency, he selected the Liverpool firm of William C. Miller and Sons to build her. Miller had years of experience constructing vessels for the Royal Navy and already had on file in his office a full set of plans for a gunboat that the yard had recently completed for the government. Since the design included most of the features Bulloch wanted, he decided to use it as the basis for his own ship, with a few minor modifications. He asked the Millers to flatten her bilge, which would allow more room for coal bunkers, and to increase her overall length amidships to give her additional speed. Like virtually all oceangoing steamships of the period, she was to be fully rigged for sailing, so that she would not be solely dependent on steam power for propulsion. Bulloch asked the Millers to increase the size of her sails, to give her a better spread of canvas when sailing close-hauled, or with the wind abeam.

One special feature Bulloch was particularly eager to incorporate in his new ship was an ingenious device called a lifting screw. This was a mechanism by which the propeller, when not in use, could be detached from the drive shaft and raised out of the water, so that it did not create drag when the ship was under sail. This unusual feature, which added significantly to the ship's speed, was typical of the high level of construction on which Bulloch was to insist for all his ships.

To disguise the fact that his ship was destined for service in the Confederate Navy, Bulloch contracted for her under his own name, and to further divert inquiries on the part of the curious, he gave the ship the name *Oreto,* which sounded Italian, and then spread the story that she was being built for a mercantile firm doing business in Palermo. To support the claim, and to further hide her true identity, he arranged for a Mr. John Henry Thomas, the Liverpool representative of the Thomas Brothers firm of Palermo, to officially supervise her construction.

Bulloch had arrived in England with neither money nor credentials, and with the law clearly against him. Now, less than a month later, he had established his credit, altered a major act of Parliament to suit his purposes, and commissioned the construction of a major vessel of war. It was a promising beginning.

THREE

Number *290*

Toward the end of June, even before the keel of the *Oreto* was laid at the Miller yard in Liverpool, Bulloch had crossed to the opposite side of the Mersey to open negotiations with the Laird brothers, proprietors of the Birkenhead Iron Works, for the construction of another, even more ambitious vessel. The Laird works, founded in 1829, was one of the largest and most modern shipyards in England, with more than four thousand workers. Many of the finest vessels in Britain had come out of its docks, and Bulloch wanted to take advantage of the company's long experience in the design and construction of steam-powered vessels.

From her very inception, there was something different about the ship that Bulloch would build at Birkenhead. She was to be larger, more powerful, more precisely designed for her ultimate calling than the *Oreto*, which had been hurriedly adapted from another design and was therefore something of a compromise.

In keeping with his solicitor's advice, Bulloch presented himself to the Laird brothers as a sea captain lately arrived in England, a private citizen of unspecified nationality, with financial ties to the firm of Fraser, Trenholm in Liverpool. He was careful to give no hint of any ties to the Confederate government, but the Lairds would readily have guessed his secret. Every knowledgeable businessman in the Liverpool area was aware that Fraser, Trenholm was funding Confederate agents, and the Lairds would have realized that their visitor was simply one of the more recent arrivals from the Southern states. If he wished to keep his allegiances private, that was his affair. They welcomed him and invited him to inspect their extensive establishment.

In the course of his tour of the yard, Bulloch made it a point to bring up the subject of wooden "despatch vessels" and described in considerable detail the specific characteristics of such vessels that appeared to him to be most desirable. The Lairds listened carefully and expressed polite interest.

Bulloch was eager to get started on a second ship, but the Confederate government still had not come through with the promised funds, and he had no money. Fraser, Trenholm had supplied the financial backing to begin construction of the *Oreto*, but ships are expensive items, and the company was not in a position to advance the cash for another such large-scale commitment. Bulloch decided to ask the Lairds for help. A few days later, when he returned to Birkenhead for a second visit, he reopened his previous conversation and made it clear that he wished to build a "despatch vessel" along the lines he had described and that he hoped to engage the services of the Laird firm for that purpose. They told him they would welcome the business. Bulloch explained that he was temporarily short of funds and was therefore not as yet in a position to sign a contract, but he assured them that he was expecting a large draft of money in the near future. Would the Lairds, in the interim, be willing to go into the necessary calculations, draw up specifications, and make drawings and a model, upon his assurance that he meant business and was ready to give them the necessary financial guarantees? The two brothers, who were strongly pro-Southern in their sentiments, saw Bulloch's proposal as something more than simply another business deal and readily agreed to his terms. The details were quickly settled, and Bulloch was soon commuting to the Birkenhead yard on a daily basis and working full-time with the Lairds' engineers and naval architects.

The new ship would be similar to the *Oreto* but more carefully thought out. Over the early weeks of summer, while Bulloch awaited the arrival

of money from Mallory, there was time to go over every aspect of the
ship's plans, to discuss alternative construction technologies, to draft
and redraft her lines until both he and his shipbuilders were satisfied
that she would be, in Bulloch's words, "as well-found as any vessel built
in Great Britain, and superior to any ship in the world in her fitness to
roam the oceans as a sea raider."

From the beginning, Bulloch had specified that the ship was to be
built of wood. The Lairds had at first tried to dissuade him, pointing
out that wood had almost entirely gone out of use among British shipbuilders. Due to the depletion of Britain's forests, they warned, it was
likely that their suppliers would run into difficulties in obtaining suitable timber for the heavy scantlings required for the ship now taking
shape on the drawing board. They were particularly concerned about
the key timbers, including the stem, keelson, and especially the sternpost, which would have to be bored through to receive the screw shaft.
They suggested to Bulloch that he could save money by building the
ship of iron. Bulloch listened thoughtfully to their arguments but continued to insist on wood. He wanted ships that could sail the world. A
damaged iron ship could be repaired only at seaports equipped with
modern facilities, but a wooden ship could be refitted anywhere on
earth or even at sea, if necessary. Besides, he knew that wooden decks
could better support the great weight of the guns he planned to install.
His ship must be built of wood, he told the Lairds. Price was not an
object.

The Foreign Enlistment Act was not the only set of legal restrictions that would affect the design and construction of Bulloch's ships.
There was another, more rigid set of rules that shaped his shipbuilding
program, embodied in a document called the Queen's Proclamation of
Neutrality, which had been issued by the British government shortly
after news of the outbreak of the American war reached England. The
proclamation was drawn up to define Britain's legal relationship to
the two belligerents. By its terms and subsequent Admiralty orders, the
vessels of both navies, Northern and Southern, were free to visit ports
within the British Empire in the normal course of their operations, but
they were forbidden from using such visits to in any way improve their
ability to wage war. Specifically they could not recruit crewmen in such

ports or change their guns or take on board any stores classed as "contraband of war" or make any repairs other than were necessary to ensure safety at sea. As to refueling, such vessels were allowed to purchase only as much coal as necessary to take them to the nearest port of their own country, and after receiving that coal, they could not again refuel at any British port for at least three months.

The restrictions made it necessary for Bulloch to design a vessel with a huge carrying capacity, a ship with room for enough crewmen, enough ordnance, enough fuel, and enough food and water to maintain herself at sea for many weeks, even months, with no source of resupply other than what she might plunder from her captured victims. The main effect, in terms of design, was to force Bulloch to construct raiders with abnormally large coal bunkers. As he commented ruefully, the design of the Laird ship was shaped as much by the limitations set by the Queen's Proclamation as it was by any principles of hydrodynamics.

Toward the end of July, Bulloch's long-awaited funds finally arrived at Fraser, Trenholm, and he could at last notify the Lairds that he was ready to commit to the construction of his "despatch boat." On the morning of August 1, he and Prioleau, along with Bulloch's lawyer, F. S. Hull, crossed the Mersey on the Tranmere Ferry to sign and witness the contract for the ship. The men were in a cheerful, even ebullient mood. According to all the reports reaching them from across the Atlantic, the war in America was going well. Even the Confederacy's commerce raiders were in the news. An item in the papers confirmed that at the end of June, Commander Semmes had made a daring escape from New Orleans in the CSS *Sumter* and was now busily spreading havoc in the Caribbean. Bulloch and the others would doubtless have been even more cheerful had they known that just days before, the Confederate Army had won a decisive victory in the first major battle of the war, at Manassas, Virginia. It was a good time to be a Southerner.

On their arrival at the Laird yards, the visitors were ushered into the

The Laird yards in Birkenhead, in 1862, one of the largest and busiest shipbuilding sites in Britain. With so many other vessels under construction, the ship known as number 290 attracted little attention.

main offices and seated around a large conference table. Prominently displayed on the table, ready at hand for reference, was a meticulously rendered model of the ship, along with a complete set of plans for the proposed vessel—sheer, body, and sail. Both model and plans were scaled to the standard Royal Navy ratio of 48 to 1, so that each inch on paper represented 4 feet in true measure. Because the model measured precisely 4 feet, 7 inches in length and 8 inches across at its widest part, it was evident that the proposed vessel was to be 220 feet in length, with a 32-foot beam.

She was to be a propeller-driven steamer, bark-rigged, with a full set of sails, so that she could operate without her engines. As with the *Oreto,* her screw was to be fitted with a lifting device. A novel feature was a telescoping funnel that could be lowered out of sight, to hide the fact that she was a steamer. No one seemed curious as to why Bulloch was willing to pay extra money for something of such marginal value as a disappearing funnel. Her draft would be about 15 feet when fully loaded, and her deadweight tonnage was listed as 1,023 $^{827}/_{940}$ tons. Importantly, there was to be room in her capacious bunkers for 350 tons of coal, enough fuel for eighteen straight days of steaming.

Because Bulloch had not specified a name for the new ship, she was referred to throughout as number *290*, which simply reflected the fact that she was the two hundred and ninetieth vessel to be built in the Birkenhead works since its founding.

———

The articles of agreement were written out by hand in the clear and unambiguous style of law clerks trained to write legibly rather than gracefully. To ensure full understanding by all parties of the terms of the agreement, the entire contract was read aloud, with the reader stopping only to answer questions, of which there were few:

> *The Hull*   *and machinery to be built in general accordance with the plans & Specifications. Everything both as to materials, fastenings and workmanship to be of the best quality.*

She was to come equipped with five boats—including launch, cutter, and whaleboat—and ample ground tackle. She was to be well supplied with hawsers and enough spare blocks, running gear, and so forth to meet all requirements for at least a year.

> *The Outfit*   *of Sails, Ropes, Shipchandlery, Anchors, Cables, Boats, Hawsers, Warps &c to be generally the Same in quantity and quality as usually Known by the term of "East India Outfit" which is in fact a double Suit of Sails (except Studding Sails and SkySails) and other Stores in proportion so that the Ship is ready for a long Voyage.*

Attached to the contract proper, page after page of detailed specifications defined the materials to be used, and the construction methods to be employed, throughout the vessel. Even a casual scan-

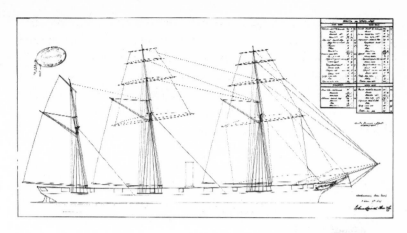

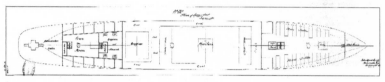

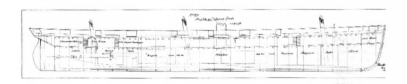

Original plans for ship number 290, *the future* Alabama. *After the war
the U.S. War Department obtained the plans, which were presented as
part of the American government's case in the* Alabama *claims
arbitration.   Source: National Archives.*

ning confirms the builders' commitment to construct a first-class
ship:

Limber Strakes	*Thick*	*4 inches*
Oak or Greenheart Bands at Floorheads	*thick*	*4 "*

English Oak or Greenheart		
Diagonal	Broad	10 "
Truss Pieces	Thick	4 "
English Oak	To be fastened with a ³⁄₄ Copper bolt in each Timber	

The ship's scantlings, those frames and cross members that made up the basic structural elements of the vessel, were to be disproportionately large for a ship of her size. What great weight were they designed to support? No one at the table chose to comment.

Elm Ing. except	" Forward	11 "
Keel	Sided in Midships	14 inches
the foremost and	" Aft	11 "
after piece which	Moulded	16 "
are to be English		
Oak	To have Six ⅞" Copper Bolts in each Scarph Lip bolts to be ½" diameter	

Two of the vessel's most distinctive characteristics—the large amount of space given over to crew quarters and the exceedingly small cargo capacity—made it evident to those at the table that the vessel under contract was a fighting ship in every respect save for her lack of guns. But no one chose to comment.

Keelson	Sided in Midships	14 inches
Teak or	" Forward & Aft	11 "
Greenheart	Moulded	15 "
	Bolted with Copper Bolts 1 ⅛" and 1 ¼" diameter	
Stem	Sided at the Head	14 inches
English Oak	" " " Fore foot	11 "

Stern pos,	*Sided at the Head*	*15 "*
English or	*" "Upper Pintle*	*13 "*
African Oak	*Sided at the Heel*	*11 inches*

Cross Pieces	*Sided in Midships*	*10 @ 11 in*
English Oak	*" Forward & Aft*	*9 @ 10 "*
	Moulded at the	
	Cutting down	*13 "*
	" " the head	*10 "*

The heavily reinforced open areas on the deck, particularly those immediately forward of the bridge and abaft the engine room skylight, which would have made excellent locations for permanent gun emplacements, went unremarked.

Iron Diagonal .	*Broad*	*4 inches*
Riders	*Thick*	*⅝ "*
	To be fastened alternately	
	with ¾ " Copper Bolts	
	and ¾ " Galvanized Iron	
Lower Deck	*Deep*	*8 inches*
Shelf		
Teak or	*Broad Amidships,*	*12 inches*
African or	*" fore and aft.*	*10 "*
English Oak	*To be fastened with ⅞"*	
or Mahogany	*Copper Bolts*	

She was to have a fireproofed magazine, metal-lined throughout. What could be the purpose of a magazine other than to store gunpowder? And why was it positioned $2\frac{1}{2}$ feet below the waterline, except to protect it from enemy fire?

Lower Deck	*Sided*	*7 inches*
Beams	*Moulded at Middle*	*7 "*
Dantzic fir	*" " Ends*	*6 ½ "*
except in wake	*To round*	*4 "*

of mast Bitts,
Engine Room
Bulkheads &c
which are to
be of Oak or
Teak over Engine
room of iron
13.5

No one seemed curious about certain other features that could only be meant for a warship. The ship was to be fitted with shot and canister racks on deck, and her sides were pierced forward, midships, and at the quarterdeck. What were the shot and canister racks to hold? Why the openings in the ship's gunwales, except for guns?

Her engines were to be equal to Admiralty standards, and the engineer's stores and spare gear were equal to those supplied to ships of the Royal Navy.

Dimensions &c	*No. of Cylinders*	2
	Diam of "	*56 ins*
	Stroke not less than	*27 "*
	No. of Revolutions	
	per Minute	*65*
	Power by English	
	Admiralty Rule	*300 HP*
		400

The Engines to be direct acting horizontal condensing Engines having the Cylinder on one side of the Crank Shaft, & the condenser, Pumps, &c on the other.

The Slide Valves to be fitted with rings on the back to relieve the pressure.

Air pump Valves to be of India rubber, with brass seals & guards.

Discharge valves at Ships side to be of Brass. Air pumps to be horizontal, double acting.

Feed & Bilge pumps, horizontal, single acting with solid plunger & india rubber valves.

Hand pump, single acting, of suitable size.

Donkey Engine Pump, double acting, of suitable size.

Bed plates with main bearings & guides, Cylinders Pistons. Cylinder Covers, Slide Valves & Valve casings. Condensers & covers, Eccentric Wheels Balance Weights, Plummer blocks for Screw, Shafting, safety & Stop Valve Boxes, all to be of Cast Iron.

She was to be propelled by a brass screw (Griffith's pattern), and equipped with an important new device, a condenser and cooling tank that would supply fresh water every day, eliminating another reason to come into port and giving number 290 even greater freedom to roam. She would be copper-fastened and coppered, and finished in every respect as a first-class ship.

In Witness whereof the said parties to these presents have hereunto set their hands the day and year first above written.

WILLIAM LAIRD JNR
JAMES D. BULLOCH

Signed by the Parties
in the Presence of
JOHN GREEN
Bookkeeper
Birkenhead

This was the ship that would eventually become world famous as the CSS *Alabama*. Her total price, including the outfit (but not including any armament, of course), was to be £47,500, or roughly a quarter of a million dollars at the rate of exchange then current, payable in five equal payments of £9,500, with the last installment payable after satisfactory trial and delivery on the Mersey. James Bulloch thought it an eminently reasonable figure and was confident the Confederacy would get its money's worth.

FOUR

Nemesis

B y any assessment, James Bulloch's accomplishments during his first two months in England were extraordinary. Along with his shipbuilding responsibilities, he was also the chief purchasing agent for the Confederate Navy. Working virtually alone and in secret, and operating on a severely limited budget, he had somehow managed to recruit a small but highly effective corps of subagents, scattered over several British ports, and by the end of the summer of 1861, in addition to initiating the construction of the two gunships now rising on either side of the Mersey, he and his team had placed orders for, and in some cases taken delivery on, multiple consignments of guns, small arms, munitions, textiles, and medical supplies, which now awaited shipment to the Confederacy. Bulloch seems to have possessed an almost infinite range of skills. He could manage people, negotiate contracts, assess ship models, process shipping manifests, parse legal briefs, analyze technical and mechanical plans, and answer, or find answers to, seemingly every question that arose. It is hard to imagine anyone else in the entire Confederacy who could have done as much.

What made his accomplishments all the more impressive was the fact that they were achieved in the face of a devastating breach of security. Soon after his arrival in Liverpool, he had been shocked to open a two-week-old New York newspaper and find his own name in it. Federal agents in Washington had learned of his presence in England, he read, and knew precisely what he was doing there. The newspaper described how Confederate agents, operating in the North, had used the public telegraph lines to communicate with other agents, in the naive belief that such messages, like the U.S. mail, were private. Federal officers had combed the telegraph company's files and uncovered extensive details of various Confederate undercover activities, including Bulloch's mission. The government had provided the newspapers with copies of some of the incriminating documents, and Bulloch, with mixed emotions of fury and dismay, was able to read the explicit, damning details of his budgets, his timetables, and virtually everything else relating to his supposedly secret operations.

There was only one saving factor in what was otherwise an unmitigated disaster: all of the incriminating telegraph messages predated his arrival in England, so that while they gave the Federal agents a good idea of what he planned to do, they provided no information as to where he was operating in England or whether he had been successful in implementing his orders. Bulloch was confident that the Yankees had not as yet stumbled upon any of the projects already initiated.

The news of his exposure forced Bulloch to exercise an even greater degree of caution. He had to assume he was being shadowed, and as far as it was practical to do so, he avoided visiting the two yards where his ships were under construction. There was little he could do to hide or disguise the ships themselves, but he took a certain comfort in the fact that there were literally hundreds of vessels under construction in Liverpool, Bristol, Portsmouth, Glasgow, and a half dozen other British shipbuilding centers, and it would be extremely difficult to spot the ones he had initiated. The *290*, which was only beginning to take shape, was being built upriver of the city and was not likely to attract much attention. The *Oreto*, however, was another matter. She was considerably further advanced in construction, which made her more conspicuous, and because she was located at the Miller yard, she was in daily view of thousands and was more likely to become the subject of public curiosity. To help guard her secrets, Bulloch arranged for all the *Oreto*'s contracts to be placed with Fawcett, Preston & Company, the smaller, less prominent firm he had hired to build her engines. Anyone who wanted to find out about his ships was going to have to search long and hard.

The *Oreto* was scheduled to be ready for sea in January 1862, and the *290* was expected to follow her two months later, in March. Since he was now forced to limit his visits to the shipyards, Bulloch found himself with unwelcome time on his hands. He was an active man by nature, and casting around restlessly for something to do, he eventually decided that rather than sitting idly by waiting for his two gunships to be completed, he would make a quick trip to the Confederacy, and personally deliver the military and medical supplies that he had amassed and that were now awaiting shipment.

With the last of his funds, he purchased a small steamer, the *Fingal,* to carry his cargo of contraband across the Atlantic and prepared to run the blockade into Savannah, Georgia. He calculated the round-trip would take no more than six to eight weeks, which would get him back to Liverpool in plenty of time to supervise the final fitting out and departure of his two ships. But Bulloch recognized that wartime plans can be notoriously unpredictable. There was always the possibility that he might be delayed or otherwise kept from returning in time, so he took the precaution of leaving detailed instructions with Prioleau for the disposition of the ships. Since Bulloch was also the owner of record of both vessels, he signed over his power of attorney to Prioleau as well. On October 15, confident that all was in order, he boarded the *Fingal* and left Britain, bound for Savannah.

Bulloch's decision to make a quick round-trip to the South seemed eminently reasonable, but it was to prove otherwise. His absence from Liverpool brought on a near disaster to the Confederate operation in England and, in hindsight, turned out to be one of his few serious mistakes.

———

Only days after Bulloch's departure in the *Fingal,* a new figure stepped ashore on the docks of Liverpool, a tall, somberly dressed American Quaker named Thomas Haines Dudley, who arrived to take up his duties as the newly appointed United States consul. Dudley was a lawyer with a lifelong commitment to the antislavery movement, a man of deep convictions and strong will. He had the thin, sharp features of a ferret and a hunting instinct to match, and he would soon establish himself as the nemesis of the Confederate procurement operations in England. He would institute a program of intelligence-gathering and legal obstruction that would sorely test the efforts of Bulloch and his people, and in the months and years to come, he and Bulloch would prove worthy adversaries, playing out an epic game of cat and mouse across the Merseyside waterfront. Time and again Bulloch's audacity and cunning would be tested by Dudley's tenacity and relentless determination. These two remarkable men, operating thousands of miles from the fields of battle, would have a unique impact on the war.

Like Bulloch before him, Dudley was quick to perceive the strong pro-Southern sentiment in Liverpool. His initial impressions were confirmed when the man he had come to replace, the acting U.S. consul, complained to him about blatant anti-Yankee activities on the part of local officials and recounted rumors about the mysterious James Bulloch and the equally worrisome and mysterious Fraser, Trenholm & Company.

The acting consul's laments about Confederate activities in Liverpool were probably accurate, Dudley guessed, but since they were based largely on hearsay and conjecture, they were of no value to him. If he ever hoped to stop Bulloch or even slow him down, he would need hard evidence; within days of his arrival, Dudley began to put together what quickly became a full-scale network of agents dedicated to unraveling the secrets of the Confederacy's operations in Liverpool. Assembling such a crew from the rough trade of Merseyside was a distasteful task for the diffident Dudley, and in a letter to the State Department in Washington, he noted apologetically, "They are not as a general thing very estimable men, but are the only persons we can get to engage in this business."

Liverpool was a large and densely developed industrial center, and it was not going to be easy to pick up the trail of Bulloch and the other Confederate agents who were operating in the area. Dudley had neither the time nor the talent to head up such an operation. He needed someone local to supervise the search, and by Christmas he had found the man for the job. His name was Matthew Maguire, a retired policeman with good contacts in the dockyards, pubs, and boarding-houses of Liverpool, a detective who knew how to bribe and cajole sailors and local workmen and sniff out promising leads.

Within days of his hire, Maguire made a major discovery. He spotted the wooden ship at the Miller yard, the one that Bulloch called *Oreto,* and was able to identify her as a gunboat destined for the Confederacy. On January 24, 1862, as the ship approached completion, Maguire even came up with a rough approximation of her name, although he garbled some of the details. "The *Oritis,* a screw gunboat is fitting out at one of the docks in this place," he wrote in a dispatch to Dudley; "she is built of iron and is 700 tons. She is reported for the Italian Government, but the fact of the machinery being supplied by Fawcett and Preston and other circumstances connected with it made me suspicious, and causes me to believe she is intended for the South."

Dudley pressed Maguire for more details and began his own investigation. By February 4 he had received important confirmation of Maguire's suspicions from a different source. The Italian consul in Liverpool informed him that his government had no knowledge of any gunboat being built in Liverpool for the Italian Navy. Two weeks later, on February 19, Maguire was able to confirm that Fawcett, Preston, the firm that had built and installed the gunboat's engines, had been paid by Fraser, Trenholm. If true (which, of course, it was), this was exactly the sort of solid evidence that Dudley needed.

He sent word of his discovery to Charles Francis Adams, the American minister in London. Adams, who had long suspected secret collusion between the British government and the Confederacy, immediately fired off a peremptory note to Lord John Russell, the British foreign secretary, relaying Dudley's information and demanding that the suspect vessel be prevented from leaving port, citing section 7 of the Foreign Enlistment Act as his justification. Russell agreed to look into the matter, and in due course the collector of customs for Liverpool, S. Price Edwards, was ordered to investigate the *Oreto.* Edwards went over to the Miller yard and interviewed the owner, William C. Miller, who told him that he knew little of the ship. It was his understanding that the *Oreto* was being built for the firm of

Thomas Brothers, of Palermo, and he had heard that the owners in-tended to sell her to the Italian government.

While Edwards was questioning Miller, he ordered his people to examine the *Oreto,* and after investigating the ship thoroughly, and taking note of her metal-lined magazine, heavy stanchions, and over-sized bunkers, they reported that she showed every sign of being a gunship, except for the fact that she carried no guns. Edwards included these findings in his report to London and explained that since she was unarmed, he could not detain her, because her builders had broken no law. Clearly F. S. Hull's somewhat idiosyncratic interpretation of the Foreign Enlistment Act had found an advocate in the British customs office.

In London Lord Russell, citing Edwards's letter, informed the American minister that he was sorry but that under the circumstances he could take no action.

Adams told Dudley to redouble his efforts.

———

By now it was March 1862. Almost five months had passed since Bul-loch's departure from Liverpool, and he had still not returned. The partners at Fraser, Trenholm had heard nothing, and Charles Prioleau was worried.

The *Fingal* had in fact arrived off Savannah on schedule, in No-vember, and Bulloch, after successfully running the blockade and de-livering his much-needed cargo to the military authorities, had made a hurried trip by rail to Virginia to meet with Stephen Mallory at the new capital in Richmond. He then returned directly to Savannah, in-tending to take the *Fingal* back out through the blockade on the first moonless night, but in this he was repeatedly thwarted by the pres-ence of Yankee cruisers offshore. After months of frustration, Bulloch was finally forced to abandon the *Fingal* where she lay and travel overland to North Carolina, where he managed to escape through the blockade by taking passage on the fast steamer *Annie Childs,* out of Wilmington.

Throughout his long period of enforced inactivity, Bulloch had heard nothing from England, and as the *Annie Childs* approached the British Isles, he was naturally eager to get back to Liverpool as quickly as possible to find out what had happened in his absence. Rather than finish the voyage by ship, he hurried ashore at Queenstown, Ireland, and caught a train to Dublin. From there he made his way by steam ferry to Holyhead, in Wales, where he caught another train and was scheduled to pull into Liverpool early in the afternoon of March 10, 1862.

Bulloch was in a sanguine mood. Despite the many frustrations caused by the blockade, he had accomplished much during his trip. The *Fingal* had carried in her hold "the greatest military cargo ever imported into the Confederacy," enough equipment to outfit ten regiments, and he had been personally gratified by the heartfelt thanks of the military authorities in Savannah. But it was his talks with Mallory that had proved particularly satisfactory. When Bulloch had originally volunteered his services to the Confederacy, he had hoped for a navy commission and was disappointed when Mallory thought it best to send him to England as a private citizen. In November, when the two men met again in Richmond, Bulloch renewed his request for a commission, and this time Mallory agreed. Bulloch was returning to England as a proper naval officer, with the rank of commander in the Confederate Navy, rather than as a civilian agent with only a shadowy and indeterminate status. Equally satisfying was the fact that Mallory had promised him command of the *290*. According to the schedule Bulloch had worked out with the Lairds the previous summer, she would be ready for sea in a matter of weeks.

During his long absence, Bulloch had of course heard nothing of the status of the *Oreto* and had assumed that she had been launched and fitted out as scheduled and that she had long since left Liverpool and gone to sea, in accordance with the instructions he had left with Prioleau. Thus, it must have come as a particularly disagreeable surprise for him to look out his window as his train sped along the banks of the Mersey and see the *Oreto*, with her unmistakable double-stack silhouette, lying in plain sight in the river, off the Egremont Ferry slip.

What could possibly have happened? All sorts of dread possibilities tumbled through his mind. Had the ship been seized by the authorities? Was she being detained by the builders for lack of payment? The *Oreto* should have gone to sea in January. What was she doing lying peacefully in the Mersey in March?

As soon as the train pulled into the station, a shaken and deeply troubled Bulloch hurried to the offices of Fraser, Trenholm, only to find an equally distraught Charles Prioleau and hear from him an anguished tale of mistakes and delays that had characterized every step in the construction and fitting out of the *Oreto*. A hundred unanticipated problems had kept the ship in Liverpool months beyond the date of her scheduled departure. Materials had arrived late, there had been confusion over her command, and most recently the United States consul had become suspicious and had tried, without success, to get the British Customs Office to seize the ship.

Bulloch listened stoically to Prioleau's litany of confusions and misunderstandings. Neither man had time for or interest in recriminations. The truth of the matter was that the only man at fault was Bulloch himself. In his restlessness and his eagerness to deliver his supplies to the Confederacy, he had assumed that others were as well equipped as he to handle the myriad mishaps and problems that were bound to crop up in any enterprise as large and complex as the construction and deployment of two oceangoing vessels.

Bulloch immediately set to work to resolve the problem. The overriding imperative was to get the *Oreto* to sea without arousing further suspicions. Sorting quickly through the details, he was able to ascertain two salient facts: first, that she had completed a satisfactory trial run, so he could assume she was seaworthy, and second, that she was fully provisioned and ready to leave, and lacked only a crew. Overnight Bulloch transformed himself into the producer, principal actor, and stage manager of an elaborate piece of theater, to be played out for the benefit of a small but vitally important audience of British officials and Yankee spies.

For Bulloch's plan to work, he had to make sure there would be no question concerning the *Oreto*'s legal identity, nothing to tie her to the Confederate States. She had to be, in every respect, an English vessel, registered in the name of an English owner, with a regular official number and her tonnage marked upon the combings of the main hatch, operating under the direction of the Board of Trade, and flying a Union Jack at the peak. No detail was to be overlooked.

The Fraser, Trenholm people could help him with the paperwork and legal documentation, but where was he to find a captain for his ship? It was a ticklish question. There was no shortage of qualified men in Liverpool licensed to command the *Oreto*, but Bulloch needed someone more than simply an English captain: he needed someone he could trust, because he would have to divulge to him the *Oreto*'s true identity, a state secret of potentially explosive nature, which could have incalculable repercussions should it ever become public. It was through the ship's builder, William C. Miller, that he found precisely the man he needed: James Alexander Duguid. Not only was Duguid a properly certified British master mariner, and therefore legally qualified to take the ship out of Liverpool, but he was also Mr. Miller's son-in-law and could therefore be trusted to keep family secrets. With Captain Duguid's help, Bulloch set about recruiting a crew and engineer's staff. He made sure that all legal formalities were observed and that each man was engaged in strict conformity to the conditions of the Merchant Shipping Act. To prospective crew members he described a fictitious itinerary for the *Oreto*, a vaguely defined voyage from Liverpool to Palermo and from there, possibly, to a port or ports in the Mediterranean or the West Indies, and back to a port of discharge in Great Britain, the entire voyage not to exceed six months. Privately he informed Duguid that as soon as he cleared Liverpool, he was to sail directly to Nassau, in the Bahamas, where he would be met by Confederate agents who would give him further instructions.

Getting the *Oreto* out of Liverpool was only part of the job. Bulloch had to find a way to get her guns out, too. He chartered a steamer, the *Bahama*, and arranged for the *Oreto*'s four 7-inch rifled guns, along with their carriages and ammunition, to be shipped to the port of Nassau, where they could be installed in the new ship.

After an exhausting week of last-minute arrangements and makeshift planning, on March 22, 1862, the *Oreto* hauled anchor and made her way down the Mersey for the last time. To give the ship's departure a more innocent look, Bulloch arranged a festive party on deck, complete with a retinue of fashionable ladies invited for the occasion, whose presence aboard suggested that the ship was on a routine trial and would be returning that same day. Once across the bar and into the Irish Sea, Bulloch transferred himself and the partygoers to another vessel for the return to Liverpool, and the *Oreto* steamed off into the St. George's Channel and the Atlantic, never to return.

———————

At the American legation in London, a furious Charles Francis Adams learned of the *Oreto*'s departure in a hurried telegram from Liverpool and suggested to Dudley that he hire more spies.

FIVE

The *Enrica*

Despite Bulloch's efforts to cloak the *Oreto*'s departure in secrecy, her story was too good to remain untold, and news of her dramatic escape from Liverpool spread quickly through the drawing rooms and clubs of England's ruling classes. The droll tale of how some cheeky Confederate agents, by cleverly manipulating the law, had managed to build a warship in England and spirit her out from under the very noses of the dim-witted Yankees was seen as an exceedingly good joke. The acerbic Charles Francis Adams, whose duties as American minister required him to attend social gatherings of the rich and powerful, could not avoid hearing the story again and again, and the well-bred laughter of England's rulers only further incensed him and increased his frustration.

Although the Americans had failed to stop the *Oreto,* not all the news was gloomy at the United States legation. If they had lost one Confederate gunship, they had found another. On March 28, just a week after the *Oreto*'s departure, Matthew Maguire identified another mysterious vessel under construction on the crowded Merseyside waterfront, this one in Birkenhead. He sent a report to Thomas Dudley, who quickly forwarded it on to Adams in London. "The gunboat now building at Lairds' yard, no person knows whom she is for, excepting Laird's themselves, and the foreman carpenter . . . declines to give any information. The information we shall endeavor to obtain from some person employed there."

Maguire reported that the numeral 290 was prominently displayed over the mystery ship's construction site and that everyone at the Birkenhead works referred to her by that number. By the following month, Maguire and his people had identified enough suspicious details relating to the 290—her copper-lined magazine, her heavy timbers, and the secrecy surrounding her ownership—to give the American minister sufficient cause to report her to the authorities. Once again Adams petitioned Lord Russell, informing him of the imminent launching of another cruiser, almost certainly destined for the Confederacy, a larger and potentially more powerful vessel than the *Oreto*. Again he demanded that the British government detain her until he could be assured that she would not be used to cruise against United States shipping. Again he cited section 7 of the Foreign Enlistment Act, and again Lord Russell promised to look into the matter.

————

Meanwhile, in Liverpool, Bulloch was at last able to turn his attention to the 290, which he had been forced to neglect while he dealt with the *Oreto* crisis. As with her sister, construction of the 290 was well behind schedule. Even under the most favorable circumstances, she would not be ready for another three months. The delay, caused in part by Bulloch's long absence, had been exacerbated by the Lairds' insistence on only the best-quality building materials. Selecting the wood for the sternpost had been a typical problem. The sternpost was the most important timber in the ship and had to be fashioned from a single piece of wood. The Lairds had rejected the first two or three timbers sent to them, and the one they finally accepted had cost them £100, an astronomical sum.

Bulloch had become increasingly conscious of the proliferation of Yankee spies since his return and noted that "a private detective named Maguire was taking a deep and abiding interest in my personal movements." Maguire and his men seemed to be everywhere on the waterfront, buying drinks, asking questions, and even attempting to recruit his own people to work for them. Although Bulloch was not yet aware that the Yankees had spotted the *290*, he took steps to divorce himself from the day-to-day supervision of her construction. He turned the bulk of the operations over to John R. Hamilton, a Confederate naval officer who had only recently arrived in England and who would therefore be unfamiliar to Maguire's men, and arranged for two native Britons, the English coxswain George Freemantle and a Scottish engineer, Angus McNair, to oversee the deck preparations and the installation of the engines.

But Bulloch could not bring himself to avoid the *290* altogether. He was human, and the fact that she would soon be his to command sparked in Bulloch a very personal interest in her progress. Sea captains traditionally adopt an intimate relationship with their ships, but Bulloch's description of his future command, as she stood still unfinished in the Laird yard, has some of the intensity of a lovesick swain. "Her comely frame had been covered in by the binding grip of the outside planking," he wrote longingly, "which had developed the graceful curves of her counter and the delicate wave lines of her bow." Any reader curious as to why ships are traditionally referred to in the feminine has only to ponder that sentence to gain some insight.

In addition to getting the *290* finished, Bulloch had legal questions to consider. His efforts to disguise his first commerce raider as an Italian gunboat had worked flawlessly, but he knew it would be only a matter of weeks before the British government learned that the *Oreto*, which had been officially cleared for Palermo, had never arrived there and had instead dropped anchor in Nassau, a British port on the other side of the Atlantic. How would Whitehall react to the fact that his ship's construction and departure had been an elaborately orchestrated charade? Would his evasion of the Foreign Enlistment Act be allowed to stand unchallenged, or would the British government, angered and embarrassed by his deception, move to curtail his shipbuilding program?

The question was a matter of grave concern to Bulloch, for he was no longer committed solely to the construction of commerce raiders. In one of his meetings with Mallory in Richmond, the secretary had given him orders to initiate the construction of two additional vessels,

not wooden cruisers this time but something of far greater consequence. Mallory wanted him to build ironclads, impregnable floating
fortresses, designed to steam across the Atlantic and punch large holes
in the blockade.

Bulloch warned Mallory that building ironclads in England was
likely to be a very different proposition from building wooden cruisers.
It was one thing to build a gunboat-without-guns, which, by stretch-
ing the meaning of words, a clever lawyer could describe as something
other than a ship of war, but it was quite another thing to pretend that
an armor-plated ship, even unarmed, was designed for any other purpose than combat. Even if he continued to hold strictly to the law, Bulloch pointed out, it would be impossible to disguise the true nature of
such ships or to claim they were anything but what they were—the
deadliest, most modern warships in the world. Mallory had waved
aside Bulloch's objections. He was confident the British government
would not interfere. As a lawyer, he had been impressed by Bulloch's
success in finding loopholes in the Foreign Enlistment Act and felt
sure that if the British government had been willing to look the other
way in the matter of wooden raiders, it was likely to continue to do so
in the matter of ironclads. Mallory knew he was taking a gamble, but
he considered it a prudent one. Like everyone else in the Confederate
cabinet, he was by that time convinced that Great Britain was as eager
as they were to break the blockade and was on the verge of recogniz-
ing the South. He assured Bulloch that a little additional tinkering
with the Foreign Enlistment Act, so long as it was handled in a judicious manner, was not going to weigh very heavily in Whitehall's deliberations.

On his return to England, Bulloch had opened the subject of ironclads with the Lairds. The two brothers were enthusiastic and immediately committed themselves, but since no money had as yet arrived,
the project remained in the talking stage, and no space had been
cleared in the yard for the construction of the new ships.

Finally, two months behind schedule, the *290* was launched on
Thursday, May 15, 1862. As workmen opened the ways, allowing the

ship to float gently into the Mersey, Harriet Bulloch, who had come over from New York to join her husband, ceremoniously christened the ship *Enrica*. It was only a temporary name, part of the disguise that would help get her out of England, but Bulloch's choice of the name *Enrica* had a sentimental origin. It was the Spanish equivalent of Harriet.

The Lairds were anxious to make up time. No sooner had the *Enrica* come to rest in the Mersey than two steam tugs, stationed at the foot of the ways, took her in tow and moved her to the entrance of the graving dock, where she was immediately warped in and placed over the blocks. She was soon high and dry once more. Even before the dockworkers had fully secured her in her new berth, one of the Lairds' giant derricks began lowering the first heavy pieces of her engines into the hold.

Maguire and his agents continued to keep a close watch on the 290 and send in reports. Three days after the launching, Dudley read, "Her planks were caulked as they were put on; is built of the best English oak that could be obtained and that was picked."

Maguire's operatives had little idea which bits of information might prove to be important, so they included everything they could glean from Laird's work crews. "Every timber in her is fastened with copper bolts 18 feet long and 2½ and 3½ inches in circumference. The stern gear is all copper and brass, in fact, the gentleman who superintended her construction says, 'they could not turn out anything better from Her Majesty's Dock Yards.'"

Sometimes Maguire's bulletins sounded more like promotional broadsides for the Birkenhead works than spy reports. "She is allowed, by nautical gentlemen, to be one of the best boats they ever saw, and the workmanship and materials are of the best that art and skill can put together."

Details, apparently insignificant in themselves, sometimes helped provide a clearer picture of the ship than the larger statistics. "Messrs. Sidderley & Company of William Street have got the order to make the copper [gun]powder cans which are of a new patent. It is a large order, and is to be completed in a month."

———————

While workmen continued to swarm over the *Enrica* (which everyone still called the *290*), busily installing the engines, boilers, and desalination system, Bulloch began the search for an escort vessel that could carry her guns out of British jurisdiction. Toward the end of May, his agents in the south of England located a 350-ton bark named the *Agrippina*, and Bulloch authorized her purchase for £1,400. He ordered her transferred to London, where she could hide in the crowded anonymity of the Isle of Dogs docklands, far from the inquiring eyes of curious Yankee investigators. As soon as the *Agrippina* arrived in London, Confederate agents began loading aboard the formidable 100-pound Blakely rifle that was to serve as the raider's principal battery as well as most of her other guns, ammunition, side arms, and uniforms for the officers and crew. An equally important addition to her cargo was the shipment of 350 tons of coal, which would be transferred to the *Enrica* when the two vessels finally rendezvoused at a location that Bulloch still held secret, somewhere beyond the 3-mile limit.

———————

As had been the case with the *Oreto*, Bulloch was determined that the *Enrica* conform in every detail to British law so long as she remained in English waters, which meant that once again he needed a British skipper in command. Captain Duguid, who had served so well on board the *Oreto*, was no longer available. And this time it was going to be even more difficult for Bulloch to find a man in whom he could place implicit trust, because it was now common talk along the Liverpool waterfront that the United States consul and his agents were offering sizable rewards for the right kind of information about the ship known as number *290* at Lairds. Without question the Yankees would be willing to pay thousands of pounds to an officer of the ship, particularly her captain, who would be willing to give testimony as to the ship's true nature.

The man Bulloch eventually came up with was Matthew J. Butcher, who was a first officer in a Cunard steamship but who had a master's certificate and was therefore qualified to serve as captain. Bulloch had heard of him through an English friend and arranged a meeting. The two men discovered they had met previously in Havana, and after a half hour's conversation, Bulloch felt confident he had found his man. He took Butcher across to Birkenhead, introduced him to the Lairds, and set him to work at once, superintending the *Enrica*'s preparations for sea, arranging for officers, and seeing to the myriad details that by law and custom fall within the office of the commander of a vessel.

Bulloch was taking a very real risk. Butcher was in a position to set himself up financially for life by selling the secrets of the *Enrica*. The fact that he chose not to would earn him Bulloch's undying gratitude and respect.

———

By the middle of June, Dudley was forwarding spy reports into the legation in London on an almost daily basis:

> About 40 or 50 gentlemen went out with her on her trial trip, which was to the Formby Lightship. The Byrnes were there also some from Messrs. Fraser Tronholm [*sic*] & Co.'s firm.
>
> There are two hundred [gun]powder cases for her, sixty of which are delivered and the remainder to be delivered by the end of the week . . . cost £2 each.
>
> Her engines are on the oscillating principle and are 350 Horse Power. . . . Is 1050 tons burthen and when loaded will draw 14 feet forward. Barque rigged, what is termed "Jackass" or "Donkey" rig. Spars &c. very light. Has a lifting fan by steam power. [A reference to the lifting device for the propeller.] Coppered and copper fastened, and is capable of going 15 knots an hour. Her mast yards &c. bright; mastheads, topmastheads, topgallantmastheads, yards &c. tipped with black.
>
> The framework in which the fan works is solid brass castings and weighs from one and a half to two tons. [Another reference to the propeller's lifting device.]

She is now bonding sail and has the ensign flying from her peak and will sail, if possible from here, before eight days from the date of this report. Her guns, if possible, will be Armstrong's patent and of the largest size they can get to work on board.

Armed with Dudley's reports, and concerned that the *290* might sail away at any moment, Charles Francis Adams sent off still another urgent note to Lord Russell. In what had by now become an almost ritualized procedure, the American minister noted that "a new and still more powerful war steamer . . . is fitting out for the especial and manifest object of carrying on hostilities by sea. . . . The parties engaged in the enterprise are persons well known at Liverpool to be agents and officers of the insurgents in the United States." It was this letter that would eventually become the first document in the bitter, decade-long controversy between Great Britain and the United States known as the *Alabama* claims.

Lord Russell once again passed along Adams's note to the Treasury, which oversaw the Customs Office, and in due course a Mr. Morgan, surveyor of her majesty's customs at Liverpool, took the ferry over to Birkenhead to inspect the ship in question. He reported that he and his men were given free access and that "there has been no attempt on the part of the builders to disguise what is now apparent to all, that she is intended to be a ship-of-war." But he found no guns in the ship, so once again the report went back to London that "at present there is not sufficient ground to warrant the detention of the vessel."

Lord Russell confirmed to Adams that the vessel in question was indeed a warship, but because she was unarmed, and was not owned by a belligerent power but by a private individual residing in the Liverpool area, he could not order her seized. The incensed American minister decided it was time to fight fire with fire. If Lord Russell was going to twist British law to suit his own purposes, then Charles Francis Adams would have to find someone who knew how to twist it back again. He engaged the services of Robert P. Collier, QC, an eminent London barrister and one of the most respected legal minds in England.

Toward the end of June, while Captain Butcher was occupied with the last-minute details, James Bulloch was equally busy preparing to assume command as soon as the ship passed beyond the marine league. He had been studying charts and weather records for weeks, weighing the advantages of alternate passages to the open sea and beyond. He had packed up his sword and his new uniforms, which he had never worn publicly, along with his official papers and his commission as a commander in the Confederate States Navy, and stood ready to send everything on board as soon as a sailing date could be determined.

It was at this moment of fulfillment that Bulloch received a crushing blow, in the form of a letter from Secretary Mallory, denying him the command of the new ship. "Your services in England are so important at this time," Mallory wrote, "that I trust you will cheerfully support any disappointment you may experience in not getting to sea. The experience you have acquired renders your agency absolutely necessary." The secretary ordered him to turn the *Enrica* over to Captain Raphael Semmes, who was already on his way from Nassau to take command.

Twenty years later, in referring to this painful letter from Mallory, Bulloch, with typical understatement, noted only that it "greatly disappointed my hopes and expectations."

SIX

The Passmore Affidavit

A
s the personal representative of President Abraham Lincoln, Charles Francis Adams had the plenipotentiary power to command United States military officers to do his bidding. Under normal circumstances, it was highly unusual for a minister to exercise such powers, but in the summer of 1862, circumstances were far from normal. The increasing likelihood that the mysterious ship known as the *290* was about to escape from England, and that the British government would do nothing to stop her, was creating a situation of such gravity that Adams felt he had no choice but to request the aid of the American navy's steam cruiser *Tuscarora*.

So it was that on the morning of July 8, 1862, in his office at the American legation in Portland Place, Adams was pleased to entertain a somewhat puzzled Captain Thomas T. Craven, commander of the *Tuscarora*. Craven had only just dropped anchor at Southampton and caught the early train up to London to learn why it was that Adams had summoned him and his ship to England.

The minister quickly explained the situation at Birkenhead and showed Craven the spy reports on the *290*. He described how the Confederates, hiding behind what he described as spurious technicalities in the Foreign Enlistment Act, had built the ship illegally, how they now planned to smuggle her out of England and arm her at some secret rendezvous, and how Lord Russell, Britain's foreign secretary, who was openly hostile to American interests, was using every means at his disposal to help the rebel ship escape.

Adams assured Craven that he would continue to press the Foreign Office to detain the *290*, but if he failed, it would be up to the U.S. Navy to do what he, as a diplomat, could not. If the *290* got out of Liverpool, would the *Tuscarora* be able to stop her?

Craven considered the matter. It would be easy enough for the heavily armed *Tuscarora* to subdue an unarmed Confederate vessel at sea, but, of course, the *290* was not a Confederate vessel, at least in a legal sense. Technically she was still British and would doubtless go to sea under British colors. It would be unthinkable to attack such a vessel on the open seas, in view of the diplomatic considerations. However, if the *Tuscarora* happened to be steaming in international waters off the west coast of England and, as if by chance, encountered the *290* as she emerged from the Mersey, there was no problem. No direct contact between the two vessels was necessary, no challenge, no confrontation, no shot across the bow, or similar dramatics. All Craven had to do was to keep his quarry within sight. So long as she remained under the guns of the *Tuscarora*, the rebel ship would be unable to proceed to her rendezvous, wherever that might be, at which point she would be forfeit. It was not a perfect plan, and the rebels might find some way to escape in a storm or in the dark of night, but it was certainly worth trying.

As was almost always the case when naval matters coincided with diplomatic considerations, there were complications. To make Craven's plan work, the *Tuscarora* would have to remain at Southampton, so as to be in constant telegraphic communication with London and Liverpool, ready to pounce the moment the *290* made her move. But legally, under the terms of the Queen's Proclamation of Neutrality, the *Tuscarora* could not remain in port longer than twenty-four hours, unless Craven could find some way to legitimately prolong her stay. He told Adams he was confident that he could arrange with the Royal Navy for permission to continue in port for minor repairs, but to do so, he might have to pull some strings. He would have to get back to Southampton immediately. With the minister's blessings, he left before lunch to return to his ship.

Adams was pleased. The presence of the *Tuscarora* strengthened his hand substantially and gave him a powerful new trump to use in the increasingly high-stakes contest in which he found himself engaged with Lord Russell.

———————

Charles Francis Adams was a dour, humorless Boston Brahmin, fifty-four years old, bald as an egg. His face wore a perpetual frown of anxious concentration. He was the scion of one of the most distinguished families in America, a man who took his patriotism with utmost gravity. His heritage was unique. He was the son of the sixth president of the United States, John Quincy Adams, and the grandson of the second president, John Adams. Therefore, he had grown up with an almost proprietary attitude toward the United States and considered America's moral welfare and political improvement a personal responsibility.

In his efforts to elevate and improve his country, he had championed many political causes. The one closest to his heart was the crusade against slavery, the South's "peculiar institution," which he saw as America's greatest evil. Like many in the North, he saw his country's current agony as the inevitable consequence of its most shameful moral flaw.

Adams had been a congressman when the war began and had actively sought the ministerial appointment to the Court of St. James's, in the belief that he was particularly well suited to the mission. Both his father and grandfather had held the same post, the nineteenth-century equivalent to ambassador, and each had met with considerable success. Adams felt he could do as well, in part because he believed he had a strong rapport with what he presumed were British sympathies. For many years he had admired Britain's unflagging efforts to stamp out the international slave trade. His voluminous correspondence with antislavery leaders in England had convinced him that Britain would sympathize with the North in its dispute with the slave-owning South and that his own antislavery record would stand well with her leaders. It therefore came as a shock, when he first arrived in London, to discover the virulence of the anti-Union sentiment he encountered. Wherever he went, the overwhelming majority of the people who actually ran Britain—even members of the intellectual and artistic communities, including the likes of Thomas Henry Huxley and John Ruskin—stood solidly against the North and, by extension, on the side of the South. Adams was astonished and dismayed. How could the same people who led the fight against the slave trade support the slave owners of America? He was appalled by what he saw as their blatant hypocrisy.

In the year since his arrival, Adams had encountered what he perceived to be active support of the South almost everywhere he looked. Nowhere had Britain's deceitful double-dealing been more apparent to him than in Whitehall's handling of the Confederate shipbuilding program. Adams, who had a deep reverence for the law, was personally outraged by what he saw as Lord Russell's deliberate misinterpretation of his own country's Foreign Enlistment Act. As Adams saw it, a clear and unambiguous act of Parliament had been deliberately distorted and misinterpreted, solely to help the South purchase a navy that it could not build for itself. American lives were being put at risk and American treasure sacrificed because of British greed.

But now Adams had Captain Craven and the *Tuscarora* on his side. With any luck a heavily armed American cruiser might help him check what he saw as the scandalous machinations of an arrogant and duplicitous Britain.

As June turned to July, James Bulloch was caught between conflicting imperatives. On the one hand, he wanted the *Enrica* gone. The longer she remained in Liverpool, the greater the chance that the American minister would find some way to force the British to detain her. His agents had alerted him to the continued presence of the *Tuscarora* in Southampton, and he had no doubt the Yankee cruiser was being held there to foil any escape. But for all his desire to get the ship away, he did not want to send her off without Captain Semmes, who had not yet arrived from Nassau.

Bulloch had long since determined that once the *Enrica* and her tender, the *Agrippina*, left England, they would rendezvous at Terceira, an obscure little island in the Azores, in the middle of the Atlantic. He considered the possibility of sending the two ships off without waiting for Semmes but decided it might be more dangerous to have them at the rendezvous, unarmed and unattended, where a passing United States cruiser might by chance fall upon them, than to keep them in England, where even if they were discovered, no enemy could touch them.

On July 21 Bulloch wrote Mallory a letter that closed with an interesting observation. "I am looking most anxiously for the arrival of Captain Semmes. His ship is all ready, and the American minister is besieging the Foreign Office with demands to stop her." How did Bulloch know of the American minister's actions? The letter confirms that Bulloch's intelligence network had actually penetrated the corridors of Whitehall and that he had an authoritative source at the highest level of the British government, who was providing him with information on American diplomatic efforts.

While he waited for Semmes, Bulloch concentrated on his other project, his two new ironclads. The money to build them had finally arrived, and the Lairds had cleared two sites in their yard and commenced construction.

Bulloch was excited by the prospect. The enormous importance of the ironclads had helped assuage his bitter disappointment at losing command of the gunboat to Semmes. The strategic potential of the new ships was impossible to overstate. They could actually be the means of winning the war. They were to be truly formidable battleships, designed under Bulloch's close supervision, after consultation with experts from the Royal Navy, who provided extensive, if unofficial, support. In size the new vessels were to be comparable to the *Enrica*—220 feet overall length, 42 feet extreme breadth, 15 feet draft, powered by 350-horsepower engines—but there the resemblance to the commerce raiders ended. The ironclads would be virtually invulnerable, sheathed in armor plate from the waterways of the upper deck to well below the waterline, and their steel skins would be up to 4½ inches thick and backed by as much as 12 solid inches of teak. Instead of the traditional broadside batteries, each vessel was to carry three gun turrets, equipped with enough firepower to destroy almost anything afloat. At the bow, hidden 3 feet below the surface of the water, each carried a 7-foot-long steel ram, or "piercer," capable of disabling and sinking an enemy ship without so much as firing a shot. With the advent of steel and steam, the most dreaded weapon of the ancient Roman triremes had been reinvented, more formidable than ever. Bulloch, who was not given to wishful thinking, was confident that nothing in the Yankee fleet could stand up to these two vessels.

Such state-of-the-art warships would not come cheap. Each ship was priced at £93,750 (unarmed), or about half a million dollars, twice as much as the commerce raiders. The Confederate government, although strapped for cash, had already forwarded the first installment, with the second promised to arrive before the actual completion dates of the ships, which were scheduled to be ready for sea in March and May of 1863.

Matthew Maguire's agents had not as yet spotted the two ironclads, but they continued to maintain their close watch on the *290*: "Captain Bullock went over to Tranmere in the same boat as I this morning (Wednesday, July 2nd, 10 o'clock boat). Went to Laird's Yard and on board the gunboat, where he seemed to be giving orders to the men, who saluted him and who went and appeared as if they were carrying his orders into effect, whatever they were."

Almost as soon as Bulloch engaged an English captain for his ship, Maguire's people knew about it: "Captain Butcher is to command her, Mr. McNair is to be Chief and Mr. Black second engineer. She may go out any tide and sail in two or three hours' notice."

In general their reports were accurate, although sometimes they got the detail wrong: "According to the chalk marks on the deck she will carry three swivel guns. She has three double ports each side:—viz, forward amidships and aft, she will carry sixteen guns in all, swivels included." In fact, the ship was designed to carry two swivels and six broadside guns, for a total of eight.

On occasion a report was dead wrong, such as the one that suggested she was shipping weapons: "On Friday, July 18th, two dozens of swords were taken on board the '290.' . . ." This was definitely inaccurate. Bulloch had issued standing orders that not so much as a penknife was to be allowed to remain on board, for fear of providing the American consul with an excuse to claim that the ship was "armed."

Increasingly the reports suggested the date of departure was imminent: "The stores are all on board. Some person of the name of Barnett is shipping the crew by direction of Captain Butcher."

Thomas Dudley continued forwarding Maguire's reports to Adams, who routinely sent them on to Lord Russell, each accompanied by another demand that the ship be forcibly restrained. His notes were met at first with polite indifference, but over time, as the information in the reports became increasingly difficult to ignore, the Foreign Office began sending them on to Sir John Harding, the queen's advocate and the government's senior law officer, for his opinion.

There the matter rested, until July 21, when Maguire came up with a bombshell: he had found a credible witness who was willing to confirm in a sworn statement that the *290* was a Confederate warship.

The affidavit of William Passmore remains one of the key pieces of evidence in the voluminous history of the *Alabama* claims and was the first document presented by the Americans that the British could not ignore.

It opened with a clear, unambiguous identification of the deponent:

> I, William Passmore, of Birkenhead, in the county of Chester, mariner, make oath and say as follows:—
>
> 1. I am a seaman, and have served as such on board Her Majesty's ship 'Terrible,' during the Crimean War.

It then defined the nature of the mysterious vessel at the Birkenhead yards and identified the English captain whom Bulloch had hired:

2. Having been informed that hands were wanted for a fighting vessel built by Messrs. Laird & Co., of Birkenhead, I applied on Saturday, which was I believe the 21st day of June last, to Captain Butcher, who, I was informed, was engaging men for the said vessel, for a berth on board her.

The third paragraph clearly established the Confederacy's connection to the ship:

3. Captain Butcher asked me if I knew where the vessel was going. In reply to which I told him I did not rightly understand about it. He then told me the vessel was going out to the Government of the Confederate States of America. I asked him if there would be any fighting; to which he replied yes; they were going to fight for the Southern Government. I told him I had been used to fighting vessels, and showed him my papers. I asked him to make me signal man on board the vessel, and, in reply, he said that no articles would be signed until the vessel got outside, but he would make me signal man if they required one when they got outside.

The next two paragraphs described an unequivocal violation of the Foreign Enlistment Act, which specifically prohibited enlisting British subjects into the service of a foreign belligerent power:

4. The said Captain Butcher then engaged me as an able seaman on board the said vessel at the wages of £4 10s. per month; and it was arranged that I should join the ship in Messers Laird and Co.'s yard on the following Monday. To enable me to get on board, Captain Butcher gave me a password, the number "290."
5. On the following Monday, which was I believe the 23rd day of June last, I joined the said vessel in Messrs. Laird and Co.'s yard at Birkenhead, and I remained by her until Saturday last.

The sixth paragraph defined the ship's warlike features:

6. The said vessel is a screw steamer of about 1,100 tons burthen, as far as I can judge, and is built and fitted up as a fighting ship in

all respects. She has a magazine, and shot and canister racks on deck, and is pierced for guns, the sockets for the bolts for which are laid down. The said vessel has a large quantity of stores and provisions on board, and she is now lying at the Victoria Wharf, in the Great Float at Birkenhead, where she has taken on about 300 tons of coal.

The seventh paragraph showed that she was seriously undermanned:

7. There are now about thirty hands on board her, who have been engaged to go out in her. Most of them are men who have previously served on board fighting ships, and one of them is a man who served on board [a vessel of] the Confederate Government, to act against the United States, under commission from Mr. Jefferson Davis. Three of the crew are I believe, engineers, and there are also some firemen on board.

In the penultimate paragraph, Passmore finally ties Bulloch into the picture:

8. Captain Butcher and another gentleman have been on board the ship almost every day. It is reported on board the ship that Captain Butcher is to be the sailing-master, and that the other gentleman, whose name I believe is Bullock, is to be the fighting captain.

To wrap things up neatly, Passmore provides hearsay evidence to support the American claim for violation of section 7:

9. To the best of my information and belief, the above-mentioned vessel, which I have heard is to be called the "Florida," is being equipped and fitted out in order that she may be employed in the service of the Confederate Government in America, to cruise and commit hostilities against the Government and people of the United States of America.

(Signed) WILLIAM PASSMORE.

Here was red meat, indeed.

Undoubtedly Passmore had been paid handsomely for his cooperation, and almost certainly he had been carefully coached and directed
by Dudley and Maguire, but such facts in no way diminished the
power of his affidavit. Here, on paper, duly sworn to, was the account
by a native Briton and a Royal Navy veteran, who was a registered
member of the 290's crew, defining the subterfuge of the ship's pur-
ported British registry, her warlike character, her direct links to the
Confederacy, and stating as fact that her captain was openly recruiting
British subjects to serve a foreign power.

S. Price Edwards, the customs official before whom Passmore had
sworn his oath, shrugged off the affidavit, repeating the ritual mantra
that since the 290 was unarmed, he could take no action. But the next
day, when a copy of the affidavit reached the American legation in
London, Minister Adams recognized its unique power and rushed a
copy over to his new lawyer, Robert P. Collier, QC, and asked for an
opinion.

Collier's response was swift and unambiguous. He wrote the American minister that it was his opinion that if the collector of customs at
Liverpool did not immediately detain the vessel described in the affidavit, "the Foreign Enlistment Act . . . is little better than a dead letter" and, importantly, that the U.S. government would have "serious
grounds for remonstrance" against Great Britain.

Adams received Collier's note on Thursday, July 24, and sent it off
triumphantly to the Foreign Office the same day, along with a nota-
rized copy of Passmore's affidavit.

SEVEN

Escape

Throughout the final week of July 1862, the ship known as the *290*, lying at dock 4 in the Laird yards, remained the primary focus of attention for numerous government officials in both Liverpool and London. Some of the officials were American, some British. All were acutely aware of the explosive diplomatic issues relating to the ship. Later those same officials would sift through the records to justify the actions they either took or did not take during that week. The Americans would uncover what they perceived as evidence of high crimes and misdemeanors, while the British would find nothing more than a few examples of innocent bureaucratic bumbling. It would take ten years to decide which interpretation would prevail.

What follows are the facts, as far as they are known.

Friday, July 25, 1862

Lord John Russell, Britain's foreign secretary, always maintained that he failed to act in a timely manner to stop the *290* from leaving England because he did not receive the note from the American minister, enclosing the Passmore affidavit and Collier's opinion, until Saturday, July 26. He claimed that the ensuing confusion and indecision on the part of the British government could all be traced to that simple fact.

Adams was always suspicious of Russell's allegation. In the 1860s the British postal system operated at a speed and efficiency far exceeding today's standards, and to suggest that a letter sent from Portland Place to Downing Street—a twenty-minute walk—should require two days for delivery strained credulity. Adams felt sure that his letter arrived at the Foreign Office on Friday, not Saturday, and that the delay in Britain's response was deliberate.

Adams was probably right about the delivery date but quite possibly wrong about the reasons for the British government's slow response. It is likely that his letter, along with its important enclosures, arrived at the Foreign Office in the early mail on Friday morning, July 25, where, under normal conditions, Russell would have read it soon after reaching his office. But as it happened, on July 25, before Russell even had the opportunity to read his mail, he was informed of a distressing and totally unexpected event. Sir John Harding, the queen's advocate and the man responsible for formulating the government's legal response to the American complaints about the *290*, had suddenly and without warning suffered some sort of severe nervous seizure. As Russell later described it to Adams, Harding was stricken "with symptoms of the brain." Whether it was a stroke or something else, Harding was completely incapacitated, and Russell was told it would have been folly to consult him on any matter until he recovered.

Later that day, when Russell finally had an opportunity to read Collier's opinion, he immediately recognized its importance. Collier directly challenged the "no guns" interpretation of the Foreign Enlistment Act that Russell and other British officials had adopted to justify their inaction, and his blunt warning that if the ship left port, her escape would give the United States "serious grounds for remonstrance" gave Russell genuine concern. That sort of thing could lead to all kinds of disagreeable consequences. Russell and his undersecretary, Austen Henry Layard, debated whether to bypass the stricken Harding and send Adams's time-sensitive letter to the Crown's other law officers, the attorney general and the solicitor general. While they debated the issue, an entire day was lost.

Saturday, July 26, 1862

British government offices were open only half days on Saturdays. When Lord Russell arrived on the morning of July 26 and learned that Harding's condition had not improved, he ordered that Collier's opinion be sent to William Atherton, the attorney general. Russell then left for the weekend, retiring to his estate outside London and leaving the undersecretary, Austen Layard, to handle the details. Layard set the office clerks to copying out the relevant papers, proofreading them, and notarizing them, all of which took time. When the paperwork was completed, he forwarded the documents to the attorney general's office by messenger, to ensure delivery, but it was too late. The attorney general had already left for the weekend and would not see Collier's opinion until the following Monday.

In Liverpool, on that same Saturday, James Bulloch received a secret message from someone in the Foreign Office, an unnamed informant whom he described only as "a private but most reliable source." The message warned him that it would not be safe to leave his ship in Liverpool another forty-eight hours. To this day no one knows who sent the message or how it reached him. Almost certainly it was the same person who had been sending him reports on the increasingly urgent American demands addressed to the Foreign Office.

Bulloch immediately hurried across the river to the Laird yards. He had been working intimately with the brothers for more than a year, and while no words of a confidential nature had ever passed between them, he knew that they were fully aware of who he was and what he was doing. But even in the emergency, Bulloch was careful to maintain the charade they had all adopted in the early days of their business relationship. He said nothing about the need to get the *Enrica* out of Liverpool, but told them only that he had decided on the need for additional "sea trials" for his ship and requested that they make the necessary preparations. The brothers were given to understand that the ship might not be returning from these particular "trials."

Bulloch then contacted Captain Butcher, with whom he could be

more open. He instructed him to complete his stores and be ready to
come out of dock on Monday's tide. Butcher pointed out that the ship
was seriously undermanned and that there were only about thirty
crewmen on board. Bulloch promised to take care of the problem.

Bulloch had decided to disguise the *Enrica*'s departure as a ship-
board party, the same ruse he had used with the *Oreto*. He spent the
rest of the day making out a guest list, hiring musicians for the gala,
and ordering sufficient refreshments.

It was not until 1884, almost twenty years after the war, that James Bulloch revealed that he had a "private but most reliable source" in Whitehall. But long before then, it had been widely rumored in London that
the Confederates had a direct link to top government officials, and
there was considerable speculation as to who the mole might be.

In 1865 Charles Francis Adams noted in his diary that there was
reason to suspect that a young clerk in the Foreign Office named Vic-
tor Buckley was the conduit by which government secrets were leaked
to the Confederates. By 1872 his suspicions had shifted to S. Price Edwards, the collector of customs in Liverpool, an official who was
known to be openly sympathetic to the Southern cause and who, it
turned out, was also a speculator in cotton and therefore eager to promote the independence of the Southern states. But by the year 1900,
long after most of the participants in these events were dead, Adams's
eldest son, a noted historian who had studied the question intensely,
was forced to admit that after a careful examination of all the relevant
papers, there was "no evidence whatsoever to support the charge"
against Edwards.

More recently it has been suggested that Austen Layard, the undersecretary for foreign affairs, may have sent the message. Layard was
an active participant in all the events leading up to the escape of the
290, and his sympathies were strongly anti-Union. He was a member
of Parliament and closely associated with leaders of the pro-Southern
faction in the House of Commons. Equally compelling, he represented
dockside London, and his constituents included English shipowners

who would profit directly from the destruction of the American merchant fleet.

But there has always been another, far more prominent suspect. Immediately following the eventful week under consideration, it was whispered in London that Lord John Russell himself may have helped the Confederates get their ship away. Over the years many have ridiculed such a possibility, declaring it unthinkable. Russell was, after all, one of the grand old men of Victorian politics, an illustrious figure, comparable to Disraeli and Gladstone. It was Russell who introduced the first great Reform Bill of 1834, the landmark legislation that initiated the gradual process by which Great Britain became a democracy. And it was Russell, an aristocrat, who led the fight to abolish the corn laws, another great popular move. He was also one of the founders of the Liberal Party. The idea that a man of such stature would secretly involve himself in the escape of a Confederate gunship appeared to many as totally out of character, and ludicrous.

Yet there is another aspect of Russell's politics that supports the suspicion that he may have found ways to secretly help the Southern cause. Russell was never a disinterested observer of the American Civil War. For months before the war actually broke out, he made it clear that he wanted the South to win its independence. It was to Britain's advantage in terms of both trade and political power to see the United States split into two competing nations, but his arguments were not based solely on national interest.

Time and again, both publicly (in his statements in Parliament) and privately (in conversations with Charles Francis Adams and others), he expressed his sincere conviction that the American republic was permanently broken and that it was folly to try to mend it. He asked, how could the North possibly hope to win? Even in the unlikely event that the Federal forces could somehow manage to conquer the enormous expanse of the Confederacy, how could the government in Washington possibly hope to reconstruct the Union? How could it return the seceded states to their former equality with those that had conquered them? The North should let the South go, he urged. All the bloodshed and suffering was in vain.

There was another overriding reason for Russell's support of the Confederacy that could be summed up in a single word: cotton. The manufacture of cotton textiles was Britain's single largest industry, and after a year of civil war in America, with no fresh supplies of raw cotton arriving from the South, the English Midlands were beginning to suffer a devastating cotton famine. Factory owners were closing their mills, and literally hundreds of thousands of operatives would soon be thrown out of work. Every week the press was filled with heartbreaking accounts of fresh suffering and privation. With the end of summer, the unemployed cotton operatives and their families would soon be threatened by starvation and cold. The British government was working diligently to alleviate the hardships and doing everything in its power to develop new sources of raw cotton in India, Egypt, and the Caribbean, but it was obvious to everyone that the best and fastest way to overcome the crisis was to reopen trade with the South. Unfortunately such a step was inimical to the interests of the Northern states, and Russell was reluctant to take any overt action for fear that Washington would respond by marching into Canada, invading the Bahamas, or initiating some other catastrophe.

But to a mind as subtle as Russell's, there were always options. He was a student of history and understood that sometimes a nation could achieve seemingly impossible goals simply by the judicious manipulation of circumstances. In his own lifetime, he had seen the little island nation of Great Britain take control of the entire subcontinent of India, with all its wealth and millions, virtually without effort, simply by having a few of the right people in the right place at the right time. Could the British government find some equally effortless way to alleviate the hardships created by the cotton famine? It was not an idle question.

For all his feigned ignorance of the provenance of the ship called the *290*, Russell knew perfectly well that she was built to be a Confederate cruiser and that she was constructed in defiance of Britain's own laws. He simply chose to look the other way, since it was to Britain's advantage for the Confederates to build a navy that might break the blockade and bring about the resumption of the flow of cotton. The only real danger lay in the risk of war with the United States, and Russell kept a close watch on that possibility.

As a trained lawyer, he understood clearly that the Passmore affidavit, and Collier's opinion on it, severely limited the British government's options. He would be forced to order the 290 seized. The only question was one of timing. The fortuitous illness of Sir John Harding had slowed the decision-making process and had given someone the opportunity to send a warning to the Southerners to get the ship to sea. In his memoirs Russell admitted that the 290 "ought to have been detained during the four days I was waiting for the opinion of the law officers," and the fact that she was not "was my fault as Secretary of State for Foreign Affairs." While his statement is hardly an admission of guilt, it can be read as a veiled admission of complicity.

That Saturday afternoon in Birkenhead, William Passmore ran into some shipmates from number 290, as he described in a subsequent affidavit:

> Met the seamen, say thirty in number, on Saturday coming down Canning Street from the ship, playing "Dixie's Land" on a fife, concertina and a cornopean and they all took 4.30 Woodside boat for Liverpool. They still kept playing "Dixie's Land" on board the ferry boat. Went up to one of the men and asked him when he thought the ship would be going out. He told me that their bed clothes and bedding were on board and the boatswain had told those who intended to go in her, to hold themselves in readiness for early next week.

The identity of the 290 could hardly be considered much of a secret if her crew knew of it and chose to advertise it through the streets of Liverpool.

Sunday, July 27, 1862

Sunday was a day of rest for most of Britain, but in certain parts of the kingdom, the crisis over the *290* continued to generate feverish activity.

At his home at 3 Wellington Street, in the outlying district of Liverpool known as Waterloo, James Bulloch spent the day on paperwork, most importantly drafting secret instructions to Captain Butcher, in Birkenhead; to Captain Alexander McQueen of the *Agrippina,* in London; and to two Confederate naval officers, Lieutenant John Low and Acting Paymaster Clarence Yonge, who would be sailing with Butcher. The four different sets of instructions, each of them long and detailed and quite unique, demonstrate very clearly just how complicated an operation Bulloch was orchestrating.

On behalf of the Confederate Navy, Bulloch was sending two British captains on a clandestine operation of extreme sensitivity and complexity. The two men, who had never met and who did not even know each other's names, were to rendezvous in a foreign port with which neither skipper was familiar. They were to find each other under circumstances of such a covert nature that it was necessary to devise not only secret signals but even false names. Once the two captains made contact and had transferred the materials from the one vessel to the other, they were to stand by and wait for still a third captain (Semmes). This third captain, whom neither of the first two knew, was to take charge. All three captains were to be helped by the two Confederate officers, Low and Yonge, who would be traveling incognito. Low and Yonge would have their own responsibilities, many of them as difficult to carry out as those assigned to Butcher and McQueen.

The fact that Bulloch managed to compose the four sets of orders in the midst of the turmoil related to getting his ship out of England says much about his skill as an administrator. The surviving letters, with their precision and seemingly effortless clarity, provide an insight into Bulloch's character and are among the most interesting documents in the crowded records of what would become the explosive international quarrel known as the *Alabama* claims.

In London, at the American legation, Charles Francis Adams, unaware that his latest note to the Foreign Office had at last moved the British government to take action of a sort, continued to study Collier's opinion, hoping to find further reasoning to bolster his case against the Confederate gunship.

Elsewhere in London, the crisis over the 290 had become the most urgent issue of state, and with Russell away in the country, his undersecretary, Austen Layard, had brought up the matter directly with the prime minister, Lord Palmerston, who decided it was imperative that Sir John Harding, the queen's advocate, be removed from the picture. Immediately after leaving 10 Downing Street, Layard rode straight to the home of the unfortunate Harding and suggested to Sir John's wife that her husband resign. She begged him tearfully not to remove him from office indelicately, as it would be a severe blow to his pride. Layard decided it could wait another day.

Outside London, amid the tranquil hills of Surrey, Lord John Russell enjoyed an untroubled Sunday.

Monday, July 28, 1862

Monday would be an exceptionally busy day for James Bulloch. It began early, at his office at Fraser, Trenholm, where he met with Captain Butcher and the two officers who were to accompany him in the *Enrica*, his clerk Clarence R. Yonge, who was to be the ship's paymaster, and John Low, a trusted aide who, despite his Scottish nationality, held a commission in the Confederate Navy and would serve as Butcher's first officer.

Bulloch gave orders to Butcher to get the *Enrica* out of dock on the morning flood tide and arrange for mooring in deeper waters, where she could escape at a moment's notice. He directed John Low to hire a tugboat for the following day, to accompany the *Enrica* on her "trials," and told Clarence Yonge to get his gear on board immediately and prepare to take up his new duties. Yonge's final assignment as Bulloch's clerk was to make copies of the numerous letters, orders, and lists that Bulloch had written over the weekend, including his own orders.

Bulloch then turned his attention to the bark *Agrippina*, lying at London with 350 tons of coal and the *Alabama*'s guns in her hold. He telegraphed his London agent, ordering him to complete final preparations for departure, and by mail sent orders to Alexander McQueen, the *Agrippina*'s captain. Bulloch was aware that he was taking a significant chance with McQueen. He barely knew the man and had no particular reason to trust him. He was forced by necessity to reveal to him highly secret information that could very easily end up in the wrong hands. He would have preferred that McQueen wait until he was in international waters before reading his orders, but that would have been impractical. Instead, in his covering letter, he directed him to keep the orders sealed until his ship had left her moorings. McQueen was a British subject, and Bulloch knew that by giving him explicit instructions, he was dangerously skirting restrictions imposed by the Foreign Enlistment Act. It would take McQueen a day to get down the Thames to the channel, during all of which time the *Agrippina* would still be in British waters, and the fate of the *Enrica* would be entirely in his hands. It was not a comfortable situation for Bulloch, but he knew that there were times when it was necessary to sail close to the wind, and this was one of them.

In London, Attorney General William Atherton arrived at his office Monday morning to find Collier's opinion on his desk, awaiting his immediate attention. As soon as he read it, he recognized that the government had to stop the *290*, but not wishing to take sole responsibility for such an important step, he asked the queen's third-ranking law officer, Solicitor General Roundell Palmer, to read the opinion as well. Early that afternoon the two men discussed the situation and agreed that, first thing Tuesday, they would press Lord Russell to seize the ship.

Tuesday, July 29, 1862

On Tuesday morning James Bulloch, accompanied by his wife, Harriet, and a scattering of other Southern agents in Liverpool, including the partners of Fraser, Trenholm and their ladies, boarded an early ferry for the journey across the Mersey, where the *Enrica* lay at anchor off the Seacombe dock. Bulloch was pleased to note that the crew was already putting up the bunting and other decorations for the party.

Soon afterward John Low arrived on board the steam tug *Hercules*, which he had engaged to serve as ship's tender for the day. With all guests on board and the *Hercules* in attendance, Captain Butcher ordered up steam. A little after nine o'clock, with flags fluttering gaily from the rigging, the *Enrica* raised anchor and made her way in stately fashion down the Mersey, across the bar, and into the Irish Sea. Because the ship was expected to return to port after her "sea trials," there were no speeches, no farewells, and none of the formalities associated with clearing customs. Thus, quietly and without ceremony, the ship that would soon become the cruiser *Alabama* departed Liverpool. Matthew Maguire, watching from shore, hailed a cab and headed for the U.S. consulate.

From late morning until early afternoon, the ship made a show of undergoing "sea trials," steaming back and forth between the Liverpool bell buoy and a lightship anchored to the northwest. Bulloch noted with satisfaction that she was making an average of 12.8 knots.

She was still seriously undermanned. There were enough hands on board for the day's exercises but nowhere near enough to handle the ship when she went into action. The lack of crew was the single most important detail still to be dealt with, and Bulloch made arrangements to take care of the matter the next day.

That same morning, in London, the attorney general and the solicitor general addressed an urgent message to Lord Russell, advising him in the strongest possible terms to immediately detain the *290*. The evidence submitted to them "makes it reasonably clear that such vessel is intended for warlike use against citizens of the United States, and in the interests of the (so-called) Confederate States. . . . We therefore recommend that, without loss of time, the vessel be seized by the proper authorities."

That afternoon, when the message was received at the Foreign Office, a telegram was promptly dispatched to Liverpool ordering the *290* detained. By that time, of course, she was gone.

───────────

Around three o'clock that afternoon, in the Irish Sea, James Bulloch announced to the assembled partygoers that due to unforeseen circumstances, it would be necessary to continue the trials overnight, and as a result the *Enrica* would not be returning to port as expected. He invited his guests to join him on board the tug *Hercules,* for the return to Liverpool.

Before transferring to the tug, Bulloch had a word with the pilot, George Bond, who had been hired to serve during the "trials," and asked if he was familiar with Moelfra Bay, a sheltered anchorage on the north coast of Anglesey, some 45 miles west of Liverpool. Bond said he was, and Bulloch told Butcher to take the ship there and wait. He would be back the next day with additional crewmen.

Later, as Bulloch and his guests were returning to port in the *Hercules,* he engaged the tug for the following day and arranged for the captain to meet him at the Woodside Landing in Birkenhead at six in the morning.

───────────

The return of the *Hercules* without the *290* was noted by Matthew Maguire's spies, who immediately relayed the alarming news to Thomas Dudley. The American consul, remembering the escape of the *Oreto,* wired the American minister in London, informing him of the facts.

Dudley was puzzled. He knew the *290* had only a skeleton crew on board. Where would she pick up the rest of the hands she would need? He guessed—correctly, as it turned out—that she might still be in the area, hidden somewhere off the coast, waiting for additional crew. If such were the case, he guessed—again correctly—that Bulloch would have engaged a shipping master (or "crimp," as they were known on the waterfront) to round up more sailors. He told Maguire to find out.

In London, Adams received the news of the *290*'s departure and immediately telegraphed Captain Craven, of the USS *Tuscarora* at Southampton, mentioning the *290*'s shortage of crewmen. Craven speculated that the rebels might pick up additional hands at the next convenient British port, which would be Queenstown on the southern coast of Ireland. He decided to head there to intercept the *290*.

Wednesday, July 30, 1862

At six o'clock on Wednesday morning, the tug *Hercules* arrived as scheduled at the Woodside Landing, on the Birkenhead side of the river, and began taking on board some assorted timbers for the *290* that had been left behind in the confusion of her hurried departure. Also on hand was the crimp whom Bulloch had hired to find extra crewmen, along with thirty or forty bleary-eyed seamen accompanied by a large and noisy crowd of women. The crimp had scoured the Merseyside brothels and public houses to find his recruits, but their women had insisted on coming with them and were demanding a month's pay in advance from the sailors before they would let them go.

One of Maguire's people took in the scene and quickly left to notify Dudley. The consul, on learning that the tug was shipping timbers, leaped to the conclusion that they might be gun mounts, which would be highly incriminating evidence. Despite the early hour, he hurried over to the office of the collector of customs and complained that the *Hercules* was loading illegal contraband for the *290*. He demanded that the tug be inspected, and grudgingly the customs officer agreed.

When Bulloch arrived at the Woodside Landing, he found a mob scene. The crimp was standing on the dock, trying to placate a crowd of groggy men and angry women, while the captain of the *Hercules* was in the hold of the tug with the collector of customs, poking around in the dark, looking for nonexistent gun mounts.

Bulloch's mind was on Moelfra Bay and the *Enrica*, which was at risk as long as she remained in British waters. After all his efforts to get his ship past the marine league limit, he had little patience with the sailors' women or with some customs official's mistaken suspicions about gun mounts. After it became evident that there was indeed no contraband on board the tug, Bulloch ordered the crimp to get his recruits onto the *Hercules,* making it clear that the women were to remain behind. The shipping master demurred and explained apologetically that it was not to be that simple. The women had a hold on the sailors, he explained knowingly, and they would not let the men go without them. It was a case of take all or none. He was powerless to interfere.

Bulloch was angry, but he was no fool. He had spent a lifetime on waterfronts and could recognize the badger game when he saw it. He could also see that in this case he was the mark. The crimp depended on the women of the docks to round up his crews for him, and he would not risk their anger by denying them their profit. Bulloch was about to remonstrate when an aide handed him a telegram alerting him to the fact that the *Tuscarora* had just left Southampton. This meant he had even less time than he had thought. Annoyed but resigned, he allowed the women on board and directed the captain of the *Hercules* to make for Moelfra Bay.

———————

For most of those on board, the six-hour voyage out to the *Enrica* must have been a particularly miserable trip. It rained most of the way, and there would have been little shelter on a tugboat that was never designed to carry passengers. The sixty or seventy sailors and their ladies would have been squeezed onto the deck, unprotected from the elements, and left to pass the time as best they could, while Bulloch found drier and more comfortable accommodations with the captain in the wheelhouse.

Around three o'clock in the afternoon, the tug at last caught sight of the *290,* riding peacefully at anchor off the pretty little Welsh village of Moelfra. Within the hour the *Hercules* was alongside of her.

There had been nothing to eat on board the tug, and the cold, miserable passengers were hungry and, as Bulloch noted, "not in suitable frame of mind for business." Bulloch needed them in a more receptive mood if he was to sign them on as crew. To jolly things along before the negotiations started, the steward was ordered to prepare a substantial supper with "a fair but safe allowance of grog, to add zest and cheerfulness to the meal."

While his guests were at dinner, Bulloch repaired to the captain's cabin with Butcher, to go over his final instructions.

At the end of the dinner hour, and after giving the men an opportunity to enjoy a pipe with the last of their grog, Bulloch called them aft and, mounting a raised platform so that he could be seen and heard by all, explained vaguely that he needed some hands for a possible run to Havana, perhaps touching at an intermediary port. Bulloch was aware that the ship was still within the 3-mile limit, so he carefully avoided any mention of the Azores or of the far more interesting future planned for the *Enrica*. But if he was indefinite about the details of the cruise, he was explicit about the money. Each man who signed on would receive one month's pay in advance, paid down on the capstan head. If the ship did not return to England, he assured them that they would be sent back free of charge or that some other satisfactory settlement would be made for them.

When he was through, the men broke up into small groups to discuss his offer. Over supper they had conferred with the older hands who had already signed on at Birkenhead and were fully aware of the true nature of the ship. After brief consultations among themselves, all but two or three agreed to sign on. Each one of the volunteers came down to the captain's cabin in turn, accompanied by his lady, to sign the articles of agreement. After each sailor was safely signed on, the woman with him received the stipulated advance "on the capstan head," as promised.

It was nearly midnight before all the paperwork was settled. The wind had shifted to the southwest and was blowing in spiteful squalls. Heavy rain fell. The tug was still lying uneasily alongside. "It seemed inhospitable to turn the ladies out on such a night," Bulloch recalled, "but there was no accommodation for them on board, and there were reasons why the *Enrica* should not be found in Moelfra Roads on the next morning."

Clutching their wages, and probably just as glad to be heading home, the women clambered on board the *Hercules* for the long, cold voyage back to Liverpool.

Thursday, July 31, 1862

Soon after the tug left, the weather grew worse, and by one o'clock in the morning, it was raining heavily, the wind blowing hard from the southwest. Bulloch stared into the blackness and thought of the USS *Tuscarora*. She would almost certainly touch at Queenstown for news and, finding none, would assume that the ship she was hunting would follow the usual route to the Atlantic and lie off Tuskar, in the St. George's Channel, to intercept her. But she would wait in vain, because Bulloch had ordered Butcher to go "north about," over the top of Ireland.

The weather continued to worsen. "It was not an opportunity such as a prudent seaman would choose to leave a safe roadstead and venture into the Irish Sea," Bulloch remembered, but he had little choice. At 2:30 in the morning, he gave the order to get under way, and the *Enrica* stood out of the bay, sails furled, under steam power alone.

By eight o'clock in the morning, with the sun hidden behind leaden clouds, the ship was off the small island known as the Calf of Man, just to the south of the Isle of Man. The sky began to clear and the wind to drop, and with a middling fresh breeze, Butcher decided to set all sail. Much to Bulloch's pleasure, the ship bowled along at 13½ knots. At noon they passed South Rock and steered north along the coast of Ireland. Eventually the wind fell, and they lost the effect of the sail. Once again powered by steam alone, they entered between Rathlin Island and Fair Head and, at six in the evening, stopped the engines off the Giant's Causeway, on the rocky shores of County Antrim. It was time for Bulloch to return to Liverpool to await the arrival of Captain Semmes. Butcher hailed a fishing boat, and Bulloch and the pilot, George Bond, went ashore in a pelting rain, leaving Captain Butcher to proceed in accordance with his instructions.

Once ashore, the fishermen directed them to a local inn, where they found lodgings for the night. "During the evening it rained incessantly," Bulloch recalled, "and the wind skirled and snifted about the gables of the hotel in fitful squalls. Bond and I sat comfortably enough in the snug dining-room after dinner, and sipped our toddy, of the best Coleraine malt; but my heart was with the little ship buffeting her way around the rugged north coast of Ireland."

Friday, August 1, 1862

On Friday morning, August 1, the USS *Tuscarora* arrived off Point Lynas and looked into Moelfra Bay. She found nothing there to engage her special attention.

Dr.? by H.B. Hall, Jr. N.Y.

Raphael Semmes, fiery captain of the Alabama. *His crews called him "Old Beeswax," in reference to his mustache.*

II

Semmes

EIGHT

Terceira

Nine days after escaping across the top of Ireland in a storm, Captain Butcher and his mystery ship had sailed more than 2,000 miles to the south and west and raised the island of Terceira, in the Azores. To the weary hands of the *Enrica*, the island presented a picturesque sight, rising, as if alone, out of the green Atlantic. Almost every square foot appeared to be under cultivation. Little white houses with red tile roofs dotted the mountainside and continued down to the water's edge. As the ship approached the land, shore breezes carried a welcoming scent of citrus and semitropical perfumes to the sailors on deck.

Terceira, like all the Azores, was a Portuguese possession. The principal harbor of the island, Porto Praya, lay open to the east, and the town itself was situated on the northern curve of the bay. In accordance with his written orders, Captain Butcher entered the roadstead and dropped anchor in 10 fathoms of water. From the quarterdeck he scanned the area for anything that might be the tender *Agrippina*. There were a number of other vessels in the harbor but nothing that fit the description Bulloch had given him. Butcher ordered a white English ensign flown from the after shroud of the main rigging, which was the prearranged signal by which he was to identify his ship to the *Agrippina*.

Butcher's arrival had not gone unnoticed on shore. Shortly after he

dropped anchor, a boat put out from the town carrying uniformed officials of the Portuguese government. Butcher watched the boat as it
approached. One of the men would be the local health officer. He
would want to know from what port the ship had sailed and whether
she was carrying any communicable diseases. The other man would
want to know the vessel's nationality and identity, and the reason for
her visit to Praya. Almost all of their questions were ones that Butcher
did not want to answer—at least, not with any degree of accuracy—lest
word get back to the local American consul. The United States government almost certainly maintained a consulate in Praya, as it did in
any port in the world where American vessels were likely to call, and
if the consul was any good at his job, he would be curious about
Butcher's arrival. He would pester the officials as soon as they returned
to shore, to learn what he could about the stranger. It was unlikely that
word of Butcher's escape from England would have reached Praya as
yet, but there was always the remote possibility that the consul had
been alerted to look for any suspicious steamer out of Liverpool, in
which case Butcher did not want to advertise the fact that he commanded the notorious vessel known variously as the *290* and the *Enrica*. As the little boat carrying the two officers came alongside,
Butcher ordered a ladder let down for them and prepared to rechristen
his ship with still another false identity.

When the officials arrived on the quarterdeck, Butcher graciously
welcomed them on board the brand-new steamship *Barcelona* (a lie),
recently built in London (another lie) for the Spanish government
(still another lie). He was on his way to Havana, he explained, to deliver her to her new owners and had stopped at Praya to resupply (three
more lies). The information was duly registered, and then the health
officer, after some preliminary questions and a quick inspection, ordered the ship placed in quarantine for four days, as a routine safety
precaution.

There was little now for Captain Butcher to do until the arrival of
the *Agrippina*. On the voyage out, he had observed some leaking in the
ship's upper works, so he gave orders to his officers to set the crew to
caulking, while he settled back in the privacy of the captain's cabin to
wait.

On August 13, the day the quarantine was lifted, an American whaling vessel, the *Rising Sun,* sailed into Praya and anchored near Bulloch's ship. In itself this was not a cause for concern. Later that day, however, when several of Butcher's officers went into town and ran into some of the *Rising Sun*'s men in a waterfront saloon, the *Barcelona*'s paymaster, Bulloch's ex-clerk Clarence Yonge, let slip the true nature of their ship. It was a clumsy mistake and could have led to serious problems, but fortunately the whaling captain took no notice and soon brought his ship back out to sea. The incident was quickly forgotten by everyone except John Low, the first officer, who would have cause to remember Yonge's lack of discretion on another, more troubling occasion, several months later.

It was not until August 18, a week after Butcher's arrival, that the *Agrippina* finally arrived in the harbor. She had been delayed by gales. Captain McQueen spotted Butcher's secret signal and hoisted his own in response. When that signal was in turn answered by Butcher, the tender came alongside, and the two British captains exchanged greetings.

The following morning, again in accordance with Bulloch's instructions, the two vessels were lashed together, and the crews were put to work off-loading the guns, gun carriages, ammunition, side arms, uniforms, and other fighting gear from the *Agrippina* into the larger ship.

Later that morning, while they were still completing the transfer, an unidentified steamer appeared on the horizon. Butcher warily trained his glass on her and followed her progress as she entered the harbor. By now there had been sufficient time to disseminate the news of his ship's escape from Liverpool, and Butcher was growing increasingly anxious for her safety. There was a real chance that the stranger now approaching might be a United States naval vessel, in which case his ship would be totally defenseless, lashed as she was to the *Agrippina,* with all her new armament scattered about on the deck, unsecured and useless. Butcher was much relieved when a signal from the stranger told him that she was, in fact, the ship for which he had been waiting.

The chartered British steamer *Bahama* stood into Praya harbor carrying both James Bulloch and Captain Raphael Semmes, along with a number of officers whom Semmes was bringing with him from his old command and thirty-seven sailors whom he had hired off the Mersey docks and hoped to enlist for service on his new cruiser.

Raphael Semmes had already gained considerable fame as commander of the *Sumter,* the Confederacy's first commerce raider. She had been a leaky makeshift, with insufficient power and a rotting hull, and Semmes had been forced to abandon her in Gibraltar when her engines gave out, but not before he had captured eighteen Yankee merchantmen and made himself a Confederate hero and something of an international celebrity.

His public reputation was that of a swashbuckler, but he was in fact a starchy, fastidious naval officer. He was fifty-two years old and carried himself with a great sense of gravity and an almost exaggerated military bearing. His fierce expression was set off by his most notable feature: a luxuriant black mustache that stood out on either side of his face to such an extent that his crews had long ago nicknamed him "Old Beeswax."

Semmes had been looking forward to his new command with undisguised excitement. Ever since their departure from Liverpool the week before, he had listened hungrily to Bulloch's descriptions of his ship, and throughout the voyage, he had pestered Bulloch like a small boy with questions on every aspect of her construction, rigging, armament, and design. When at last the *Bahama* reached Terceira and Semmes caught sight of his ship for the first time, he was instantly enchanted and did not take his eyes off her from the moment her hull rose above the horizon. "She was indeed a beautiful thing to look upon," he would later rhapsodize. "Her model was of the most perfect symmetry, and she sat upon the water with the lightness and grace of a swan." Here was a vessel to quicken his fiercely partisan spirit, a ship in which to perform noble deeds for his beloved South.

Raphael Semmes was a man of deep and abiding passions, and none was deeper or more abiding than his hatred and loathing of the North-

ern states, their people, and their institutions. His disdain for the
North bordered on obsession. Yankees, he pointed out, were the descendants of Puritan Roundheads, and they had produced a society of
narrow-minded, money-grubbing people of limited taste and imagination. The South, on the other hand, had been founded by English cavaliers, blue-blooded members of a nobler race, who had created a
genteel, cultivated society, centered on an appreciation of the finer
things in life. His highly romanticized, blinkered faith in the superiority of Southern values, combined with his great energy, keen intelligence, and hunger for glory, would soon burnish his reputation and
add fresh luster to his fame.

About 11:30 that morning, as soon as the *Bahama* dropped anchor,
Captain Butcher came on board to bid the Confederates welcome to
Terceira. He reported that his crew had already transferred all the
heavy guns and many of the paymaster's stores out of the *Agrippina*
and into the ship that he could now openly refer to as the *Alabama*. It
was a matter of considerable satisfaction to be freed from the con-
straints of the Foreign Enlistment Act and the shadowy presence of
Yankee spies, but everyone was aware that the need for secrecy remained. Publicly the ship would have to retain the temporary name of
Barcelona as long as she stayed at Terceira, and Butcher would have to
continue to serve as her nominal captain, at least until she was properly armed and manned. But those were transitory restrictions.

Semmes was naturally eager to go on board his new command, and
he and Bulloch arranged to return to the *Alabama* with Butcher. Once
they were on deck, the *Alabama* exhibited little of the serene beauty
Semmes had admired from afar. She may have looked like a swan at a
distance, but she was hardly swanlike that afternoon. The whole ship
was in a state of chaotic disarray, with guns, gun carriages, crates of
shot and shell, coils of rope, barrels of beef and pork, and boxes and
bales of paymaster's, gunner's, and boatswain's stores stacked carelessly
on the deck.

Semmes ignored the confusion. He was delighted with the ship itself. With Bulloch as his guide, he went over the *Alabama* fore and aft,

stopping to examine a piece of unfamiliar machinery or to ask a question or to peer into some storage space.

He was highly appreciative of the disappearing funnel, which would allow him to disguise his ship at will, and equally impressed with the desalinization equipment, which would provide fresh drinking water without the need for frequent landfalls. He watched with great interest a demonstration of the retracting screw, which would improve the ship's performance under sail. He complimented Bulloch on the superb workmanship throughout and was grateful for one very modern personal luxury, a flushing toilet. He was particularly charmed by the motto set into the large double steering wheel just forward of the mizzen: AIDE-TOI ET DIEU T'AIDERA ("Help yourself and God will help you"). Semmes, who considered himself something of a linguist, found the motto particularly appropriate. When it came to Yankee ships, he indeed planned to help himself.

It was highly satisfactory to have such a fine ship beneath his feet, but Semmes was fully aware that he still had problems to contend with and the most pressing one was that of manpower. The *Alabama* had plenty of officers ready and eager to give orders, but there was as yet not one sailor on board to obey them. Semmes decided to address the situation then and there. On returning to the *Bahama*, he called together the thirty-seven sailors he had brought out from England for a feigned voyage in a nonexistent vessel. After formally releasing them from the contract they had previously entered into with him, he invited them to sign up again, this time for a voyage in the Confederate cruiser *Alabama*. He waved proudly toward his new ship, anchored nearby. He spoke of the war the South was fighting for independence, explained his plans for commerce raiding, and described the good pay and the chance for prize money.

Not all of his listeners were impressed. At least some of them were aware that for all of Semmes's victories in the *Sumter*, not one of his captures had been brought before an admiralty court and declared a legal prize, which meant the *Sumter*'s crew had received no prize money whatsoever. Semmes had been forced to burn his captures, in the hope that a grateful Confederate government would award prize money after the war . . . which, of course, presumed that the South would gain its independence.

In spite of Semmes's patriotic blandishments and his rosy picture of future riches, only about half of the sailors he had brought out in the *Bahama* agreed to ship with him. The others hung back, and Semmes could only hope they were simply angling for a better deal. Disconsolately he noted in his journal, "There are perhaps some sea lawyers among them influencing their determination."

Toward evening Semmes moved his baggage to the *Alabama* and took over the captain's cabin, directly below the quarterdeck. Once in his quarters, he carefully unpacked his trophies from his cruise in the *Sumter,* including the eighteen American flags he had taken from his victims, each marked with the name of the unhappy vessel and the date of capture, as well as their chronometers, which had the twin advantages of being valuable instruments and easily transportable.

For the next two days, while Semmes familiarized himself with the details of his new ship, Bulloch supervised the installation of the guns. There were six 32-pounders, so called because they fired projectiles of that weight, and two larger-caliber pivot guns. The 32-pounders were mounted on wheeled carriages and could be moved about the deck, although only with considerable effort, since each one, with its carriage, weighed more than 2 tons. The even heavier pivot guns required permanent installation. One, the 7-inch Blakely rifle, was positioned directly before the bridge. The other, an 8-inch smoothbore, was placed between the main and mizzen masts. The forward gun fired 100-pound projectiles, 7 inches in diameter, and its bore was rifled, or grooved, to increase range and accuracy. The aft gun was unrifled and fired 68-pound projectiles, 8 inches in diameter. While the boatswain and his gang fitted train and side tackles to the 32-pounders, Bulloch supervised the carpenter and gunner, who, with the assistance of the chief engineer, put down the circles, or traverses, for the two big guns.

The rest of the men were set to the necessarily filthy and onerous work of coaling the *Alabama*. Her 350-ton fuel supply had been nearly exhausted in the flight from Liverpool, and it would be necessary to re-fill her bunkers almost entirely, in part from the *Agrippina* and in part from the *Bahama*. The men formed into a bucket brigade, which snaked from the hold of the *Agrippina* down into the *Alabama*'s bunkers. It took them three days, working long into the night, to com-plete the job, by which time every surface of the ship was covered with coal dust.

All day Saturday it rained, as the crew continued to sort out the mess on deck and down below. There was grime and rubbish every-where. By evening, by dint of hard labor and perseverance, the crew had at last brought some sort of order out of chaos. The guns were now properly mounted and secured, the stores had all been unpacked and distributed to the different departments, and the coal bunkers were once again replenished. The *Agrippina* had been sent on her way.

Now that she had her guns, the *Alabama* had at last assumed her in-tended configuration. The great weight of her battery and provisions lowered her silhouette and deepened her draft, and she had finally be-come the warship that she was designed to be. The aliases that had served to mask her true identity for more than a year—*290, Enrica, Barcelona*—were now something that belonged in her past.

The following morning, August 24, dawned bright and clear. Semmes ordered all hands turned out, and after a few hours of scrubbing and holystoning the deck, the ship was shining and spotless. As Semmes described his new command, echoing the same gender-specific lan-guage Bulloch had employed when he still expected to become her skipper, "she looked like a bride, with the orange wreath about her brows, ready to be led to the altar."

Semmes wanted one more ceremony to confirm the transformation of his glamorous new warship. He ordered up steam, and the *Alabama*, still wearing the Union Jack at her peak and protected by the British registry that had guarded her on the open seas, moved out to sea un-der a cloudless sky, accompanied by the *Bahama*.

When the vessels were safely past the marine league and therefore beyond the authority of the Portuguese government, Semmes ordered his ship hove to and piped all hands to the quarterdeck. Dressed for the first time in his formal gray uniform, he mounted a gun carriage and read aloud to his respectful audience his commission from Jefferson Davis, appointing him captain in the Confederate Navy. He then read the orders from the secretary of the navy, Stephen Mallory, directing him to assume command of the *Alabama*.

While he read, two small lashed bundles were raised slowly and with great ceremony, one to the peak and the other to the main royal masthead. A quartermaster stood by the British colors, while a gunner, lock-string in hand, stood by the weather bow gun, and a band of musicians stood at the ready on the quarterdeck, all eyes on Semmes as he spoke. At the conclusion of his reading, Semmes signaled dramatically with his hand. The gun went off with a bang, the British flag was respectfully lowered, and the lashings were jerked free from the two bundles, revealing the Confederate Stars and Bars at the peak and the ship's pennant at the main royal masthead. The air was rent by a deafening cheer from officers and men alike, and the band broke into a stirring rendition of "Dixie." A short distance away, the *Bahama* fired her own signal gun and cheered the men on board the *Alabama*.

The purpose of the commissioning rites had been more than ceremonial. Semmes was anxious to get the crew in a proper mood for another recruiting speech. He was very much aware that without the cooperation of almost all of the crewmen on board, his ship would be hopelessly undermanned and his position perilous in the extreme. Most of the men had come out from Liverpool in the *Enrica*, a ship that no longer existed, and, by the terms of the articles they had signed, were now free to return to England. Semmes was only too aware that, of those he had brought out in the *Bahama*, only half had responded to his call for volunteers the previous Wednesday. As matters stood, he had fewer than twenty crewmen under contract to handle a ship designed for a crew of 120. He needed to convince almost all the remaining sailors now on board to sign up with him. Even then the ship would be undermanned.

Most of his listeners had not heard his previous enlistment speech, so he went over much of the same material, but this time with more details, as if to win their hearts as well as their minds and to appeal as much to their sentiments as to their self-interest.

He told them of the war in America and described in some detail how the long-suffering Southern states, weaker than the overbearing Northern states, had dissolved the ties that bound them to the North and declared themselves sovereign and independent. The *Alabama*, he told his audience, would be fighting the battles of the oppressed against the oppressor. He enumerated the advantages they might expect to reap from enlisting to serve on the *Alabama*. The cruise would be one of excitement and adventure, he promised. There would be good food and grog twice a day. They had a fine, British-built ship beneath them, and she would visit many parts of the world, where they could expect liberty on proper occasions. The ship would undoubtedly destroy many of the enemy's vessels.

Semmes was understandably nervous when it came time to bring up the subject of money. Both he and his listeners were aware that the sailors had him pretty much where they wanted him. If they chose not to accept his offer, he had no place else to go. He sensed that many had been unimpressed with the pay he had offered the previous Wednesday, so now he announced a considerably sweetened package, which was almost double that of the Royal Navy. He offered seamen £4 10s a month; petty officers £5 and £6, depending on rank; and firemen £7—and was much relieved when the announcement was greeted with shouts of "Hear! Hear!"

He invited all those desirous of signing new articles to report at once to the paymaster, Mr. Clarence Yonge. To his delight and relief, almost all the sailors hurried forward. In the end, Semmes managed to sign up a total of eighty-two men. He could have used more, but it was a very good start.

What Semmes described dismissively as his "stump speech" was the first and last time he ever addressed the crew in anything other than an authoritarian manner. "Democracies may do very well for the land," he noted dryly, "but monarchies—and pretty absolute monarchies at that—are the only successful government for the sea."

The remainder of the day was spent making out half-pay tickets for the sailors' wives and sweethearts, drawing drafts for small amounts payable to relatives and dependents for such of the sailors who wanted them, and paying advance wages to those who had no pay ticket to leave or remittances to make.

It was eleven o'clock at night before everything was in order and Bulloch could step over the gangway for the last time to return to the *Bahama* and to England. He and Semmes bid each other farewell, and as soon as the *Bahama* had turned away, Captain Semmes mounted to the bridge and directed the engineer to let his fires go down. For the present they would proceed by wind alone. He ordered the propeller hoisted out of the water and drawn up into its specially built well, and set the ship on a course to the northeast.

A contemporary sketch of the Alabama, *certified as accurate by Raphael Semmes. She displays the Stars and Bars, which was subsequently replaced by the more familiar Southern Cross (Confederate battle flag), quartered on a white field.*

NINE

First Blood

Dawn on the morning following the departure of the *Bahama* broke cloudy, with a fresh wind and rough sea. The *Alabama* was rolling and tumbling about, to the discomfort of everyone on board, none more so than her captain, who, like the great Nelson, was subject to seasickness.

There was still much to do on board ship. Semmes ordered the *Alabama*'s first lieutenant, John McIntosh Kell, to supervise the berthing, messing, quartering, and stationing of the men, while he went belowdecks, where everything was still in disarray. Spare shot boxes and other heavy articles were sliding about unsecured, and the ship continued to leak considerably through her upper works. Despite the efforts of the Lairds to use only the best materials throughout, some improperly seasoned wood had found its way into the decks, which had then been caulked at Birkenhead in the cold northern winter. Now, in the warmer climate of the Azores, the ship's seams were beginning to gape. Semmes had his officers organize the men into teams to secure the materials belowdecks and stuff the leaks with fresh caulking. The eternal clanking of the pumps, which could be heard throughout the ship, made everyone aware that their new vessel continued to take on water.

Observing the general sense of confusion, Semmes decided he needed a little more time to set things right before going on the hunt. He gave orders that for the next few days the *Alabama* should avoid those areas where she would be most likely to come across other vessels.

Organizing the gun crews was a top priority. Training the men, which might have been a difficult and time-consuming process, turned out to be a simple matter. A goodly number of the ship's hands were veterans of the Royal Navy, and some were even familiar with the very guns on board the *Alabama*. Semmes was pleased to see crews exercising the pivot rifle with an ease and efficiency that could be gained only from long experience.

During the *Alabama*'s brief shakedown cruise, Semmes was also gratified to discover that his new ship proved a good sailer under canvas. This augured well, for it meant he would be able to use his engines sparingly. He was very aware that the *Alabama* carried enough coal for about eighteen days of steaming. Bulloch had specified oversized bunkers in order to get around the restrictions on refueling set out in the Queen's Proclamation of Neutrality, but Semmes had his own reasons for avoiding going into port. His experience in the *Sumter* had taught him that frequent port stops for refueling left a trail that made it easy for the enemy to track him down. By relying primarily on his sails, Semmes could avoid such frequent landfalls and was free to remain at sea for months on end, crossing thousands of miles of ocean, without the American navy having a clue as to his whereabouts.

A week or so after her commissioning, Semmes finally felt ready to take the *Alabama* into action. Bulloch had selected Terceira as his rendezvous point because of its remote location, but the Azores had another distinction as well, and Semmes now planned to take full advantage of it. During the late months of summer, the waters around the islands were the primary feeding grounds for many of the whales of the North Atlantic, and as a result, the area was a magnet for the whaling ships that preyed upon them. Almost all of the whalers were American, and Semmes knew that they would be concentrated east of the Sargasso Sea. He decided to take the ship there, to see what he could find.

On the morning of September 5, with the weather cloudy and the wind light and from the east, the *Alabama* lay off the islands of Pico and Faial. The lookout, high overhead, called down to report that he had spotted a ship on the horizon, lying to with her foretopsail to the mast. Semmes, who made it a practice to sail under false colors, ordered the flag of the United States hoisted to the ship's peak and approached within a few hundred yards of the other vessel. As expected, she was a whaler. A huge sperm whale, recently caught, had been made fast alongside and partially hoisted out of the water by the ship's yard tackles. The crew was busily flaying blubber and rendering it in huge pots on deck. The captain, who was supervising, paid only cursory attention to the *Alabama* as she approached. In answer to Semmes's flag, the whaler identified herself by running up her own Stars and Stripes and thereby sealed her fate.

It was as simple as that. Without a chase, with hardly any effort or ingenuity whatsoever, other than the simple trick of displaying false colors, the *Alabama* prepared to claim her first victim. It was less a conquest than a mugging. In what would soon become a familiar ritual, Semmes sent his second lieutenant, Richard Armstrong, off in a boat to bring back the unfortunate captain of the whaler along with his ship's papers. She turned out to be the *Ocmulgee,* out of Edgartown on Martha's Vineyard. Nothing could exceed the blank stare of astonishment on the face of the Yankee skipper as he climbed on board the *Alabama* and saw the United States colors come down and the Confederate flag unfurled. Semmes described the man as a genuine specimen of the Yankee skipper: long and lean, "and as elastic apparently, as the whalebone he dealt in." The crestfallen captain told Semmes that when he saw the *Alabama* approaching wearing U.S. colors, he assumed she was a gunboat sent out by the American government to protect the whale fleet. Semmes sympathized and ordered his men to remove the *Ocmulgee*'s crew.

Semmes had reason to ponder the captain's comment. America's whaling fleet represented a major national industry, and it was indeed remarkable to him that the United States Navy offered no protection to it. Unlike ships of commerce, whalers were obliged to congregate within small, well-known spaces of ocean and remain there for weeks at a time, while the whaling season lasted. Such vessels, clustered together, would naturally attract the attention of Confederate cruisers. There were not more than a half dozen principal whaling stations on the entire globe, and it would have taken only a single U.S. warship at each of those locations to provide sufficient protection.

———————

It took several hours to ferry the *Ocmulgee*'s crew of thirty-seven men over to the *Alabama* and to loot the captured vessel of some beef, pork, and small stores that the paymaster decided he could use. Semmes made a special point of preserving the ship's flag and her chronometer. Both were sent down to the captain's cabin, to join the similar souvenirs of earlier conquests.

As a final step before destroying his capture, Semmes sent his first officer, Lieutenant Kell, across to the *Ocmulgee* to estimate her value. Semmes was confident that a grateful Confederate Congress would award him and his men the prize money they had earned, as soon as the South won the war, and in order to support the claim he planned to present to the Congress, he made it a practice to assess the value of each of his victims before burning them.

Kell returned with a combined estimate of $50,000 for the ship and the barrels of whale oil in her hold. Some of the other officers, undoubtedly with an eye to their own share of the prize money, protested that $50,000 was a far too conservative figure and argued that the oil alone was worth more than $100,000, but Semmes accepted Kell's figure.

———————

It was nine o'clock at night by the time all details had been properly attended to, including the housing of the prisoners, and Semmes decided to wait until morning to burn the *Ocmulgee*, since the light from the flames might alert other whalers in the area to his presence. Shortly after dawn on September 6, he sent a team of experienced "incendiaries" across to the captured whaler, which still had the carcass of the dead sperm whale hanging from her side. The men, armed with axes, fanned out to either end of the ship and began chopping up whatever furniture they found and forming it into two piles, one in the cabin, the other in the forecastle. They added whatever bedding and other combustible material they could find and then poured butter and lard from the galley pantry over the rubbish. The officer in charge, after ordering everyone back to the boats, threw a match into the piles and dashed for safety.

The *Ocmulgee,* her timbers saturated with whale oil from years of service, went up in a spectacular blaze. Even before the boat carrying the incendiaries reached the *Alabama,* the flames from the fire were licking the topsails of the doomed ship. Any other whalers that might have seen the smoke from over the horizon would have assumed it to come from a passing steamer.

Later that day the lookout spotted another sail, and the *Alabama* immediately returned to the chase. Once more Semmes ordered the American flag hoisted, and as they approached the intended victim, he directed his helmsman to bring his vessel to her windward side, to give him the weather gauge, in case the other captain tried to make a run for it. In an earlier age Semmes would have forced the stranger to heave to by firing a shot across the bow, the time-honored means of demonstrating that the chasing vessel had the other ship under her guns. But modern technology had made such proof irrelevant. With the advent of steam power and long-range guns, the traditional shot across the bow was a waste of ammunition. Instead, Semmes simply fired a blank cartridge. It was less expensive, and as he knew would be the case, it immediately brought the stranger about.

In response to the *Alabama's* Stars and Stripes, the stranger hoisted the tricolor of France. Now it was up to Semmes to decide, was she really French, or was her flag simply a ruse, like the one fluttering over the *Alabama?* He drew close enough to speak to the other ship, which as it happened was indeed French and bound for Marseilles. Semmes wanted to keep the identity of his own ship a secret for as long as possible, so as not to alert the American shipping interests, so he identified himself as a United States cruiser. The two vessels parted company, with the Frenchman continuing on an easterly course, while the *Alabama* bore away to the north, headed for the island of Flores, the westernmost of the Azores.

One of the major problems Semmes had to contend with as a commerce raider was the housing and feeding of his prisoners. The captured vessels of the enemy, as well as their cargoes, were legitimate prizes of war and could be sold or otherwise disposed of in any way the raiding captain chose. But the crews of such vessels were another matter. By the internationally accepted rules of war, they were to be treated humanely and returned to freedom as quickly as possible. The crew of the *Ocmulgee* had been on board the *Alabama* for only two days, a relatively brief period, but Semmes was eager to get rid of them. On reaching Flores, he brought his ship close in to the little village of Lagens, on the south side of the island, and hove to. The prisoners were bundled into the *Ocmulgee*'s three whaleboats, which had been brought away from the prize specifically for that purpose, and sent into the land. Semmes knew they would be able to sell their boats to the islanders, which would give them enough cash to get by until they made contact with the American consul on the neighboring island of Faial.

Hardly had Semmes managed to disembark his prisoners when there was a cry of "Sail ho!" from the masthead. He immediately wore away in pursuit of what looked like a schooner, fast disappearing over the horizon. For a change he ordered English colors hoisted to throw the stranger off guard. The *Alabama* was about to take her second prize.

During her first two weeks of active hunting, the *Alabama* was a fox among the chickens, moving relentlessly from one victim to the next, in an almost wanton display of destructive ferocity. In that brief period, all of it spent in and around the Azores, she captured and burned a total of ten American vessels, mostly whalers, with an aggregate value of $232,000, an amount virtually equal to her entire purchase price. Any further conquests would be in the profit column.

The tenth victim was another whaler, the *Elisha Dunbar*, twenty-four days out of New Bedford. The capture was made in foul weather, and

Semmes's description of the burning of the *Elisha Dunbar* provides a vivid word picture of what must have been a sight worthy of Dante.

The scene was "wild and picturesque beyond description," he wrote.

> The black clouds were mustering their forces in fearful array. Already the entire heavens had been overcast. The thunder began to roll, and crash, and the lightning to leap from cloud to cloud in a thousand eccentric lines. The sea was in a tumult of rage; the winds howled, and floods of rain descended. Amid this turmoil of the elements, the *Dunbar*, all in flames, and with disordered gear and unfurled canvas, lay rolling and tossing upon the sea. Now an ignited sail would fly away from a yard, and scud off before the gale; and now the yard itself, released from the control of its braces, would swing about wildly, as in a madness of despair, and then drop into the sea. Finally the masts went by the board, and then the hull rocked to and fro for a while, until it was filled with water, and the fire nearly quenched, when it settled to the bottom of the great deep, a victim to the passions of man, and the fury of the elements.

The description tells us as much about Semmes as it does about the fiery end of the *Elisha Dunbar*.

TEN

The Grand Banks

By the end of September, Raphael Semmes had left the mid-Atlantic far behind and moved the *Alabama* 1,200 miles to the west and north, where she was now crusing off the coast of Newfoundland. She was alternately battling the region's stormy winds, and ghosting in and out of the patches of thick, wet fog generated by the arctic air coming off the Canadian landmass, and interacting with the perpetual warmth of the Gulf Stream.

The *Alabama's* fiery debut in the Azores—during which she had, in the course of a fortnight, crippled the American whaling fleet operating in the North Atlantic—was a source of considerable satisfaction to Semmes. But it had only whetted his appetite for even richer and more valuable plunder. After struggling with the frustrations and inadequacies of the *Sumter* for the better part of a year, he was eager to make up for lost time. Now, with a proper warship under his feet, he meant to make the most of his opportunities.

Semmes had come north to ambush the Yankee grain ships, the fleet of cargo vessels that would soon be parading up the coast on their way to Europe, laden with the recent harvest from the western states. He knew they would pass the Grand Banks before turning east, and he was eager to catch as many as possible before word of his presence on the high seas reached New York and Boston and caused the shipowners to take evasive action.

So eager was Semmes to get the *Alabama* on station in time to catch the grain ships that he left the Azores still carrying fifty or sixty prisoners and was now looking for someplace to dump them. Prisoners were always a nuisance, and the large number he was now carrying was particularly irksome. They had to be fed and looked after, and their presence kept the ship from operating efficiently. There was nowhere on board to put so many men, and in consequence they were always in somebody's way. The obvious place to house them was the berth deck, but that was already given over to the ship's crew, and it would be inconvenient and possibly dangerous to set aside a portion of that space as a holding pen for a lot of angry and miserable passengers. Instead, Semmes had ordered his men to stretch out some spare sails amidships, forming a large, open-sided tent, under which the prisoners could huddle for shelter. There he kept them, night and day, manacled and with an armed guard placed over them. They were provided with makeshift bedding, and those who could ignore the chill air and constant dampness slept on gratings laid on the deck. If the shelter was not entirely waterproof, most of the prisoners, who were accustomed to a rough life, managed well enough. Semmes, whose disregard for Yankees was matched by his casual disdain for sailors in general, considered it adequate protection. "Ordinarily they were very comfortable," he observed dismissively, but admitted with amusement that "sometimes, during the prevalence of gales, they were, no doubt, a little disturbed in their slumbers by the water."

Early on the morning of the third of October, after several days without sighting another ship, two sails were simultaneously reported by the lookout at the masthead—one directly ahead, the other on the lee bow. Both vessels were standing in toward the *Alabama*, and all Semmes had to do was to await their arrival. There would be no need for a chase. As the strangers' hulls lifted above the horizon, he was pleased to note that they were both large ships, with a profusion of tapering spars and white canvas. Better still, each one exhibited the distinctive hull design, rigging, and cut of sail that was recognized around the world as characteristic of Yankee ships. Semmes was confident they were both Americans.

The wind was light, and the ships came on with all sails set, from truck to rail. Semmes made no effort to alter course. Both vessels would pass sufficiently near with no effort on his part. Semmes remarked to one of the officers on the bridge that the strangers apparently had no suspicion of their danger. He ordered a British flag raised to the peak and waited. When the vessels were nearly abreast, and only a few hundred yards distant, the *Alabama* suddenly wheeled, fired a gun, and hoisted the Stars and Bars. There were immediate indications of surprise and confusion on board both vessels. The Confederates could see men running about the decks, and for a few moments there was an evident indecision as to what steps to take. But with the *Alabama's* guns pointed at them, it did not take the masters of either ship long to get a realistic view of the situation. The only sensible option was to surrender, and this they did by hoisting their colors, in both cases American flags, and heaving to their ships.

Semmes called out to his own men to shorten sail, and the boarding crews lowered a couple of quarter boats and set off to the prizes. One of them proved to be the *Brilliant,* out of New York and bound for London, laden with flour and grain; the other, the *Emily Farnum,* also from New York, was bound for Liverpool, with a similar cargo.

––––––––––

Raphael Semmes was able to bring a unique set of skills to his command of the *Alabama.* Not only was he a highly qualified naval officer, he was also a lawyer. As a young man he had discovered that life in the peacetime United States Navy included long periods on shore without assignment, and without pay. To make ends meet, and to take care of his family, he had read law and was eventually admitted to the Maryland bar. For much of his life, he had alternated between a life at sea and a life in the law courts, and was equally adept at both.

As it happened, his deep knowledge of legal matters proved to be a highly practical asset for a commerce raider and made it possible for him to navigate the intricacies of international law at sea, which were often subtly obscure.

As was his regular practice after a capture, Semmes turned his cabin into a private admiralty court, where he could interview the ships' captains, examine their official papers, and decide their fate. Semmes sat at a large table, with his law books within easy reach, and with his personal clerk, William Breedlove Smith, standing by to take notes, and prepared to sort through the various titles of ownership, bills of lading, consular certificates, and other legal papers documenting the ownership not only of the ships but also of their cargoes.

There were three factors that would govern his judgment. If it was discovered that a ship and her cargo were owned by Americans, he would declare her fair prize and destroy her. If, on the other hand, a ship's papers showed that she was owned by neutrals, he would have to let her go, even if her cargo was American-owned. But if the ship turned out to be American, while the cargo she carried was owned by neutrals, the ship might be fair prize, but he could not destroy her, since doing so would involve destroying the neutral cargo. He would be forced to release the ship "on ransom bond"—that is, he would get the ship's master to sign a legal document attesting to the value of the ship and promising, at the end of the war, to pay to the Confederate government a sum equal to the value.

Captain Hagar, of the *Brilliant,* was the first to be ushered into Captain Semmes's cabin to have his ship's papers examined. Semmes leafed through the documents and announced cheerfully that since they showed that the ship was American, and that her cargo was also apparently American, he was taking her as prize and would destroy both ship and cargo.

Captain Hagar remonstrated, claiming that the tons of flour, wheat, beef, pork, bacon, and butter on board his vessel had been purchased in New York by British nationals, for delivery in London, and were therefore neutral-owned. Semmes understood Hagar's personal situation in regard to the *Brilliant.* He knew that the captain was part owner of the ship, that he had invested everything he had in her, and that she represented all his worldly goods. Hagar had designed his ship, supervised her construction, and served as her only captain. Semmes listened briefly to Hagar's entreaties but quickly ran out of patience.

"Do you think I am only a damned fool, not to burn the ship?" he countered sharply, cutting Hagar short and dismissing him impatiently.

The papers presented by Captain Simes of the *Emily Farnum* showed unequivocally that she, too, was an American ship, but Semmes was irritated to see that the documentation on her cargo told a different story. There was no question that the goods she was carrying were on English account. Semmes was particularly anxious not to upset the British government, so with the greatest reluctance, he was forced to release the *Farnum*, but only after getting her captain to sign a ransom bond payable at war's end.

Although he could not burn the *Farnum*, Semmes was able to make use of her as a passenger ship. He transferred all his prisoners to her, including the crew of the *Brilliant*. (Three members of the *Brilliant*'s crew, all Englishmen, elected to remain with the *Alabama*, tempted by the high pay and chance for adventure on board a Confederate raider. Semmes noted that the new recruits were "more valuable to us than the prizes, shorthanded as we are.")

At sunset Semmes sent off his team of incendiaries to the *Brilliant* to set her on fire, and by seven in the evening, she was in flames fore and aft. The wind fell still, and the sea, as glassy as a millpond, reflected the light from the blaze to the horizon and beyond. Both the *Alabama* and the *Farnum* were becalmed and remained in the area until the following morning.

George Fullam, the English master's mate on board the *Alabama*, wrote in his journal, "I never saw a cargo burn with such brilliancy, the flames completely enveloping the masts, hull and rigging in a few minutes, making a sight as grand as it was appalling." Fullam had been unmoved by the burning of the whale ships off the Azores, which he saw as straightforward acts of war. But the *Brilliant* was a different matter. She was carrying food for his countrymen. His thoughts were on the unemployed English textile workers who faced starvation in the winter ahead. He wrote, "It seemed a fearful thing to burn such a cargo as the *Brilliant* had, when I thought how the operatives in the cotton districts would have danced with joy had they shared it amongst them."

Because Semmes wanted to keep his presence on the North Atlantic trade routes a secret as long as possible, he made Captain Simes promise to continue in the *Emily Farnum* directly to Liverpool and not put back into an American port to spread the news of the *Alabama*'s presence.

———————

As the *Farnum* slipped over the horizon, Semmes turned back to resume the hunt. The *Alabama* was still short a full crew, and Semmes was concerned that too many jobs on board were going undone or being executed poorly. The three volunteers from the *Brilliant* had been an unexpected bonus, and he was exceedingly glad to get them, but he knew he would need considerably more than that to run his ship properly. Within the next week, he would add two new hands, perhaps the two most singular recruits the *Alabama* ever came up with.

The first he found in the act of capturing the *Dunkirk*, out of New York, bound for Lisbon with a cargo of grain. In the process of transferring her crew to the *Alabama*, Semmes was disagreeably surprised to come across an old troublemaker who had served under him in the *Sumter*. His name was George Forrest, and he was a sailor from one of the Northern states who had for some reason decided to throw in his lot with the Confederacy in the early days of the war. After several months under Captain Semmes, Forrest had a change of heart and jumped ship in Cádiz. Now Semmes ordered him thrown into double irons and scheduled a court-martial, which promptly found him guilty of desertion. Semmes briefly considered hanging Forrest, an act that might serve as a useful message to his crew, but eventually decided that his need for extra hands outweighed his need to give his men an object lesson, so he put Forrest to work as an unpaid member of the *Alabama*'s crew.

Two days later Semmes picked up another recruit from his next capture, the packet ship *Tonawanda*, out of Philadelphia and bound for Liverpool. His newest hand was a seventeen-year-old black slave named David White. White was the property of a citizen of Delaware, a young man who was on his way to Europe to escape the Federal Army draft. Semmes, the consummate Southern gentleman, was amused at the idea of taking as lawful prize a slave—slavery was still legal in Delaware and the other Border States that had remained in the Union—and appointed him a wardroom orderly. David White's name was duly entered on the books of the *Alabama* as a member of the crew, and he was paid at the same rate as others of his grade.

Two new "Yankees" to help fill out his meager crew.

ELEVEN

Off the Georges Bank

By the twenty-third of October 1862, the *Alabama* had moved considerably to the south and west and was now off the New England coast, near latitude 39°35′ and longitude 63°26′. Around four o'clock in the afternoon, a large ship was sighted in the northwest, running toward her. Semmes noted that though the wind was sharp, the stranger had her royals and fore-topmast studding sails set and was, in consequence, running before the wind at great speed. The large ship, as she ran down toward them, presented a beautiful picture—all the more beautiful because she had the look of a Yankee.

Semmes needed to know as early as possible whether a distant vessel was likely to be an enemy merchantman or not. Like most experienced sailors of his day, he had a good eye for spotting the nationality of a vessel by the cut of her jib, but whenever he was in doubt, he could call upon the help of his master's mate, a Savannah pilot named James Evans, who had a remarkable ability along those lines. He could usually make his identification even when the ship was so far away that her lower rigging and hull were still hidden below the horizon. It was a highly valuable skill that had already saved Semmes from wasting countless hours chasing the wrong ships. Evans was so good at spotting Yankees that Semmes trusted his judgment implicitly.

That afternoon, when Semmes called for Mr. Evans, the little master's mate took the captain's glass and studied the stranger carefully for a minute or two, then confirmed, "She is a Yankee, sir." Semmes had been calculating the stranger's speed and recognized that he might have to spread more canvas if he meant to catch her. He ordered his topmen to prepare to set the topgallants if it should be necessary, and moments later the *Alabama*, with the English colors at her peak, filled away, moving into the path of the stranger.

Semmes stood for a time by the mizzen backstays, watching with anticipation as what he hoped would be his next victim gradually ran down toward him. She was "a picture, with her masts yielding and swaying to a cloud of sail, her tapering poles shooting skyward, even above her royals." She came on, rolling gracefully to the sea, and as her hull rose over the horizon, Semmes spotted her flaring bows, a distinctive feature of ships built in New York. The sea foam thrown up before her as she cut through the water gave her what sailors called admiringly a "bone in her mouth." The ship made no change in her course and was soon under the *Alabama*'s guns, at which point a blank cartridge from one of the forward guns brought her promptly to the wind.

On boarding, the prize proved to be the *Lafayette*, out of New York, laden with grain, destined chiefly for Irish ports. As was his custom, Semmes immediately sought out any newspapers on board the capture and was annoyed to learn from them that despite his efforts to conceal his presence on the northern trade routes, his secret was splashed all over the New York press. For all his promises to continue on his journey to England, the master of the *Farnum* had apparently doubled back to America to alert shippers on the east coast of the *Alabama*'s presence, and news of the capture of his ship and of the *Brilliant* had already reached the United States. Semmes cursed the perfidy of Yankees, complaining that even the promise of a ship's captain could not be trusted.

It was typical of Semmes that he allowed himself the right to practice every sort of subterfuge—false flags, disappearing funnels, and the like—but took umbrage at anything that he saw as inappropriate behavior on the part of his enemies.

With the element of surprise lost, Semmes recognized that his job would likely become considerably more complicated. American ship-

pers, now that they were aware of the *Alabama,* would use every means
to disguise their property and make it look as if it were owned by foreign nationals. Semmes knew that from now on he would have to rely
more on intellect than seamanship to wage his war and would be using case law and precedent as his principal weapons.

When he examined the *Lafayette's* papers, he discovered that the
process of legal obfuscation had already commenced and that the shippers had used a variety of devious stratagems to obscure the fact that
their cargoes were American-owned.

There was no question as to the nationality of the *Lafayette* herself.
She was American-built and American-owned—in part by her master,
Alfred T. Small, of Freeport, Maine—and therefore a legal prize. But
as to her cargo, the issue was, to say the least, clouded. Semmes examined various certificates presented to him by the *Lafayette's* captain, all
of which indicated that the cargo was owned by British nationals.
Semmes knew that if he accepted these documents at face value, he
would be forced to release the ship on bond. But he was particularly
keen on burning the *Lafayette.* Lieutenant John Low had examined her
carefully and had estimated the combined value of ship and cargo at
$100,337, which made her one of the most valuable of all the *Alabama's*
captures. It would be most disappointing to let her go.

The certificates, sworn to before the British consul in New York,
claimed that the goods enumerated—chiefly wheat, corn, and lard—
had been purchased and shipped on neutral account. Semmes was
skeptical. "These *ex parte* statements are precisely such as every unscrupulous merchant would prepare, to deceive his enemy, and save his
property from capture." He dictated this to his clerk, in a judgment
that would become part of the official records of the *Alabama.*

There were two New York shipping houses involved: Craig and
Nicoll and Montgomery Brothers. Semmes examined first the bills of
lading covering the cargo shipped by Craig and Nicoll, which indicated that the grain belonged to two different firms in Belfast—the
Messrs. Shaw and Finlay and the Messrs. Hamilton, Megault, and
Thompson. Semmes leafed through the papers. Everything appeared
very much in order, but as every experienced lawyer knows, the devil is
in the details. After close scrutiny, Semmes noted that the grain was

not consigned to either of the Irish parties, and under the wording of the bills of lading, neither one could demand possession of it when the ship reached Belfast. "It is, on the contrary, consigned to the order of the shippers; thus leaving the possession and control of the property, in the hands of the shippers," he dictated. With obvious relish he pointed out that "even if the property were purchased, as pretended, by Messrs. Craig & Nicoll, for the parties named, still, their not consigning it to them, and delivering them the proper bill of lading, passing the possession, left the property in the possession, and under the dominion of Craig & Nicoll, and as such liable to capture." The cargo, by Semmes's reckoning, still belonged to the Yankee shippers.

In a final flourish, he cited as his authority one of his law books. "See *3 Phillimore on International Law,* 610, 612, to the effect, that if the goods are going on the account of the shipper, or subject to his order or control, they are good prize. They cannot even be sold, and transferred to a neutral, *in transitu.* They must abide by their condition, at the time of the sailing of the ship." So much for Craig and Nicoll. They were Yankees, the goods were theirs, and so the goods were forfeit.

With a single summary judgment, Semmes had managed to condemn most of the cargo in a satisfactory manner, but the rest of it represented a somewhat different legal issue. "The property attempted to be covered by the Messrs. Montgomery Bros., is shipped by Montgomery Bros. of New York, and consigned to Montgomery Bros., in Belfast. Here the consignment is all right. The possession of the property has legally passed to the Belfast house."

But just because Montgomery Brothers of Belfast was within the British Isles, was it therefore truly British? Semmes pointed out that the two trading houses, both doing business under the same name in different countries, were in fact partners, so that the property now owned by the Irish traders was also in part owned by the American house and therefore subject to capture. Delighted by his own ingenuity, Semmes concluded triumphantly, "To this point, see *3 Phillimore,* 605. Cargo condemned."

Late that night Semmes ordered his incendiaries to set fire to the *Lafayette* and watched with satisfaction as the ship, like so many before her and so many yet to come, burst into a glorious blaze that lit up the night seas. Years later he would admit that as he watched her go up in flames, he was not *quite* sure that the *Lafayette*'s cargo belonged to the shippers rather than the consignees, but he was confident enough to enjoy the spectacle without qualms.

———

Semmes's fussy precision over points of law may seem abstract and somehow irrelevant, but in fact it was central to his effectiveness as a naval commander. The *Alabama* was operating in an international arena. He and his ship were being watched by a global audience. He was acutely aware that a single misstep on his part could seriously damage Confederate hopes for recognition by the European powers. In a way, Semmes was carrying on a war by jurisprudence not all that different from the legal contest being waged in London between Lord Russell and Charles Francis Adams.

———

By the end of October 1862, after two full months at sea, the *Alabama* had captured twenty-one vessels, with a total estimated value of more than a million dollars, a huge figure for the time. Her final victim for the month was an old brigantine, the *Baron de Castine* of Bangor, Maine, loaded with lumber and bound for Cuba. On inspection she proved to be of little value—a mere $4,000—and with his ship once again overcrowded with forty-four prisoners, Semmes decided to release her on ransom bond and send her into New York with his unwilling passengers. As he watched the *Baron* depart into the night, Semmes pictured in his mind the merry mess on board, with the masters and mates of three burned ships trying to squeeze into a single cabin, all of them celebrating their release.

Semmes toyed with the idea of taking his ship into New York harbor and laying the city under ransom but decided against such a spectacular sortie when the *Alabama*'s engineer reported the ship had only four days of fuel remaining. Semmes decided instead to run down into the West Indies, to meet his tender, the *Agrippina*, and renew his coal supply.

In the back of his mind, Semmes had another goal that lured him south. In a recently captured copy of the New York *Herald*, he had come across information concerning future operations of the U.S. Navy off the coast of Texas, and he decided he might like to be present on the occasion. As he noted wryly, "Perhaps this was the only war in which the newspapers ever explained, beforehand, all the movements of armies, and fleets, to the enemy." He would make good use of such freely offered military intelligence.

TWELVE

The Pirate Semmes

F ragmentary reports of Raphael Semmes's depredations in the Azores began filtering into the Navy Department in Washington in early autumn. The first accounts were confused and contradictory. While it was abundantly clear to Secretary of the Navy Gideon Welles and his staff that the whaling fleet had suffered a grievous blow at the hands of the Confederate Navy, it was not immediately evident whether the destruction had been the work of one gunboat or a number of vessels.

Semmes had deliberately created the confusion by varying his tactics and disguising his ship's appearance in order to give the impression that more than one ship was involved. On occasion he made use of the *Alabama*'s telescoping smokestack, collapsing the funnel so that the ship looked like a peaceful merchant sailer laden with cargo. At other times he erected a false second funnel, made from a black wind sail, which made his ship look like a swift British two-stacker. As often as not, he would display a British flag to intended victims and use English boarding officers dressed in Royal Navy uniforms to complete the deception. Many of the neutral vessels that he stopped and then released never suspected that they had been compelled to heave to by a Confederate warship.

Semmes's tactics might have continued to confuse the American

Navy for several more precious weeks had he not found it necessary to off-load so many prisoners onto the *Emily Farnum* after his first successful captures off Newfoundland. Although Semmes cursed Captain Simes of the *Farnum* as a liar, the Yankee had in fact honored his pledge to continue toward England, thereby keeping the *Alabama*'s presence a secret. But soon after parting from Semmes, Captain Simes found himself facing a serious predicament. With sixty-eight unexpected passengers on board, the *Farnum* was quickly running out of water. To alleviate the problem, Simes arranged to transfer his passengers, a few at a time, to the westbound American vessels he encountered as he continued his passage to Liverpool. It was Semmes's own prisoners who first reached the United States and spread the news of the *Alabama*'s presence off the Grand Banks.

One of the first to arrive in America was Captain Hagar of the *Brilliant*. His lurid account of events caused a sensation throughout the Northern states, and particularly in New York, the *Brilliant*'s home port. Hagar had a score to settle with Semmes. He had lost his entire fortune in the destruction of his ship, and he was determined to give back to Semmes as good as he got. Immediately on landing, he launched a campaign designed to blacken the *Alabama* and vilify her captain in the darkest and most damning terms.

His angry account of Confederate duplicity and the cruel mistreatment of sailors on the high seas won him instant sympathy. In a letter published by the New York *Journal of Commerce,* he provided a precise and accurate description of the cruiser for the benefit of those in the U.S. Navy who might find themselves hunting the *Alabama,* as well as a guide for his fellow sea captains, to help them avoid her. Hagar had spent his brief sojourn on board the cruiser asking numerous questions and observing the ship closely: "The *Alabama* was built at Liverpool or Birkenhead, and left the latter port in August last," he reported. "She is . . . propelled by a screw, copper bottomed . . . carries three long 32-pounders on a side . . . has a 100 pound rifled pivot gun forward . . . a 68 pound pivot on the main deck . . . is represented to go thirteen knots under canvas and fifteen under steam. . . . General appearance of the hull and sails decidedly English. . . . Her crew are principally English, the officers chivalry of the South." His long and detailed description of the cruiser closed with an accurate listing of her officers, by name and rank.

The reaction of Wall Street and the New York shipping interests was instantaneous. Insurance rates on American bottoms skyrocketed, and those fortunate owners of foreign vessels, which were immune to Confederate capture, found themselves besieged with orders and requests for cargo space and discovered they could charge top dollar with no loss of trade, while American ships found it increasingly difficult to compete, even at discount rates.

———————

A frightened New York Chamber of Commerce convened a special session to consider the *Alabama* question. Out of its well-publicized deliberations emerged a characterization of Semmes that was to remain virtually unchanged during the rest of the war and beyond. Throughout the meeting, he was repeatedly branded a "pirate," a deliberately insulting epithet. The clear implication was that he was not a legitimate naval officer, practicing a recognized form of war at sea, but an outlaw carrying out illicit thievery. In that era the word *pirate* carried none of the romantic or adventurous overtones that it does today and was closer in meaning to the modern *terrorist*. A measure of the power of the accusation is that Semmes himself was outraged by it and continued to rail against it for years.

In a pamphlet issued immediately after the meeting, the vice president of the New York Chamber of Commerce, Mr. A. A. Low, made much of the fact that Semmes, after capturing the *Brilliant*, waited until dark before setting fire to her and then remained near the blazing hulk throughout the night. Fire was a constant maritime menace in the age of wooden ships, and Mr. Low pointed out that it was the universal practice among sea captains, on sighting a vessel on fire, to rush to the rescue. He charged that Semmes, by waiting until evening to burn the *Brilliant* and then remaining in the area throughout the night, had deliberately used the burning *Brilliant* as a lure to attract further victims.

The pamphlet argued that as a result of the barbarous tactics em-

ployed by the "rebel pirate" Semmes, American captains, mindful of
their responsibility to protect their ships, could no longer afford to
hurry to the rescue of burning vessels, since by doing so they were
likely to put their ships in jeopardy of a Confederate trap. The safety
of the seas, charged Low, was being recklessly compromised by the deceitful practices of the *Alabama* and her unscrupulous captain.

It was a dramatic accusation and established the character of
Semmes as he would henceforth be presented in the Northern press: a
heartless, calculating villain who would stop at nothing to further his
evil cause. Soon after the pamphlet appeared, the New York *Commercial Advertiser* picked up the theme in an article describing Semmes's
subsequent capture of the American merchant vessel *Lauretta*, bound
for Madeira and Messina. According to the newspaper, the entire shipment of flour and wooden staves was owned by neutrals and legally
covered by various certificates from the Portuguese, Italian, and British
consuls in New York. The newspaper's account of Semmes's confrontation with the captain of the *Lauretta* describes him in almost
comical terms, a mustache-chewing stage villain:

> Captain Wells' account . . . gives an excellent idea of the pirati-
> cal intentions of the commander of the *Alabama*. . . . Semmes took
> first the packet which bore the Portuguese seal, and with an air
> which showed that he did not regard it as of the slightest conse-
> quence, ripped it open, and threw it upon the floor, with the remark
> that "he did not care a d—n for the Portuguese." The Italian bill of
> lading was treated in a similar manner, except that he considered it
> unworthy even of a remark.
>
> Taking up the British bill of lading and looking at the seal,
> Semmes called upon Captain Wells, with an oath, to explain. It was
> evidently the only one of the three he thought it worth his while to
> respect.
>
> "Who is this Burden?" he inquired sneeringly. "Have you ever
> seen him?"
>
> "I am not acquainted with him; but I have seen him once, when
> he came on board my vessel," replied Captain Wells.
>
> "Is he an Englishman—does he look like an Englishman?"

"Yes," rejoined the captain.

"I'll tell you what," exclaimed the pirate. "This is a d——d pretty business— it's a d——d Yankee hash, and I'll settle it," —whereupon he proceeded to rob the vessel of whatever he wanted, including Captain Wells' property to a considerable amount; put the crew in irons; removed them to the *Alabama;* and concluded by burning the vessel.

Mr. Low's speech to the Chamber of Commerce did much to establish the image of Semmes as a deep-dyed villain, but it also made clear that he was not acting alone. "I do not desire to bring any reproach against Great Britain," he announced solemnly, and then proceeded to do just that, accusing her of complicity, "in view of the startling fact now made known to us, that a steamer has sailed from a British port, which has burned and destroyed a dozen of our ships at sea, committing their crews to chains, and, in all respects, treating them in a cruel and inhuman manner."

He then framed the argument that was already a State Department litany: "I do not make the charge against Great Britain that she is herself fitting out these piratical vessels. But this I do say, that the departure of the *Alabama*, known as the 290, was as distinctly shadowed forth as if she had been publicly advertised in the papers to sail as a cruiser of the seas for the so-called Confederate States of America."

In closing, Mr. Low left his audience with a sobering vision of even more frightening mayhem to come: "I do know that it has been reported over and over again . . . that other vessels are being built in the waters of Great Britain for the so-called Southern Confederacy." And more ominously, "It is said also that a ram, or iron-clad ship is being built for the rebel service. . . ." The fact that the British were building ironclads for the South was still largely a rumor. The American consul in Liverpool had not yet identified the two new ships under construction at the Laird works in Birkenhead. But no one in the audience failed to understand the import of the last revelation. If the *Alabama* was a pirate ship, an ironclad was something a great deal more sinister.

In Washington the anti-British sentiments voiced publicly in New York were echoed privately by Gideon Welles, who noted in his diary,

Semmes Motto "I am here"

"The pirate Semmes," as portrayed by cartoonist Thomas Nast. Throughout the Civil War, the Northern press claimed the Confederacy's commerce-raiding activities were illegal.

"the ravages of the roving steamer 290, alias *Alabama,* are enormous. England should be held accountable for these outrages."

———————

As the case against his "piracy" began to take shape in the enemy camp, Captain Semmes, at ease in his cabin in the *Alabama* and perusing the most recently captured examples of the Yankee press, was pleased to come across an agreeable item in the business pages of a Boston newspaper:

ADVANCES ON MARINE INSURANCE.—In consequence of the destruction caused at sea by the privateer steamer *Alabama,* the officers of the insurance companies of Boston have fixed the present war rates on different voyages as follows:—To the north of Europe, 4@5 per cent.; Mediterranean, 5@6; India, 4 ¹/₂; Gulf ports, 4; California gold steamers, 4; West India risks, 5; coastwise, ¹/₂ @ 1 ¹/₂. These rates are liable to be altered according to the necessary requirements of the times, consequent upon the unusual hazards to which commerce is now exposed.

And a New York paper confirmed that his predations were having precisely the effect ashore that he had hoped they would:

The damaging effect of the *Alabama's* raid on our shipping upon the maritime interests of this port were as conspicuous to-day as yesterday. It was next to impossible for the owner of an American ship to procure freight unless he consented to make a bogus sale of his ship.

As the storms of the northern winter moved in, the *Alabama* continued south, to see what further mischief she might stir up.

THIRTEEN

"An Instance of Sublime Christian Heroism"

Almost from the moment of her departure from Liverpool, the *Alabama* had become an object of intense interest to the newspaper readers of Great Britain. In large measure their interest reflected a sense of local pride. The Merseyside origins of the ship were well known, and the English were naturally curious about the exploits of a warship—even one in the service of a foreign government—that had come out of a local shipyard.

Week after week the papers reported the exploits of the dashing Captain Semmes and his crew, tracking the growing number of captures, noting the ship's mysterious comings and goings, and documenting the amusing frustrations of those American officials charged with hunting her down. Far from characterizing Semmes as a pirate, English editors presented him as a high-seas cavalier, a nautical Robin Hood of bold initiative and adventurous spirit. The generally biased presentations of the newspapers simply reflected the prejudices of their aristocratic owners, almost all of whom favored the South over the North.

It is difficult to overstate the animosity that the upper classes felt toward the United States and its citizens. A man named Cowell, a representative of the Bank of England who had lived in the United States for several years, and therefore might be thought to know Americans at first hand, wrote a description of the Yankee character that expresses the general disdain felt by the ruling classes: "The narrow, fanatical, and originally sincere puritanism of their ancestors has, in the course of six generations, degenerated into that amalgam of hypocrisy, cruelty, falsehood, unconsciousness of the faintest sentiment of self-respect, coarseness of self-assertion, insensibility to the opinions of others, utter callousness to right, barbarous delight in wrong, and thoroughly moral ruffianism, which is now fully revealed to the world as the genuine Yankee nature."

Given such an intense level of dislike, it is not surprising that there were many within the aristocracy who felt strongly that Great Britain must come to the aid of the Confederacy and use its influence to help bring about Southern independence. Even those in high political authority made no attempt to hide their bias. Typical was William Gladstone, the chancellor of the exchequer and future prime minister, who gave an impassioned speech in Newcastle in October 1862, calling for official recognition of the Confederacy. "Jefferson Davis and other leaders of the South have made an army," he declared, to loud cheers, and then, in a sly reference to Bulloch's Merseyside shipbuilding program, "they are making, it appears, a navy" (more cheers and general laughter), "and they have made what is more than either, they have made a nation!" (resounding applause).

The same sentiment was more bluntly expressed by another member of Parliament, John Arthur Roebuck, in a speech at a banquet in Sheffield in which he praised Southerners in the most exemplary terms, ending with the ultimate compliment, claiming that "they are Englishmen." In contrast, he contemptuously dismissed their counterparts in the North as descendants of "the scum and refuse of Europe."

Conspicuously present at the banquet, and sitting at the same high table, was Lord Palmerston, Britain's prime minister, who raised no objection either to Roebuck's proposal to help the South or to his characterization of Yankees. Palmerston's lifelong dislike of America and Americans was well known, but his desire to help the South win its freedom was not based on personal animus alone. As prime minister, his first responsibility was to consider the national interest, and there were obvious economic and political advantages to Great Britain if the

United States could be be permanently split into two nations, and he had already discussed these opportunities at some length with Queen Victoria.

There was, in addition, an even more pressing reason to help the South win its war, and that was the need to alleviate the terrible suffering brought on by the cotton famine. The piteous plight of unemployed factory workers in the English Midlands was becoming more evident every day. The statistics told the story. In the first half of 1862, at a time when England would normally have imported more than 1.5 million bales of cotton, only 11,500 bales reached Liverpool, less than 1 percent of the usual figure. As the resulting shortage grew worse, the price of raw cotton rose from 7 pence per pound to 30 pence—a full half crown—at which point those mill owners fortunate enough to have a stock of cotton on hand found it more profitable to shut down, because they could make more money as speculators than as spinners. Massive unemployment ensued. In Lancashire half the spindles were idle. Of the seventy-four mills in the town of Blackburn, only eighteen were running full-time, and thirty were closed completely.

Every day the situation grew more desperate. Vast armies of workingmen and their families were reduced to pauperism. Children, naked and starving, roamed the streets. Millions who had long since pawned their clothing and blankets were now totally dependent on charity. The strain on the poor laws was so severe that their modification was considered. With winter on the way, the question of what to do about the cotton famine was debated in both Houses of Parliament.

Palmerston felt compelled to do everything in his power to end the distress. If that required him to meddle in America's war, he would not shirk his responsibilities. Shortly after Roebuck's "scum of Europe" speech, Palmerston consulted with his foreign secretary, Lord Russell, and together they agreed that, as soon as it was feasible, they would make a public appeal to both the North and the South on humanitarian grounds and negotiate some sort of armistice. Once the guns were silent, the trade in cotton could resume, and the famine would be over.

In retrospect it was an incredibly reckless and naive idea, but the two statesmen managed to convince themselves that it might work. The South, they knew, was bound to welcome such a step, since the Confederacy had everything to gain and nothing to lose. On the other hand, the North was equally bound to object. The plan offered the Union no advantages and would almost certainly result in Southern independence. The government in Washington was sure to respond negatively. If that happened, Palmerston was prepared to force the issue and offer immediate diplomatic recognition to the South. Russell pointed out that the United States was sure to see such a move as not only hostile but tantamount to an act of war and might retaliate by seizing Canada. But would the North dare to make war on British possessions while it was still battling the South? In the autumn of 1862, Palmerston and Russell paused to consider their options.

For Russell it was a complicated issue, fraught with moral ambiguity. He was as ready as Palmerston to help the South. He had demonstrated as much by his blithe inattention to the warnings of Charles Francis Adams concerning the *Oreto* and the *290*. But there was one important aspect of the matter that distressed him immensely—namely, the South's adherence to slavery. Russell had spent a lifetime leading Great Britain's efforts to suppress the international slave trade. He was proud of his and his country's record, and he worried that national honor might be seriously compromised if his government pursued the plan he and Palmerston were contemplating. Britain would be seen not only as actively supporting a slave-owning society but as supporting it in order to guarantee a commerce based almost entirely on slave labor.

Palmerston had no such scruples. The morality or immorality of slavery was irrelevant to his calculations. His philosophy was simple. If something was good for England, that was sufficient rationale. He had shown this in the 1840s, when he led the country into the Opium War, turning a deaf ear to the anguished pleas of Chinese leaders and forcing them to import opium from India, simply to improve the trade balance of the British Empire.

Throughout the closing months of 1862, the two men plotted. Under ordinary circumstances, secret discussions on such a highly sensitive subject would have been handled in private meetings, where the leaders could explore their options frankly and openly, with no written record to embarrass them at a later time. But in the late summer and early autumn of 1862, such private meetings proved impossible. The queen had expressed a desire to spend the season at her ancestral home in Germany, and Russell had accompanied her to Gotha. He and Palmerston were forced to carry on their deliberations by correspondence, and as a result, they left a paper trail that, when finally made public in the twentieth century, shows just how close Whitehall came to forcing a Southern victory. By October 1862 Palmerston was determined to recognize the South. The only question was when to announce it. Because of his concern for the security of Britain's North American possessions, he decided to postpone his move until warmer weather. "As regards possible resentment on the part of the Northerners," he wrote, ". . . we should have less to care about that resentment in the spring when communication with Canada is open, and when our naval force could more easily operate upon the American coast."

Had Palmerston and Russell ever carried out their plan to recognize the South, it would have radically altered the subsequent history of the United States and of the world. The fact that they did not carry it out is due in large part to the courageous stand of thousands of anonymous cotton operatives in the English Midlands. Their story, long overlooked by most historians, impacted directly on British governmental policy, on the Civil War itself, and eventually became a factor in the tangled web of bluster and deceit known as the *Alabama* claims.

———————

Their story begins in October 1862, when the news first reached England of Abraham Lincoln's intention to sign an Emancipation Proclamation on New Year's Day. The reaction of the English press to Lincoln's announcement was almost universally negative. The *Times* was outraged, damning it as a diabolical scheme by which Lincoln proposed to foment a slave rebellion, replete with wholesale butchery of all whites. "Mr. Lincoln . . . proposes to excite the Negroes of the Southern plantations to murder the families of their masters while these are engaged in the war. The conception of such a crime is horrible," thundered the Thunderer. The editors pictured Lincoln as nothing short of Satan incarnate, and warned, "He will appeal to the black blood of the African; he will whisper of the pleasures of spoil and of the gratification of yet fiercer instincts; and when blood begins to flow and shrieks come piercing through the darkness, Mr. Lincoln will wait till the rising flames tell that all is consummated, and then he will rub his hands and think that revenge is sweet."

Echoing the satanic metaphor, *Blackwood's Edinborough Magazine* charged that "the North would league itself with Beelzebub" and that Lincoln, having failed to conquer by any other means, "seeks to paralyse the victorious armies of the South by letting loose upon their hearths and homes the lust and savagery of four million Negroes."

The outpouring of invective aimed at the Emancipation Proclamation continued throughout the remaining months of the year, but not everyone was paying attention. By then there was other American news that was of more immediate interest. In November, word reached England of American charitable institutions, stirred by accounts of the suffering caused by the cotton famine, fitting out relief ships in New York, laden with clothing and foodstuffs for the distressed victims. Soon afterward the promised supplies arrived in Liverpool on board the *Hope,* the *George Griswold,* and the *Achilles* and were greeted with heartfelt thanks in the Midlands. It did not go unnoticed that the *Griswold* had been accompanied on her journey by a warship provided by the U.S. Navy, to protect her against capture by the *Alabama.*

Ordinary Englishmen were impressed that Americans, in the midst of the cruelty and horrors of their own war, should seek to help those beyond America's borders who had been hurt by it.

A few members of Parliament—most notably Richard Cobden, William Forster, and John Bright—had been actively supporting the

North since the outbreak of the war and saw Lincoln's proposed proclamation as an important means of defining the goals of the Civil War more clearly to their constituents. They organized mass meetings of unemployed workers, led by church leaders and antislavery advocates, to examine the underlying causes of the American war, so that they might more fully grasp the reasons for their own economic distress. The workmen, gathered in various Nonconformist chapels and Quaker meetinghouses, debated the meaning of Lincoln's proposed proclamation at length and came to see what the privileged classes chose to ignore: that the antislavery movement was essentially their own cause—namely, the right of a workingman to his own share of the results of his toil. Lincoln had promised to sign his proclamation on New Year's Day, and as the date approached, the anonymous and voteless cotton operatives of England became an important voice in the increasingly public debate on the slavery issue.

On January 2, 1863, Charles Francis Adams and his secretary, Benjamin Moran, were at the American legation in Portland Place, going over the dispatches to be sent to Washington the following day, when they were interrupted by a servant, who informed them that a gentleman from Manchester was waiting below and wished to see the minister briefly on a matter that he was sure the minister would find of interest.

To Adams, the fact that the unexpected visitor came from Manchester was of immediate significance. He could only assume that the visit had something to do with the cotton famine or possibly the relief ships. The unexpected visitor, a clergyman, was ushered into Mr. Adams's office and, after introducing himself, presented Adams with a long letter composed and endorsed by the unemployed cotton operatives of Manchester. It was to be forwarded to President Lincoln.

Adams read through the text with interest. It began in a straightforward enough manner:

December 31, 1862

> *To Abraham Lincoln, President of the United States:*
> *As citizens of Manchester, assembled at the Free-Trade Hall, we beg to express our fraternal sentiments towards you and your country. We rejoice in your greatness as an outgrowth of England, whose blood and language you share, whose orderly and legal freedom you have applied to new circumstances, over a region immeasurably greater than our own. We honor your Free States, as a singularly happy abode for the working millions where industry is honored.*

Adams wondered who had actually written the address. It was the work of an educated person, he assumed, almost certainly a man of the cloth, and in all likelihood a member of the British Emancipation Society or one of its local chapters. But if the words were those of the organizers, Adams reflected, the signatures at the bottom, the often cramped and ill-formed names of unlettered workmen, were genuine and represented their endorsements of the sentiments expressed.

> *One thing alone has, in the past, lessened our sympathy with your country and our confidence in it—we mean the ascendancy of politicians who not merely maintained Negro slavery, but desired to extend and root it more firmly.*
> *Since we have discerned, however, that the victory of the free North in the war that has so sorely distressed us as well as afflicted you, will strike off the fetters of the slave, you have attracted our warm and earnest sympathy. We joyfully honor you, as the President, and the Congress with you, for many decisive steps toward practically exemplifying your belief in the words of your great founders: "All men are created free and equal."*

Adams was struck by the total lack of self-pity in the document. There was no bitter reference to the suffering the workers were forced to endure as a direct result of the war raging in America. Nothing of the starvation, of the desperate cold, of the despair that shrouded the

Midlands. Here was nothing of a self-serving nature whatsoever but simply a statement of support, from desperate men, for the cause of freedom and personal liberty. Cool and analytical as he was by nature, Charles Francis Adams could not help but be greatly moved by the document in his hands.

> *Human beings should not be counted chattels. Women must have the rights of chastity and maternity, men the rights of husbands, masters the liberty of manumission. Justice demands for the black, no less than for the white, the protection of law—that his voice be heard in your courts.*

For perhaps the first time since his arrival in England, Adams, the stuffy, taciturn, intellectual Bostonian, felt the warmth of a people who recognized and understood what it was that moved him and animated his deepest impulses.

> *Our interests, moreover, are identified with yours. We are truly one people, though locally separate. And if you have any ill-wishers here, be assured they are chiefly those who oppose liberty at home, and that they will be powerless to stir up quarrels between us, from the very day in which your country becomes, undeniably and without exception, the home of the free.*
>
> *Accept our high admiration of your firmness in upholding the proclamation of freedom.*

Adams examined the many signatures at the bottom of the page and marveled at the spirit and integrity of those who had placed them there. He thanked his visitor profusely and, later that day, recorded the incident in his diary, in his typically bloodless and almost comically disinterested style. "It was quite a strong manifestation of good feeling," he noted primly, "and I was glad to seize the occasion to express my satisfaction with it."

Within days Adams was to discover that the Manchester letter was simply the first of many such declarations of support from the working classes. In meeting after meeting, laborers from every part of En-

gland had voted strong resolutions in support of the Emancipation
Proclamation and had signed pledges of sympathy to the cause of the
North. The addresses began to pour into the legation in an ever-
swelling stream. Adams would eventually receive, and forward on to
Washington, similar addresses and open letters from Chester, Der-
byshire, Crophills, Salford, Cobham, Ersham, Weybridge, Bradford,
Stroud, Bristol, Glasgow, Liverpool, South London, Bath, Leeds,
Bromley, Middleton, Edinburgh, Birmingham, Aberdare, Oldham,
Merthyr Tydfil, Paisley, Carlyle, Bury, Pendleton, Bolton, Newcastle
upon Tyne, Huddersfield, Ashford, Ashton-under-Lyne, Mossley,
Southampton, Newark, and York. The letter from Birmingham was
signed by 13,500 people.

The resolutions were much like that adopted at Sheffield on January 10, 1863:

> Resolved: that this meeting being convinced that slavery is the
> cause of the tremendous struggle now going on in the American
> States, and that the object of the leaders of the rebellion is the per-
> petuation of the unchristian and inhuman system of chattel slavery,
> earnestly prays that the rebellion may be crushed, and its wicked
> object defeated, and that the Federal Government may be strength-
> ened to pursue its emancipation policy till not a slave be left on the
> American soil.

The letters were just one expression of the outpouring of approval
of the Emancipation Proclamation from the middle and working
classes of Britain. On January 29 a great mass meeting was held in
London at Exeter Hall, unprecedented in attendance and enthusiasm.
It had been advertised for seven o'clock, but long before that hour, the
hall was jammed and the corridors filled. A second meeting was
promptly organized for the lower hall, but even the extra room was not
sufficient to hold the crowd. The people seeking admission filled Exeter Street and stopped traffic in the Strand. Outside the hall crowds
gathered, straining to hear reports of what was going on inside and
cheering the speakers. A few Southern sympathizers who attempted to

heckle the speakers were quickly shouted down. Adams noted that the Exeter Hall meeting was "reported as one of the most extraordinary ever made in London." Working-class Britain was making its voice heard in support of the North. "It will not change the temper of the higher classes," Adams predicted, "but it will do something to moderate the manifestation of it."

Richard Cobden, who was one of the sponsors of the demonstration, wrote excitedly to a friend in America, "I know nothing in my political experience so striking, as a display of spontaneous public action, as that of the vast gathering at Exeter Hall. . . . That meeting has had a powerful effect on our newspapers and politicians. It has closed the mouths of those who have been advocating the side of the South. And I now write to assure you that . . . if an attempt were made by the government in any way to commit us to the South, a spirit would be instantly aroused which would drive that government from power."

Two days after the meeting at Exeter Hall, the *Morning Post*, widely recognized as Palmerston's mouthpiece, editorially referred to it as "a great disgrace to the Christian religion, and an egregious blunder as a step towards emancipation."

In the meantime Abraham Lincoln had responded to the original address from the Manchester workers, expressing his deep appreciation for their sympathy, in a letter that was widely published in both Britain and America:

> *I know and deeply deplore the sufferings which the working-men at Manchester, and in all Europe, are called to endure in this crisis. It has been often and studiously represented that the attempt to overthrow this government, which was built upon the foundation of human rights, and to substitute for it one which should rest exclusively on the basis of human slavery, was likely to obtain the favor of Europe. Through the action of our disloyal citizens, the working-men of Europe have been subjected to severe trials, for the purpose of forcing their sanction to that attempt. Under the circumstances, I cannot but regard your decisive utterances upon the question as an instance of sublime Christian heroism which has not been surpassed in any age or in any country. It is indeed*

*an energetic and reinspiring assurance of the inherent power of truth
and of the ultimate and universal triumph of justice, humanity, and
freedom. I do not doubt that the sentiments you have expressed will be
sustained by your great nation; and on the other hand, I have no
hesitation in assuring you that they will excite admiration, esteem, and
the most reciprocal feelings of friendship among the American people. I
hail this interchange of sentiment, therefore, as an augury that whatever
else may happen, whatever misfortune may befall your country or my
own, the peace and friendship which now exist between the two nations
will be, as it shall be my desire to make them, perpetual.*

Abraham Lincoln

England, in 1863, was still a long way from being a democracy. Only
a tiny fraction of the population had the vote. In Lancashire, for example, only one adult male in twenty-seven had the franchise. But
while the lower classes had no direct say in selecting those who would
rule over them, the upper classes, in general, were guided by a strong
sense of noblesse oblige and recognized a responsibility to those over
whom they ruled. The Palmerston government might prefer to set its
own course and support the South, but it knew it had to pay attention
to the significant upwelling of sentiment on behalf of the Northern
cause. That the antislavery movement was now supported by precisely
those who were suffering most directly from the war in America gave
their cause a nobility that the leaders of England dared not ignore.

Palmerston was forced to back away from his plan to involve his
country directly in the war. Nothing marks the critical shift in policy
more clearly than a letter dated February 14, 1863, from Lord Russell
to Lord Lyons, the queen's minister in Washington. In an unambiguous redefinition of Britain's policy, he wrote, "Her Majesty's Government have no wish to interfere at present in any way in the Civil War."
Superscribed above the message, in the copy in the Foreign Office's
records, is the notation "Seen by Lord Palmerston and the Queen."

In a famous aphorism, Frederick the Great declared, "War is decided
only by battles, and it is not decided except by them." Perhaps so. But

there are battles of blood and steel, and there are battles for men's minds, and there is no question that the dignified stand taken by some desperately cold and hungry workers in the English Midlands over the bitter winter of 1862–63 marks a critical turning point in the American Civil War.

USS *Hatteras*

For two months after leaving the New York area to head south into the Caribbean, the *Alabama* continued to play havoc with the American shipping trade, although her increasing notoriety had alerted Yankee captains, and made it impossible to maintain the almost feverish rate of captures that marked her early hunting. Even so, by Christmas she had overhauled a total of twenty-six Yankee merchant ships; twenty-two of these she destroyed, and the others she released on ransom bond. After less than four months at sea, the aggregate value of her captures stood at $1,542,211, or six times her own cost.

In compiling such a record, she had caught the imagination and won the hearts of armchair adventurers the world over. They saw in Captain Semmes a dashing and zealous David, humbling the mighty Yankee merchant fleet and making a fool of the blundering Goliath of the U.S. Navy. Semmes was delighted by all the attention, not only for personal reasons but because his exploits publicized the Confederacy to a world audience and helped generate sympathy for the Southern cause. Almost every time he overhauled another vessel, he would find some mention of his ship among the newspapers on board. Semmes was conversant in several languages and was pleased to read of his exploits in French, Spanish, Portuguese, and Dutch as well as English and American papers. The only part of the *Alabama*'s notoriety that rankled the proud and thin-skinned captain was the label of "pirate" that the Northern press pinned on him. The implications of illegitimacy irked him, along with the suggestion that he represented some sort of rogue government. But Semmes was even more irritated when the Yankees ignored the Confederacy altogether and referred to his ship as a "British pirate," defining her in terms of where she was built and the nationality of most of her crew.

It undoubtedly galled him to remember that he had made the same distinction some years earlier, in a book he had written about his adventures in the Mexican War. At the time he had asserted that, under the law of nations, for a commerce raider to be considered a legitimate ship of war, "it was necessary for at least a majority of the officers and crew [to] be citizens." Any cruiser that failed to meet that standard would, by his own definition, be a pirate. The fact that the *Alabama* could not meet his own standards undoubtedly heightened his sensitivity to the charges in the press.

Semmes and his crew spent the holiday season refitting and recoaling in the agreeably warm and sunny Arcas Islands, desolate little coral strands off the coast of Mexico. From their newspaper reading, they knew that Lincoln planned to sign his Emancipation Proclamation on New Year's Day, and to mark the event, the steerage officers climbed to the most prominent site on the largest island and mounted a mock tombstone that proclaimed,

IN MEMORY OF ABRAHAM LINCOLN,
PRESIDENT OF THE LATE UNITED STATES,
WHO DIED OF
NIGGER ON THE BRAIN.
1ST JANUARY, 1863.

It was signed simply "290." An accompanying note, written in Spanish, asked anyone finding the tablet to forward it to the nearest U.S. consul.

A few days later, on January 5, 1863, Semmes once more ordered up steam and pointed the *Alabama* northward, toward Galveston, Texas, bent on a novel and daring mission. In November, while still off New York, he had learned from a newspaper report that a U.S. Navy expedition had captured Galveston and that a Union general, Nathaniel P. Banks, was preparing to use the port as a base from which to invade Texas. The article reported that Banks was fitting out an army of some thirty thousand troops, including cavalry and artillery, to take part in the operation. In one of those casually shocking breaches of military secrecy common during the Civil War, the newspaper indicated that the army would be arriving off Galveston around the tenth of January. Semmes calculated that it would require many vessels, perhaps a hundred or more, to transport such a large force, and from his years of service in the U.S. Navy, he knew that the mouth of Galveston harbor was too shallow for most transports to enter and that the vast majority of them would be forced to anchor outside and transfer their passengers, horses, guns, and field equipment onto shallow-draft lighters to move them to shore. "Much disorder and confusion would necessarily attend the landing," he wrote. "My design was to surprise this fleet by a night attack, and if possible destroy it, or at least greatly cripple it."

Semmes was fully aware he was disobeying orders by planning an attack on General Banks's forces. Stephen Mallory had specifically directed him to avoid combat with any enemy warships, but those same orders had given him wide discretion in interpreting his mission, and the opportunity to play havoc with a major enemy troop movement, and possibly destroy it, was simply too tempting to ignore.

What made the opportunity even more irresistible was that the same newspapers that had alerted him to the upcoming invasion of Texas had reported confidently that the *Alabama* was thought to be on her way to the coast of Brazil and to the East Indies. No one suspected that a Confederate raider might be cruising the Gulf of Mexico.

Semmes had recently improved his ship's ability to fight a battle. He had found his forward pivot gun, the big Blakely rifle, unacceptable. "Indeed, the gun is too light for its caliber," he wrote. To compensate, he shifted his other guns, so that the midships 32-pounders could double up on either side, which gave him a more powerful broadside. Rather than the original five guns, he now had six: the two large pivot guns and four 32-pounders. "My crew was well drilled," he wrote, "my powder was in good condition, and as to the rest, I trusted to luck, and to the 'creek not being too high.' "

On January 11 they were approaching Galveston. It was a Sunday, and in the morning, as was customary on board the *Alabama*, Lieutenant Kell marked the day by reading the Articles of War to the assembled crew. By noon they were only about 30 miles from their goal. Semmes instructed the lookout at the masthead that he was looking for a large fleet of transport vessels anchored off a lighthouse. Eventually, as expected, the lookout cried "Sail ho!" followed by "Land ho!" but when Semmes questioned him, he reported that he could see no fleet of transports but only five steamers that looked like ships of war.

Semmes was puzzled. Where was General Banks's armada, and what was a squadron of steam warships doing off the city? Presently a shell, fired by one of the steamers, was seen to burst over Galveston, and suddenly Semmes understood. He turned to the officer of the deck and said, "There's been a change of program here. The enemy would not be firing into his own people, and we must have recaptured Galveston." Semmes's interpretation was correct, although he would not learn the details until much later. The Confederate Army, under General John Magruder, had recaptured the city on New Year's Day, and General Banks's Union troops had been forced to rendezvous at New Orleans. The five Yankee warships standing off Galveston were not there to protect an invading army but to prevent blockade-runners from supplying the Confederates who now held the city.

By now the Yankees had spotted the *Alabama*. Semmes was faced with the prospect of dealing with an entire squadron of Union steamers, most of which undoubtedly outgunned him. He could not very well plunge into such a hornet's nest. While he pondered his options, the lookout called out. "One of the steamers, sir, is coming out in chase of us."

Semmes was excited by the news. "The *Alabama* had given chase pretty often, but this was the first time she had been chased," he wrote. "I at once conceived the design of drawing this single ship of the enemy far enough away from the remainder of her fleet, to enable me to decide a battle with her before her consorts could come to her relief."

AMERICA
ANOTHER FEDERAL
DEFEAT

VERY PROBABLE.

Lord Punch. "THAT WAS JEFF DAVIS, PAM! DON'T YOU RECOGNISE HIM?"
Lord Pam. "HIM! WELL, NOT EXACTLY——MAY HAVE TO DO SO SOME OF THESE DAYS."

Throughout the war, English political cartoons, such as this one from
Punch *suggesting that the Palmerston government offer diplomatic*
recognition to the Confederacy, tended to support the South.

He wore ship, as if attempting to flee from the approaching Yankee, and like a skilled angler, lured his quarry south and away from the land. Semmes always kept the water in the *Alabama*'s boilers warm, and now he ordered the engines fired up. They would be ready in ten minutes, and he used the time to lower the propeller and engage the drive shaft, then gave his ship a small head of steam to prevent the stranger from overhauling him too rapidly. He wanted to get as far away from the other Union warships as possible before challenging the vessel that was drawing closer by the minute.

The stranger was a large side-wheeler, and Semmes could see by her build and rig that she was not a warship by design. She belonged to neither the class of old steam frigates nor that of the new sloops. She was, in fact, the USS *Hatteras,* one of the many passenger vessels that had been converted into gunboats by the Federal Navy in a hurried effort to build a blockading fleet. As subsequent events would confirm, she was no match for the *Alabama.* Her top speed was only 7 or 8 knots, her exposed paddle wheels made her a highly vulnerable target, and her armament—four 32-pounders, two 30-pounders, and a 25-pounder howitzer—was far inferior to that of the Confederate ship.

By early evening, when Semmes judged he had drawn the side-wheeler some 20 miles from the rest of the Yankee squadron, he gave the order to furl sail and beat to quarters. The sun had sunk below the horizon, and darkness was descending. The *Alabama* wheeled to meet the enemy, and the two ships now approached each other rapidly. When they were about 100 yards apart, both captains stopped their engines. The *Hatteras* hailed the stranger. "What ship is that?"

"This is her Britannic Majesty's steamer *Petrel*," came the reply, spoken by one of Semmes's English officers, to add a touch of authenticity.

Then the *Alabama* demanded the stranger's identity. The reply was not clear, but they caught "This the United States ship . . ." That was all Semmes needed to know. He turned to his first lieutenant, John Kell, to assure himself that his gunners were ready.

The stranger hailed again. "If you please, I will send a boat on board of you." His object, as Semmes knew, was simply to confirm that the ship he was addressing was indeed one of her Britannic majesty's cruisers. Semmes's English officer replied, "Certainly, we shall be happy to receive your boat."

By now it was quite dark. From the deck of the *Alabama*, they could hear a boatswain's mate call away a boat and could hear the creaking of the tackles as she was lowered into the sea.

Semmes decided to wait no longer. He turned to Kell. "Tell the enemy who we are, for we must not strike him in disguise, and when you have done so, give him the broadside!"

Kell took the speaking trumpet from the English officer and shouted, "This is the Confederate States steamer *Alabama*!" and gave the signal to fire. Instantly the starboard side of the raider erupted in a sheet of flame, and the air was rent with the roar of six heavyweight cannon fired almost simultaneously. The *Alabama* shook from the recoil.

The Federal response was immediate but far less effective, and the two ships, now less than 100 yards apart, began exchanging fire as rapidly as they could reload. There was no moon, but the starlight was sufficient to enable the two ships to see each other distinctly. At one point during the action, the distance between them was not more than 40 yards, and both ships supplemented their heavy weapons with musket and pistol fire.

George Fullam would write in his journal, "'Twas a grand though fearful sight to see the guns belching forth, in the darkness of the night, sheets of living flame, the deadly missiles striking the enemy with a force that we could feel. Then, when the shells struck her side, and especially the percussion ones, her whole side was lit up."

Semmes conducted the attack while standing on the horse block, a raised platform on the quarterdeck over the well that housed the propeller. Fullam was impressed by his captain's coolness under fire. As the shots whizzed past him, he would call out, "Give it to the rascals!" "Aim low, men!" "Don't be all night sinking that fellow!" The crew was equally enthusiastic. "That's a British pill for you to swallow!" shouted the boatswain, after a shot from the *Alabama* tore open the Yankee's side.

The action was intense. Some of the *Alabama*'s shells went completely through the *Hatteras* before exploding, while others burst inside, setting her afire in three places. One shot exploded in her steam chest, scalding all within reach. About seven minutes into the engagement, a shell from the 100-pounder Blakely entered the *Hatteras* at the waterline, exploding in the sick bay. A shot from a 32-pounder struck the walking beam, knocking the engine out of use and causing it to vibrate badly.

The *Alabama* received only seven minor hits during the engagement and was only lightly damaged. One shot struck under the counter, penetrating as far as a timber, then glancing off. A second struck the funnel; a third went through the side, across the berth deck, and into the opposite side; while others buried themselves harmlessly in the coal bunkers.

Only one shot came close to seriously damaging the *Alabama*, when it penetrated the lamp room and ricocheted. Had it passed through the glass window into the magazine, it would in all likelihood have blown up the ship.

Thoroughly beaten, the *Hatteras* made a desperate but ineffective attempt to ram the *Alabama* and board her. Thirteen minutes after the action commenced, the *Hatteras* began to sink. She hoisted a light and fired an off gun as a signal of surrender.

It was the first time in naval history that a steam warship sank another steam warship.

Boats from both ships were deployed to rescue the *Hatteras*'s crew, and eventually 17 officers and 101 seamen were brought on board the *Alabama*. The *Hatteras* had suffered two dead and five wounded, while the *Alabama* had only one casualty, a man slightly wounded in the cheek. The Yankee crewmen were put in irons, and the officers were escorted under guard to the wardroom. While the *Alabama*'s crewmen were busy trying to find space for so many passengers, a triumphant Semmes told Kell to order up an extra tot of grog for the men.

Although it was too dark to see them, Semmes knew that by now the other Union warships, drawn by the flashes of gunfire, would all be steaming toward the *Alabama*, and he planned to be long gone by the time they arrived. The Gulf of Mexico has only two exits: the Florida

Strait, leading eastward into the Atlantic, and the Yucatán Channel, leading south into the Caribbean. He did not want to be caught in a trap, and within forty-five minutes of the surrender, his ship was heading south toward the Caribbean and the British colony of Jamaica, where he was confident he could count on a friendly reception.

FIFTEEN

Straws in the Wind

By the early spring of 1863, six months after her dramatic escape from Liverpool, the *Alabama* had taken on an almost mythic stature. For millions of newspaper readers the world over, she was the elusive ghost ship of the Confederacy, at once threatening and inspiring, a modern Flying Dutchman, with neither home nor destination, restlessly wandering the seas in search of Yankee prey.

But not every reader was enthralled. At the American legation in Portland Place, Charles Francis Adams paged gloomily through the stack of London newspapers on his desk, as he did every morning, trying to gauge the level of pro-Southern bias in that day's press. It had been a long and wearing winter for Adams, and through it all, issues relating to the *Alabama* had remained a particularly bitter source of distress.

His pain had only increased when word reached England at the end of January of the warm welcome the *Alabama* had received in the British port of Kingston, Jamaica, after her attack on the *Hatteras*, news that was quickly followed by headlines announcing that the *Oreto*, after months of inaction, had at last joined the *Alabama* on the high seas under her new name, the CSS *Florida*, and together, the two raiders were now capturing and burning Yankee merchantmen with infuriating regularity.

The success of the Mersey-built cruisers weighed heavily on

Adams. In late 1861, when he first became aware of Bulloch's ship-building operations, he had discussed the situation with Henry S. Sanford, the head of the United States secret service in Europe, who was in the process of putting together an extensive network of agents throughout Britain. Adams asked him whether such a network could be used to stop Bulloch. Sanford answered in the affirmative, and when Adams asked how, Sanford's response was simple and blunt: he could arrange to have Bulloch disappear without a trace. Adams was aghast. He knew precisely what Sanford meant, and he objected strenuously. Such a solution was intolerable, he told Sanford, and insisted that no such activities were to be carried out in Britain as long as he was head of the American legation. Reluctantly, Sanford assented.

Adams's objection to Sanford's veiled suggestion of assassination was not based solely on the Bostonian's rigid moral principles. He was realistic enough to appreciate Sanford's argument that the permanent removal of a key figure like Bulloch could result in the saving of many hundreds of lives in battle, but as a statesman operating in a foreign land, he deplored cutthroat solutions for the very practical reason that if the facts ever got out, the diplomatic consequences would be disastrous.

After almost two years in London, Adams was still ill at ease with the English. For all their politeness, he could sense the almost universal antipathy toward his country, whether in the casual chat at ruling-class dinner tables or the carping tone of the editorials of the national press or, most galling of all, in the honeyed insolence of the government leaders with whom he dealt. He had long since grown used to the constant sense of isolation and disdain, and it no longer bothered him particularly. He could take comfort in the fact that his job in Great Britain was not to befriend the English but simply to keep them out of the war.

Part of Adams's frustration arose because he was operating in a world that was in large part shrouded in secrecy. He had two primary responsibilities. One was to try to impede Confederate operations in

Britain; the other, to keep tabs on British policy as it affected the United States. The Confederate operations were of course secret, but he could rely on Maguire's spies and Sanford's agents to help ferret out information on rebel activities. But it was much more difficult to divine the shifting intentions of Britain's policies. His efforts were limited to the close reading of newspapers and the examination of parliamentary debates in *Hansard,* and trying to deduce from such straws in the wind which way the Palmerston government was likely to move and why.

Sometimes the straws in the wind were clear and unequivocal. The Exeter House demonstration in favor of the Emancipation Proclamation, for example, had been an unambiguously positive indicator, just as Lord Russell's continuing evasions concerning the *Alabama* matter had been unambiguously negative. At his most recent meeting with Russell, shortly after the debut of the *Florida,* Adams came close to charging the British government with outright criminality for its disregard of his warnings about the two Confederate cruisers. Couching his charges in appropriately deferential language, he warned Russell that the United States would demand restitution "for the grievous damage done." The foreign secretary airily rejected any responsibility for the Confederate raiders and told Adams not to bring up the subject again.

Adams was not particularly surprised by Russell's curt dismissal. As he recorded in his diary, the foreign secretary's denial of responsibility was consistent with a British foreign policy that was historically "selfish and grasping in all periods . . . and never moreso . . . than now."

But not every straw in the wind was easy to interpret. What, for instance, was Adams to make of the resolution of thanks voted by the Liverpool Chamber of Commerce for "the noble gift" of food and other emergency supplies sent from New York to the cotton operatives? That such a testimonial should come from the center of rebel support in Britain was ironic, even amusing, but was it significant?

If Adams had been inclined to see the Liverpool tribute as a hopeful sign, Lord Russell would quickly have dashed any sense of optimism with the speech he made in the House of Lords on February 5, declaring that it would be "a calamity" if the North won the war and restating his government's desire for a Southern victory. No ambiguity there, certainly.

Soon after, Adams was pleased to note that there had been a heavily attended meeting at Plaistow, at which it was resolved that "the Chairman be requested to write to the Prime Minister of our Queen, earnestly entreating him to put in force, with utmost vigilance, the law of England against such ships as the *Alabama*." Was that a straw indicative of a wind shift?

Apparently not, for in March the wind had clearly shifted back again, when William Gladstone, one of the senior members of the cabinet, made a great public show of helping to oversubscribe the £3 million of Confederate cotton bonds offered on the exchange, the gold to be used exclusively for the purchase of war goods in Europe.

By the end of the winter, Adams was convinced that nothing had changed. Despite all the hopeful signs suggesting a shift in policy, the Palmerston government was not going to budge from its long-held hostility toward the United States and would continue to sanction whatever activities helped the South.

And then, quite suddenly in late March, with no hint that a change might be in the offing, Lord Russell gave a speech about the American war in Parliament that was so reasonable in its tone, and so conciliatory toward the Lincoln government, that Adams was quite taken aback. In a letter to the State Department, he described it as "the most satisfactory of all the speeches he has made since I have been at this post." But was Russell signaling a shift in policy?

Three days later, when Adams had occasion to meet with the foreign secretary, he complimented him on his speech and described the favorable report on it that he had sent to Washington. Russell was all congeniality and anxious that Adams understand that the speech had been more than a personal statement, that it represented the British government's views. He told Adams he had received a note from the prime minister "expressing his approbation of every word."

And then the meeting took a surprising turn. Russell, on his own volition, brought up the subject of Bulloch's cruisers and admitted candidly to Adams that "the cases of the *Alabama* and *Oreto* were a scan-

dal" and that it was important that such not happen again. The normally skeptical Adams could only wonder what had brought about
such a sea change. Or was it a sea change?

Adams fervently hoped so, for he was about to present Lord Russell with a grievance of such transcendent importance as to make the
arguments about the *Alabama* and *Florida* look no more significant
than petty squabbles.

SIXTEEN

Brazil

The *Alabama* had long since left the Gulf of Mexico and the Caribbean and was working her way down the coast of Brazil when she crossed the equator for the first time on March 29, 1863. By that date, in addition to sinking the USS *Hatteras* in battle, she had overhauled a total of thirty-nine American merchant ships. The estimated value of her victims—and it was a conservative estimate—had now climbed to $2,327,242, a figure almost ten times the cost of her own construction.

Equally satisfactory to her captain was the fact that his ship was at last properly manned. He had left the Azores still short some thirty hands but had managed since then to enlist enough volunteers from his captures to fill out the *Alabama*'s complement. She now finally had a more or less full crew, and this despite the seven desertions the ship suffered during the riotous celebration in Kingston, Jamaica, that followed the sinking of the *Hatteras*.

Jamaica had been a triumph. The *Alabama* had arrived as a conqueror, with a tale of victory at sea and more than a hundred manacled Yankee prisoners on board. Semmes and his men were treated as heroes by the British colonials, and after almost a week of drunken carousing and riotous celebration, it was only by dint of hard work that the officers of the *Alabama* were able to round up as many of the crew as they did before heading back to sea, and they counted themselves lucky to lose only seven.

There had been another, more serious personnel loss at Jamaica, involving one of the *Alabama*'s officers, Clarence Yonge, the Georgia-born paymaster recruited by Bulloch. Yonge had been sent on shore by Lieutenant Kell, with £400 in ship's funds to pay some bills. When he failed to return, Kell learned he was still in Kingston, fraternizing with the Yankee sailors and spending the money on drink, and most troubling of all, was reported to have made contact with the U.S. consul. Kell immediately ordered him returned to the ship under arrest, and he was subsequently dismissed from the service by Semmes, who took his sword from him and had him drummed out of the ship.

As might be expected of a crew recruited primarily from the Liverpool area, the vast majority of the hands were British nationals, but there were also enough Frenchmen, lascars, and other Continentals and Asians to give the forecastle a cosmopolitan character.

Semmes held no illusions about his men. To his eyes they were waterfront riffraff, "the scum of Liverpool," and it never occurred to him to try to change or improve them. They would remain, he was sure, lazy, morally corrupt, and disloyal. "The sailor is as improvident, and incapable of self-government as a child," he wrote dismissively.

The only man of color on board was David White, the young slave Semmes had taken out of the *Tonawanda* as "contraband," to serve as mess orderly in the wardroom. White, who drew regular pay as a registered member of the crew, quickly became a favorite of the officers. Soon after joining the ship, he had attached himself to Dr. Galt, the ship's surgeon, and so was serving as the doctor's attendant, in addition to his wardroom duties.

The captain's own private steward was an Italian, named Bartelli, "a pale, rather delicate and soft mannered young man," as Semmes described him. Bartelli was an alcoholic when he first came aboard, but under Semmes's stern but gentle guidance, he became a teetotaler. Bartelli worshiped Semmes and served diligently as his majordomo, supervising his table, taking charge of his laundry and cleaning, and overseeing every aspect of the captain's personal comfort. Semmes usually dined alone in his cabin, with the faithful Bartelli as his only companion. The young man provided a touch of elegance and style to the otherwise spartan life on board the *Alabama*. "When guests were expected, I could safely leave the the arrangements to Bartelli," Semmes wrote, "and then it was a pleasure to observe the air, and grace of manner and speech, with which he would receive my visitors and conduct them into the cabin."

Semmes ran a tight ship, with an emphasis on formality. Officers were expected to wear their uniforms at all times, and respect for discipline and proper military decorum was the rule throughout. The Yankee accusation that he was a pirate continued to rankle, and he was anxious to establish the fact that he and his men served on a ship of war, not a privateer.

The crew was kept on a short rein, with little opportunity for getting into mischief. They had long since settled into a regular routine, designed by Semmes to promote efficiency, but equally, to keep all hands employed. "My crew were never so happy as when they had plenty to do, and but little to think about," he wrote.

On weekdays the men were mustered at their quarters twice a day, at nine o'clock in the morning and again at sunset. When the weather was suitable, they were exercised at the big guns or sometimes with small arms, in case they might be called upon to board another vessel in order to effect a capture.

On Sundays there was a general muster on the quarterdeck at eleven o'clock in the morning. This was a more formal ceremony than the daily muster, with officers in dress uniform and epaulets and the sailors turned out in freshly laundered duck frocks and trousers, well-polished shoes, and straw hats. There was no chaplain on board the *Alabama*. Many naval officers in those days conducted their own Sunday service, but Semmes, who was a Roman Catholic, chose not to. After roll call and inspection, there was a reading of the Articles of War, after which the ship received a thorough cleaning below as well as topside, until the decks were shining white and the brass and ironwork glittered "like so many mirrors in the sun."

Semmes was a great believer in the efficacy of cleanliness, both for his ship and for the men who sailed in her. As with most warships in the age of sail, his crew included a number of boys, or "powder monkeys," youngsters who worked with the gun crews and took care of odd jobs. They were waterfront toughs, for the most part, and Semmes thought them "a set of scamps" but claimed that many of them became "very respectable young fellows, for which they were indebted almost entirely to the free use of soap and water."

By far the most important single factor in terms of maintaining discipline, in Semmes's eyes, involved keeping alcohol out of the *Alabama*. This was an ongoing concern, because the *Alabama*'s crewmen, in the normal course of their duties, regularly found themselves on board captured vessels replete with generous supplies of spirituous liquors. None of the *Alabama*'s sailors were allowed to take any property out of captured vessels, and most particularly alcohol. One of the first duties of his boarding officers was to obtain the keys to the liquor lockers and either destroy the contents or throw it overboard.

One time, when the *Alabama* captured a vessel with a hold entirely filled with French brandies, champagne, and other wines, Semmes was so worried that the crew might get hold of the cargo that he would not allow a single bottle to be brought on board the *Alabama*, even for the officers' mess.

Semmes was not averse to the consumption of alcohol; it was just that he wanted to make sure he controlled its use. He issued tots of grog, the traditional Royal Navy mix of rum and water, twice a day. "I was quite willing that Jack should drink," he noted starchily, "but I undertook to be the judge of how much he should drink."

For all his strict by-the-books discipline, Semmes was no martinet. While he worked hard to ensure that his men were kept busy and generally sober, he left time for relaxation. He saw to it that there was always an adequate number of violins, tambourines, and other instruments on board to provide musical diversion, and after the duties of the day were over, the crew would generally assemble on the forecastle for dancing. Those taking the woman's part indicated so by tying handkerchiefs around their waists. "The favorite dancing-tunes were those of Wapping and Wide Water Street," Semmes noted, "and roars of laughter . . . would come resounding aft on the quarterdeck."

Sometimes, instead of dancing, the evening's entertainment took the form of songs and storytelling, and there was never any shortage of yarn spinners. Semmes, in one of his more poetic flights, described how "the sea is a wide net, which catches all kinds of fish, and in a man-of-war's crew a great many odd characters are always to be found. Broken down gentlemen . . . defaulting clerks and cashiers; actors who have been playing to empty houses; third class musicians and poets, are all not infrequently found in the same ship's company. These gentlemen . . . take a high rank among the crew . . . when fun and frolic are the order of the day—or rather night."

The rigid formality on board ship gave Semmes few opportunities to relax. He deliberately maintained his distance, even from his officers. He messed alone, walked the quarterdeck alone, and even when talking with his first lieutenant or the officer of the deck, he rarely discussed anything except official ship's business. The only exception he made to this strict code was during the evening entertainment, when it was his custom to go forward to the bridge, which at that time of day was a sort of lounging place for the officers, where he would smoke his single cigar and observe the antics of the performers below. Always a lonely man, he wrote feelingly of those opportunities when he could "gather my young officers around me, and indulge in some of the pleasures of social intercourse." But he always made sure that such informal moments never led to familiarity and made it a point to seek out the officers he had joked with the previous evening, "to tighten the reins, gently, again, the next morning."

As the hour grew late and the festivities on the forecastle had run their course, there was always a somewhat surreal moment when the singing and the storytelling came to an end, and the entire ship's company arose to close out the evening with an enthusiastic rendition of "Dixie," with sometimes a hundred voices joining in the chorus. Semmes described the scene in a droll word picture of his foreign-born crew, most of whom had never set foot in the seceded states, "all joining in the inspiring refrain,—'We'll live and die in Dixie!' and astonishing old Neptune by the fervor and novelty of their music."

An 1863 Winslow Homer drawing in Harper's Weekly *shows anxious passengers on board an American ship watching "the approach of the British pirate* Alabama.*"*

All merriment came to an end at eight o'clock, when the officer of the deck raised his speaking trumpet to his lips and sang out, "Strike the bell eight—call the watch!" In an instant all was still. The shrill call of the boatswain's whistle was followed by his hoarse shout, "All the starboard watch!" or "All the port watch!" as the case might be, and whichever watch was scheduled to be on deck would immediately assemble for muster, and those men who were off duty would tumble below to their hammocks. A profound stillness would reign on board during the remainder of the night, broken only by the occasional order to make sail or take it in, or by the whistling of the gale and the surging of the sea, or by the half-hourly cry of the lookouts at their posts.

———

In the three months that she cruised off the coast of Brazil, the *Alabama* overhauled twelve more Yankee merchant ships, all but one of which she plundered and burned. Numerically she was no longer maintaining the blistering pace she had established in the North Atlantic, but even so, her latest conquests raised the total value of her captures to a stunning $3.5 million.

The Southern Hemisphere winter had grown increasingly cold and stormy, and Semmes and his crew had taken to wearing their stoutest woolen gear when working on deck. Everyone on board was aware that the hunt was becoming more difficult. There were simply fewer Yankees out there to be caught. The activities of the Southern commerce raiders, as well as the consequent sharp increase in insurance rates, were forcing Northern shipowners to close up shop and go out of business, selling their vessels to neutrals, usually at a loss, rather than braving the open seas and risking the likelihood of capture.

Just a few days previously, the *Alabama* had overhauled two ships, both of which Evans had positively identified as Yankee-built, only to discover that, while Evans had been correct in both cases, each ship was now sailing under British colors and carried British registration. The perpetually suspicious Semmes had examined their papers minutely, searching for any questionable detail that might justify his condemning the ships, but he could find nothing out of order. In both cases he was forced to recognize that the ships were bona fide transfers from the American merchant marine. Reluctantly he released them. He could take some comfort in the fact that by their sale to British owners, the ships had decreased the size of the American merchant fleet in precisely the same degree as if he had burned them.

The dramatic shrinkage of the Yankee merchant fleet was likely to continue, Semmes knew, because of the pressure he and the other commerce raiders were exerting. The previous month, while refueling in Bahia, he had been greatly pleased to encounter another Confederate cruiser, the CSS *Georgia,* which had lately arrived from Dumbarton, Scotland. Along with the *Florida,* which Semmes knew was off the Brazilian coast, there were now three cruisers in operation. Lieutenant Arthur Sinclair wrote proudly in his journal, "Now we can boast of the Confederate Squadron of the South American Station."

Despite the paucity of Yankee merchantmen, Semmes remained undiscouraged, and at around eleven o'clock on the morning of June 20, his perseverance was rewarded. The *Alabama* was sailing a little below Rio, at 25°48´ south by 40°18´ west, when a lookout spotted a sail on the horizon. Semmes immediately wore ship to intercept her. The stranger made every effort to escape, and Semmes was forced to make extensive use of the *Alabama's* steam power to gain on her. Finally, after a six-hour chase, he managed to overhaul her. She was a small bark of about 350 tons, and when Semmes challenged her, he was cheered to see her hoist American colors.

Semmes sent a boarding officer over, who soon returned with her captain and the ship's papers. As usual, Semmes used his cabin as his prize court. His latest capture turned out to be the *Conrad,* of Philadelphia, bound from Buenos Aires to New York with part of a cargo of Argentine wool. The ship, with its American registration, was clearly a legitimate prize, but her captain produced certificates showing that the cargo was owned by British merchants and was therefore protected against seizure. Semmes found himself in a familiar quandary. If the goods in the hold were indeed British, he would be forced to release the ship on bond. But he knew that by destroying the ship, he was doing more to help the Southern cause than he was by extracting IOUs from Yankee captains. He examined the bills of lading covering the cargo and finally decided with a shrug that they were counterfeit and condemned both ship and cargo out of hand. The *Conrad* became his fifty-third victim.

But for the first time, Semmes's decision to condemn did not carry with it a death sentence. Rather than burn the *Conrad,* Semmes decided to transform her into still another Confederate raider. She was too small to serve independently, at least on a permanent basis, but he decided she would make a superb auxiliary vessel. He would arrange for her to sail in company with the *Alabama,* on a parallel course about 10 or 12 miles away from the mother ship. At that distance the two vessels would be hidden from each other by the curvature of the Earth but still visible to the lookouts high in the rigging on each ship. By operating in tandem with another vessel, Semmes could almost double the width of ocean that could be observed, a priceless advantage for a hunter in search of prey.

The *Conrad*'s valuable and nonperishable cargo represented another advantage. Should she become separated from the *Alabama* in a storm, or otherwise find it necessary to strike out on her own, her captain could raise cash quickly in any port in the world simply by selling the wool in the hold.

The *Conrad*'s size was also an advantage. She was small enough to require only three or four officers and a dozen hands, and now that his own ship was fully manned, Semmes felt he could easily spare that number from his complement. The last details were resolved before breakfast the following morning, and Semmes recorded the event in his journal:

> Sunday, June 21.—The shortest day in the year. Weather clear with some haze; wind light from the northward. To-day I commissioned the prize bark *Conrad* as a Confederate States cruiser and tender to this ship, under the name of the *Tuscaloosa,* sending Acting Lieutenant Low on board to command. We supplied her with the 2 brass 12-pounder rifled guns captured from the *Talisman,* 20 rifles, 6 revolvers, ammunition, etc. Her total crew consists of 15 persons, which is quite enough for a bark of 350 tons. The crew being transferred, and all arrangements complete, at 5 p.m. Lieutenant Commanding Low hoisted his flag, firing a gun simultaneously, and

cheered. We hoisted our colors and cheered in reply, and shortly af-
terwards the two vessels separated. May the *Tuscaloosa* prove a
scourge to Yankee commerce!

With the addition of the *Tuscaloosa,* there were now four Confederate commerce raiders, all operating in the South Atlantic. That
seemed to Semmes a little too much of a good thing, and he decided
it was time to turn the *Alabama* eastward, toward Africa.

SEVENTEEN

The Laird Rams

Reports on the *Alabama* and her fellow commerce raiders continued to appear regularly in the English press throughout the spring and summer of 1863, but by now a significant number of readers no longer found their exploits quite so entertaining. For one thing the sheer number of cruisers diminished their appeal. A single gunship could be seen as a plucky underdog, but a squadron of them looked more like a pack of wolves. Besides, the fact that all the cruisers seemed to come from England or Scotland lent substance to the American complaints about British complicity and made some readers decidedly uncomfortable.

But the growing disenchantment with cruisers stemmed only in part from vague perceptions of unsportsmanlike behavior. Probably far more significant were the political and economic realities. The United States Congress was noisily debating whether to launch a fleet of privateers to attack British merchant vessels in retaliation for the depredations of Captain Semmes and Company, and alarmed Englishmen, following the news from the other side of the Atlantic, began circulating resolutions condemning the government for its part in the creation of the cruisers.

One widely circulated pamphlet, published in London, went so far as to demand that Lord Palmerston apologize to the United States for his government's part in allowing the raiders to "escape" and pay resti-

tution to the injured parties. The pamphlet featured a quote from Harriet Beecher Stowe that repeated the familiar litany of complaints
against the *Alabama:* "Yes, we have heard on the high seas the voice of
a war steamer, built for a man-stealing Confederacy with English gold
in an English dockyard, going out of an English harbour, manned by
English sailors, with the full knowledge of English government officers, in defiance of the Queen's proclamation of neutrality."

Stowe's reference to "English gold" reflected the erroneous belief,
held by millions in both Britain and America, that the construction of
the *Alabama* had been secretly financed by a consortium of 290 British
businessmen, which served to explain her mysterious name, number
290.

Charles Francis Adams could take a certain comfort in England's dis-
illusionment with the Confederate raiders, but he had been in public
life long enough to know that popular opinion was capricious and
that it was naive to attach too much significance to such apparent
shifts in mood. Besides, he now had a far weightier issue to deal with
than commerce raiders—namely, the two ironclads that Captain Bulloch was building at the Lairds' yard in Birkenhead. Construction
had started the previous July, and American officials had been nerv-
ously aware of the two ships since shortly after the escape of the *Alabama.*

Rumors that they were for the South had surfaced in the New York
press as early as October 1862, and Maguire's reports, linking them to
Bulloch, had virtually confirmed the fact, although he had not been
able to come up with any hard evidence to support such a claim.

The two ships were not large, but they represented an enormous
threat to the Yankee blockade. They were floating fortresses, virtually
bombproof and capable of smashing the wooden ships of the U.S.
Navy's blockading squadrons like eggshells. They were built to carry
9-inch guns, which made them powerful enough to threaten Northern
seaports. The American government was terrified of them, and naval
experts in Washington warned that the two ironclads, if allowed to
leave Liverpool, could literally turn the tide of war.

The ships incorporated all of the most recent developments in the rapidly changing technology of naval design. Their armored topsides were virtually impervious to enemy shot and shell. Their large guns were to be housed in rotating turrets on deck, as with the Union Navy's monitors. Protruding from the bow of each vessel, unseen below the waterline, was a steel "piercer," designed to tear into wooden hulls and sink them in minutes. It was this relatively novel feature, copied from the ancient Roman triremes, that gave the ships their popular designation as "the Laird rams."

Of particular concern to Union naval officers was the fact that the Birkenhead warships, unlike the shallow-draft U.S. Navy ironclad monitors, were oceangoing vessels. They were designed to cross the Atlantic under their own power and to cruise up and down the North American coastline, where the Union's ironclads, designed specifically for harbor defense and river operations, would be powerless to defend against them.

For months Adams had been receiving urgent notes from Washington, couched in increasingly shrill tones, demanding that, no matter the cost, the Laird ironclads must be stopped. But how could he stop them, when the British government had reduced the Foreign Enlistment Act to an impotent and totally unworkable instrument of law? There was apparently no further legal machinery in Britain to keep the rams from steaming down the Mersey and out to sea.

To add to Adams's concern, the news from home was grim. With a sinking heart, he read the newspaper accounts of Robert E. Lee's Army of Virginia, fresh from its victory at Chancellorsville, moving boldly into Maryland and Pennsylvania. And the news from London was no better. On July 4, James M. Mason, Jefferson Davis's personal representative in England, drew cheers from a large company at Lord Wynford's table when he announced that he had no doubt that at that very moment, General Lee was in Washington. And in Parliament William Gladstone once again proclaimed that the restoration of the American Union was no longer possible. On the same day, Prime Minister Palmerston was even more explicit, declaring flatly that the Union no longer existed. His words immediately excited speculation that Great Britain was about to recognize the South.

On July 9, as if to emphasize the sudden Confederate ascendancy, the first of the two Laird ironclads was launched at Birkenhead. It was the news that Charles Francis Adams had dreaded. Shaken but determined, he sent a strong note to the Foreign Office demanding that the British government stop the vessels. There was more than a whiff of hysteria in his argument. The Laird rams represented the most formidable kind of steam warships, he protested, charging that "all the appliances of British skill to the arts of destruction appear to be resorted to for the purpose of doing injury to the people of the United States. . . . It is not unnatural that such proceedings should be regarded by the government and people of the United States with the greatest alarm, as virtually tantamount to a participation in the war by the people of Great Britain." These were hardly the measured words of a cool and dispassionate diplomat. Adams was becoming an increasingly frightened man, willing to risk everything in a last-ditch attempt to save his country.

Russell chose to overlook the hysterical tone in Adams's note and promised to look into the matter. The American, who had experienced too many volte-faces from the Foreign Office to believe any of Russell's promises, held out little hope.

And then, in another of the abrupt and unexpected turnabouts that characterized that summer in London, news finally reached Britain of the spectacular Union victory at Gettysburg. Only days later came the news of Grant's equally dramatic capture of Vicksburg. With General Lee's battered army reeling back to Virginia, and the Confederacy split in two by a Mississippi now totally under Union control, the impact of the news sent shock waves through the British establishment. The leaders of both major political parties had taken a Southern victory for granted and shaped their policies to reflect such an assumption, but two such major triumphs, coming one on top of the other, proved beyond question that the Union was growing stronger, the Confederacy weaker.

Adams was profoundly moved by the war news, seeing in it an instance of heavenly intervention. On a more worldly level, he recognized that the double victory strengthened his position with the authorities on the issue of the Laird rams. Lord Russell would be forced to take him more seriously, but would that make him any more cooperative? Before he could find out, matters took a new and totally unexpected turn.

British customs officers had been busy at Birkenhead, investigating the American claims that the two ironclads were earmarked for the Southern navy, when they made a remarkable discovery. The ships could not possibly be Confederate property, because papers at the Laird works showed convincingly that they were owned by a French firm, Messrs. Bravay & Company, a shadowy but legitimate commercial house in Paris. To add to the surprise, the ships were apparently being built for the pasha of Egypt to patrol the Nile, under the names of *El Tousson* and *El Monassir*.

It was a stunning turn of events. There was apparently no doubt as to the authenticity of the Bravay brothers' contract with Laird's or other papers certifying ownership. Adams could barely contain his frustration. He had been tricked again. It was clear enough to him what had happened. Bulloch had initiated the construction of the two ships. Of that Adams had no doubt. Affidavits of numerous eyewitnesses placed Bulloch at the building site from the earliest days, and the design of the ships, so precisely adapted to the continental shelf off the east coast of North America, was further evidence of their ultimate destination. But apparently Bulloch had negotiated a deal with some French businessmen, giving them temporary ownership. Doubtless, as soon as the ships were completed and had left England, Bulloch would pay off the Frenchmen and once again take possession. It was a clever scheme, but how could Adams prove it? The fact was, he could not. Once more Adams had been outfoxed by the endlessly resourceful James Bulloch.

Toward the end of July, Lord Russell politely informed Adams that the Crown legal advisers could find no evidence of illegality in the papers covering the ironclads, that the ships apparently belonged to the Bravays, and that since France was not at war with anyone, the restrictions of the Foreign Enlistment Act did not apply. His office could therefore take no action. Adams despaired.

Could the British not see that the Laird rams represented something more than a narrow legal issue? That the ironclads were a hundred times more dangerous than the commerce raiders had ever been? Naval experts, not only in the United States but in Britain, were convinced that the Laird rams could break the blockade. The whole outcome of the American war seemed to be in the balance. Could Lord Russell not see that war between the United States and Great Britain might very well break out over what was little more than Whitehall's legalistic hairsplitting?

The threat of an Anglo-American war was real. Adams knew that the Lincoln cabinet was so afraid of the rams that it was seriously considering the possibility of flouting Britain's self-styled "neutrality" and sending a squadron of U.S. Navy steamers up the Mersey, guns blazing, to destroy the rebel ships at anchor. Such a move would unquestionably mean war with Britain.

Adams continued to pepper the Foreign Office with demands for the detention of the rams. He knew that the affidavits that Dudley had been collecting to support the American claims of Confederate involvement were weak and inconclusive, but they were the only evidence he could scrape up, and he presented them without apology.

In August, when the reports from Liverpool suggested that the first ram was preparing to depart, Lord Russell chose to leave London and go off to Scotland on holiday. An increasingly despondent Adams met with the duke of Argyll, a member of the Palmerston cabinet and one of the few British aristocrats who had been a steadfast supporter of the North. Adams expressed his anxiety over the deepening crisis and described the highly bellicose instructions he had received from U.S. Secretary of State William Seward, couched in intemperate language and including such highly inflammatory demands that Adams had not dared share them with Russell. Perhaps Argyll, as a fellow cabinet officer, might be able to write a letter to Russell and explain the situation with less heat. Argyll promised to do so.

But Russell had already made his decision. Crudely but accurately, it could be summed up: the United States be damned. He would not stop the Laird rams if they attempted to leave England. There were bound to be perils in such a step, Russell knew, but he could see great promise as well. In a letter to Mr. Adams, he loftily dismissed the minister's claim that the ships were built for the Confederacy and made his position clear:

> Her Majesty's Government are advised that the information contained in the depositions is in a great measure mere hearsay evidence and generally not such as to show the intent or purpose necessary to make the building or fitting out of these vessels illegal under the Foreign Enlistment Act. . . . Her Majesty's Government are advised that they cannot interfere in any way with these vessels.

While Russell's explicit refusal to seize the rams was making its way from Scotland to London, Charles Francis Adams was frantically gathering additional affidavits and writing further letters to the foreign secretary, begging him to take some action. His notes had taken on a pleading quality: "It is my painful duty to make known to your lordship . . . the grave situation in which both countries must be placed in the event of an act of aggression against . . . the United States by either of these formidable weapons."

On September 4, Adams received Russell's blunt refusal to seize the rams. After a sleepless night, he responded in a last, heartfelt letter that contained the single most famous sentence he ever wrote: "It would be superfluous in me to point out to your lordship that this is war." He wrote not in a threatening tone but as a desperately frightened diplomat convinced he was seeing his world fall apart. But the message was heard.

There was no immediate response from the Foreign Office. Adams kept in constant touch with Liverpool, his only solace being that neither of the rams had made a move to leave England and both remained at the Laird yards. Finally, on September 8, he received a note from the

Foreign Office: "Lord Russell presents his compliments to Mr Adams, and has the honour to inform him that instructions have been issued which will prevent the departure of the two ironclad vessels from Liverpool."

The crisis was over.

To his dying day, Lord Russell always insisted that his decision to seize the Laird rams had not been influenced in any way by Adams's "this is war" note and made the startling assertion that he had already decided to seize them on September 1, the very day he wrote Adams an unequivocal letter saying exactly the opposite.

His lordship's statement should be taken with a grain of salt. It flies in the face of reason. If he had decided to seize the rams, why did he write Adams informing him that he would not do so? Why did he wait a full week before letting Adams know he had changed his mind?

What seems more likely is that on September 1 he decided not to seize the rams and so informed Adams. Then, six days later, when he read Adams's response, he realized that he had gone too far, the situation had grown way too dangerous, and the game was no longer worth the candle. He could not bring himself to admit publicly that he had changed his mind as a result of the American's letter, so he concocted a highly suspect story that he had made the decision independently. To support the claim, he arranged for half a dozen predated letters and office memorandums to be furtively prepared and salted in the Foreign Office files, to cover his tracks. By such a stratagem, John Russell was able to emerge not as a trigger-happy adventurer but as a wise counselor, a man of principle, determined to put national honor before national aggrandizement. History can get pretty murky when statesmen seek to hide their transgressions and have the means to do so.

Wherever the truth lies in the decidedly ambiguous denouement of the Laird rams affair, it is abundantly clear that the underlying reason that Russell could not let the two ironclads "escape" is the fact that he had played that same card twice before, with the *Oreto* and the *290*, and had been exposed as a cheat each time. In the end he dared not play that game again.

EIGHTEEN

Simon's Bay

Raphael Semmes was in a melancholy mood. It was September 24, 1863, and the *Alabama* was anchored in Simon's Bay, on the east coast of the Cape of Good Hope. Nearby lay a number of other vessels, including the China station paddle wheeler *Kwan Tung,* HMS *Narcissus,* and other Royal Navy warships permanently stationed in Great Britain's most southern African colony.

The reason for Semmes's low spirits was easy enough to trace. He had captured only three ships in the three months since he had overhauled the *Conrad* off Brazil and commissioned her as the CSS *Tuscaloosa.* In the last seven weeks, he had captured nothing at all. It was not for lack of effort. He had chased down and overhauled dozens of vessels, but all proved to be owned by neutrals. The shortage of enemy merchant vessels clearly demonstrated that the *Alabama* and her sisters were successfully carrying out their mission and driving the Yankees from the seas. He should have been pleased, but after the brilliant success of the *Alabama*'s first year at sea, when his capture rate averaged better than one a week, the sudden dearth of prey had a depressing effect. He was tired and homesick. He had not seen his family for more than two years. He wrote in his journal, "I am supremely disgusted with the sea and all its belongings. The fact is, I am past the age when men ought to be subjected to the hardships and discomforts of the sea. . . .

The very roar of the wind through the rigging, with its accompaniments of rolling and tumbling, hard, overcast skies, etc., gives me the blues."

Semmes had come into Simon's Bay to refuel, only to be told that there was no coal to be had, because the U.S. Navy's *Vanderbilt* had recently come into port and bought up all the coal on hand. The American warship, a huge fifteen-gun side-wheeler, was cruising off the cape specifically to hunt down the *Alabama*. Semmes was neither surprised nor worried by news of her presence in the area. He had been operating in African waters for months now, and he knew the local U.S. consul would have long since alerted Washington. He had been expecting the enemy to show up for some time.

The arrival of the *Vanderbilt* meant it was time for the *Alabama* to be off for the Far East. Semmes was eager, even anxious, to depart, but he needed a complete resupply of coal before he could leave, and in order to get it, he had to sit idly by in Simon's Bay for over a week, while the coal was shipped in from Cape Town, on the other side of the cape. There had been another delay while Malay laborers transshipped it from the coal lighters to his bunkers. Coaling was always a filthy job, coating every surface of the ship with black, sooty dust and requiring extensive cleanup.

The men had eventually managed to scrub down the *Alabama*, but not without their usual grumbling, complaints, and malingering. "The fact is, I have a precious set of rascals on board," Semmes wrote, "faithless in the matter of abiding by their contracts, liars, thieves and drunkards. There are some few good men who are exceptions to the rule, but I am ashamed to say of the sailor class of the present day that I believe my crew to be a fair representation of it."

Semmes's pessimistic frame of mind had been further depressed by the news of the two catastrophic Southern defeats at Gettysburg and Vicksburg. "Our poor people seem to be terribly pressed by the Northern hordes of Goths and Vandals," he noted gloomily in his journal, "but we shall fight it out to the end, and the end shall be what an all wise Providence shall decree."

————————

The generally somber spirit that seemed to hang over the *Alabama* in late September was in stark contrast to the optimism and sense of purpose that had characterized the ship almost two months earlier, when she first appeared at the cape on August 5, 1863. It was the day she made her last capture. She had been approaching Table Bay that morning, when a cry from the lookout had alerted the officer of the deck to the presence of a strange sail. Spirits rose when Evans was called on to study her and positively identified her as an American bark.

Semmes ordered the men to their stations, ordered English colors hoisted, and with steam up, closed with the stranger, some 5 or 6 miles from land. When she displayed an American flag, he immediately ordered the Confederate colors raised. It was no longer the old Stars and Bars flying at the main but the newly authorized naval flag, the Southern Cross quartered on a white field. It was likely the Yankees did not even recognize it. They would learn to soon enough. He sent a boarding officer over, and when he returned with the master and his papers, the stranger proved to be the *Sea Bride* out of New York, bound with assorted cargo along the east coast of Africa. Semmes immediately claimed her and threw a prize crew on her, ordering the prize master to stand off and on the cape, while he took the *Alabama* into harbor. He could not bring his capture along with him, because the Queen's Proclamation of Neutrality forbade bringing prizes into British ports.

The capture, made within sight of land, had caused great excitement on shore, where it was witnessed by thousands of Cape Town citizens crowded onto the hills overlooking the water. The local newspaper, the *Argus,* ran a long and glowing account of the event the following day, describing how

crowds of people ran up the Lion's Hill, and to the Kloof Road. All the cabs were chartered—every one of them; there was no caviling about fares. . . . As soon as our cab reached the crown of the hill, we set off at a break-neck pace, down the hill, on past the Round-house, till we came near Brighton, and as we reached the corner, there lay the *Alabama* within fifty yards of the unfortunate Yankee.

The writer gave an enthusiastic description of the capture, taking pains to present it as a dashing example of derring-do upon the high seas:

As the Yankee came around from the south-east, and about five miles from the Bay, the steamer came down upon her. The Yankee was evidently taken by surprise. The *Alabama* fired a gun and brought her to. . . . [L]ike a cat, watching and playing with a victimized mouse, Captain Semmes permitted his prize to draw off a few yards, then he up steam again, and pounced upon her. She first sailed round the Yankee from stem to stern, and stern to stem again. The way that fine, saucy, rakish craft was handled was worth riding a hundred miles to see. She went round the bark like a toy. . . . This done, she sent a boat with a prize crew off, took possession in the names of the Confederate States, and sent the bark off to sea.

The sudden appearance of the world-famous cruiser, performing an actual capture in full view of the land, was enough to empty the city. The day turned into a carnival.

As we came, we found the heights overlooking Table Bay covered with people; the road to Green Point lined with cabs. The windows of the villas at the bottom of the hill were all thrown up, and ladies waved their handkerchiefs, and one and all joined in the general enthusiasm; over the quarries, along the Malay burying ground, the Gallows Hill, and the beach, there were masses of people— nothing but a sea of heads as far as the eye could reach.

As the *Alabama* made her way into the bay, scores of dinghies, cargo boats, gigs, and wherries—each one crammed with excited admirers— came out to greet her. The *Argus* reporter gushed:

She was surrounded by nearly every boat in Table Bay, and as boat after boat arrived, three hearty cheers were given for captain Semmes and his gallant privateer. This, upon the part of a neutral people, is, perchance, wrong; but we are not arguing a case—we are

First Lieutenant John Kell, standing by the Alabama's *after pivot gun during the ship's first triumphal visit to South Africa.*

recording facts. They did cheer, and cheer with a will, too. It was not, perhaps, taking the view of either side, Federal or Confederate, but in admiration of the skill, pluck, and daring of the *Alabama,* her captain and her crew, who afford a general theme of admiration for the world all over.

For Semmes and his crew, it was a moment of supreme triumph. Throughout the rest of the day, and for nights thereafter, he and his officers were feted and lionized by what he described as "the better classes" of Cape Town. After a few days, the *Alabama* raised anchor and sailed around the cape, to Simon's Bay, on the east side, where the ship was protected from the strong winter gales blowing out of the Atlantic.

The partying continued. They were sumptuously entertained by Rear Admiral Sir Baldwin Walker, commander in chief of British naval forces at the cape. Semmes ordered liberty for the crew, and the waterfront became a continuous scene of revelry for days on end. The townspeople humored and spoiled them. All the sailors overstayed their liberty and dribbled back days late, in twos and threes, torn, bedraggled, and hungover, with bruises and more grievous wounds as souvenirs of their spree.

Lieutenants Arthur Sinclair and Richard Armstrong posing by one of the Alabama's *32-pounders, at Cape Town, South Africa.*

Eventually, with the ship recaulked and minor repairs completed, the *Alabama* set out to cruise the waters of the cape and, not incidentally, to transact some clandestine business. Semmes had deliberately refrained from burning the *Sea Bride*. He had kept her off the cape, in the hands of her prize crew. She was one capture that he hoped to sell, if he could find a way around the law that made it illegal to sell a prize within the British Empire. At the Cape Colony he met with a local businessman who was not averse to a little off-the-books trading and who agreed to buy Semmes's prize for £3,500. The price was about a third of the ship's value and a bargain for the buyer. They arranged to make the transfer at a remote spot on the Namibian coast, beyond the reach of British law, a barren, forsaken place called Angra Pequena, a rockbound harbor surrounded by desert, a place that no ship ever visited except in quest for shelter in bad weather.

The £3,500 in gold for the *Sea Bride*, paid in "good English sovereigns," was immediately turned over to Dr. Galt, who, ever since the banishment of Clarence Yonge, was serving as the *Alabama's* paymaster as well as surgeon. It was the only prize money Semmes ever managed to raise in the war, and on his order the entire amount was put into the ship's operating funds.

While still at Angra Pequena, the engineers brought Semmes some bad news. The ship's condenser, which provided fresh drinking water for the crew, and which had been working only intermittently for weeks, had finally broken down. The pipe joints had worked loose and could not be repaired until they returned to the cape. The loss of the condenser would be a serious inconvenience, since it was in large part the ready availability of fresh water that made it possible for the *Alabama* to remain at sea for such extended periods. Its failure was not crucial. It could be repaired. But it was an indication that the *Alabama*, which had been at sea for well over a year by that time, was beginning to show the effects of overuse, with only limited replacement of parts.

Two weeks later, when the *Alabama* returned to Simon's Bay for recoaling, it was evident that something else had occurred at Angra Pequena that was likely to adversely affect the operations of the ship.

The *Alabama*'s officers, for the most part, had signed on to the ship for patriotic reasons, along with a thirst for adventure, but the crew, to a man, had enlisted for the "lots of prize money" that Semmes had promised them back at Terceira. The crew never forgot that for a moment. For months everyone in the forecastle had kept a careful tally of the estimated value of each capture and had reckoned their own share of the prize money, under a complex formula by which half the total value of the captured vessel and its cargo was divided between the officers and men. By the time the *Alabama* reached South Africa, even the least of those shares amounted to several thousands of dollars.

The men had not as yet seen one dollar of actual prize money, because Semmes had not been able to sell his captures and had been forced to destroy them or ransom them. For a year he had time and again assured the crew that a grateful Confederate government would award them large sums of money as soon as the South won the war.

But at Angra Pequena, for the first time, the *Alabama* had actually earned some prize money from the sale of the *Sea Bride*, and the crew, not unreasonably, expected a down payment on their share of the booty. When Semmes assigned the entire £3,500 to the ship's operating fund, the crew took it personally, and the result was a sullen anger that made itself evident in various acts of disobedience and rebellion.

When they arrived back in Simon's Bay, and Semmes learned that the USS *Vanderbilt* had taken the last coal and that it would be at least a week before a new supply could be lightered in from Cape Town, he realized it would be asking for trouble to keep his surly and restless crew cooped up on board while they waited. The men had already raised hell and caused considerable trouble on their first liberty in Cape Town, but reluctantly he yielded to their petitions and granted them another liberty. The results were predictably disastrous. On September 19 Semmes noted, "Liberty men drunk and few return," and on the following day he reported, "Liberty men returning in greater numbers today; the money is giving out and the drunk is wearing off."

One of the perennial problems Semmes had to face when he came into port was the presence of American consuls. Wherever he stopped, be it the Azores or Martinique or Jamaica or the backwaters of Brazil, inevitably there was a United States consular official on hand, ready to entangle him in legal snares or limit his coaling, and trying to persuade his crewmen, often with tempting offers of cash, to jump ship. In the Cape Colony, the troublemaker was one Walter Graham, a particularly energetic consul whom Semmes referred to as a "gadfly" and who had thrown one obstacle after another in the captain's way throughout his stay in South Africa and surrounding waters.

On September 22, Semmes, writing again of his crew, noted, "The Yankee consul, with usual unscrupulousness, is trying to persuade them to desert, and the drunken and faithless rascals will, many of them no doubt, sell themselves to him. With one or two exceptions, the whole crew have broken their liberty—petty officers and all."

The next day, with coaling completed and Semmes ready to leave, he found himself still short some twenty men who had failed to return from liberty. He needed the men, but he could not afford to wait for them to show up. Royal Navy friends had alerted him that the *Vanderbilt* was off Cape Agulhas, and should she get news of the *Alabama*, she would almost certainly blockade her in Simon's Bay.

With nearly one-sixth of his crew missing and presumed gone for good, Semmes had no recourse but to contact the crimps, the boardinghouse keepers who specialized in finding crewmen when all else failed. It was strictly against the law for Semmes to ship a crew in a British port, but he knew he had the sympathy of local authorities, and he trusted them to look the other way while he recruited a few hands in contravention of the Queen's Proclamation of Neutrality. Semmes talked to "one of those Shylocks who coin Jack's flesh and blood into gold" and managed to come up with eleven recruits—"ragged, whiskey-filled vagabonds"—to augment his diminished company of adventurers.

On the night of September 24, the *Alabama* left her anchorage and, near three o'clock the following morning, cleared the cape in the teeth of a southeast gale and headed into the Indian Ocean.

———

Semmes's departure did not of itself raise the sense of gloom that hung over the captain's cabin. The South African experience had been a mixed bag. There had been pitifully few captures and the loss of too many hands—he would particularly miss Michael Mahoney, the Irish fiddler who brought so much cheer to the evening concerts—but to balance the bad, there had been the hero's welcome from the "better classes" of the cape and an equally warm reception from the Royal Navy. Both were good memories, and both were evidence that the British, at least in the colonies, still supported the *Alabama* and her mission.

———

Behind him he had left another memory, in the form of an Afrikaans song, "Daar Kom die *Alabama, Alabama* Kom oor die Sie," a folk memory of a great event that would be remembered well into another century:

Here comes the *Alabama,* the *Alabama* comes over the sea.
Here comes the *Alabama,* the *Alabama* comes over the sea.
Girl, girl, the reed-bed girl,
The reed-bed is made up for me,
On which I can sleep.
Here comes the *Alabama,* the *Alabama* comes over the sea.

NINETEEN

Singapore

On leaving the cape, the *Alabama* turned south, in search of the fortieth parallel, where Semmes planned to catch the Agulhas Current and the prevailing westerlies that would blow him eastward toward Asia.

He was still in a pensive mood on September 27. It was his fifty-fourth birthday, and alone in his cabin, he marked the occasion privately, in his journal:

> Weather partially clear. A heavy, confused sea, with a falling barometer. . . . To-day is the fifty-fourth anniversary of the birth of the unworthy writer. How time flies as we advance toward old age! May God in His mercy protect us and preserve us and restore us . . . our beloved country I feel certain He will protect and preserve . . . but it may be His pleasure to scourge us severely for our past sins and unworthiness, and to admit us to His favor again only when we shall have been purified.

The Roaring Forties proved as good as their reputation, with almost perpetual gale-force winds and strong currents pushing the ship inexorably eastward. The principal problem was keeping dry. "The constant straining of the ship, in the numerous gales she had encountered, had opened the seams in her bends, and all our staterooms were leaking...keeping our beds and clothing damp," Semmes complained.

In the vast emptiness of the southern Indian Ocean, with no land-masses to impede the natural forces of wind and wave, the *Alabama* proceeded apace. Twenty-four days after leaving the cape, she had run, under sail alone, a remarkable 4,410 miles. On October 21, 1863, she crossed the tropic of Capricorn and reentered the calmer waters of the southern trades. Semmes set a course for the Sunda Strait, the narrow passage between the islands of Java and Sumatra that led into the South China Sea. This was the gateway to the east Asian mainland, and there was always a heavy traffic of Indiamen and clippers crowding through. It seemed a likely place to find Yankees.

As they drew farther north, they came across increasing numbers of sails moving into and out of the strait, and on November 6 the *Alabama* made her first capture since the *Sea Bride,* four months earlier. She was the 598-ton bark *Amanda,* bound for Queenstown from Manila. Her papers indicated that her cargo of sugar and hemp was owned by British merchants, but Semmes found flaws in the certificates. He ordered the ship burned.

A week later the *Alabama* overhauled two large clipper ships on successive days—the *Winged Racer,* bound for New York with a cargo of sugar, hides, and jute (the *Alabama's* fifty-seventh capture), and the *Contest,* which almost managed to get away, failing to do so when the wind died, and the steam-powered *Alabama* was able to make good her capture. The fact that the *Contest,* powered only by sail, came close to escaping was an indication of the toll that time and weather had taken on the *Alabama.* She had been subjected to every sort of hard usage since her commissioning in the Azores—storms, bitter cold, extreme heat, and the rough handling that any ship of war must undergo—all of which had very much impaired her strength. So constantly had she been under way that the passage of seawater under her hull had actually worn the copper on her bottom so thin that it was daily loosening and dropping off in sheets. This severely diminished her speed. Because the *Alabama* had to be ready at any given moment to chase down a potential victim, Semmes had rarely allowed the fire in her furnace to go out, except for a few hours at rare intervals to enable the engineer to remove the encrusted salt from the bottom of his boilers. After eighteen months the constant interaction of fire and salt had nearly destroyed them.

Another problem, equally serious but of a very different nature, was the attitude of the crew. Morale was low, and ill feelings palpable. The weary drudgery of months at sea, the continuing anger over the lack of prize money, and the dawning realization that they might be fighting on the losing side and would never see the money owed them had all contributed to an increasing sense of discontent among the men. They made little effort to hide their resentment. Gestures of goodwill on the part of the officers were met with disdain. Two days after the capture of the *Winged Racer*, Semmes ordered that the cigars that had been salvaged from her be divided between officers and men. A number of crew members made a point of ostentatiously throwing their cigars overboard in a show of such calculated insolence that the ringleaders were arrested and later court-martialed as an example to the rest.

The first mate of the *Contest*, John Bigelow, who was forced to spend ten days on the *Alabama* as a prisoner, wrote a report on his experiences that was far from flattering but probably accurate. He described the ship as

manned by 23 officers and 130 men, crew much dissatisfied, no prize money, no liberty, and see no prospect of getting any. Discipline very slack, steamer dirty, rigging slovenly. Semmes sometimes punishes, but is afraid to push too hard. Men excited, officers do not report to captain, crew do things for which would be shot on board American man-of-war; for instance, saw one of crew strike a master's mate; crew insolent to petty officers; was told by at least two-thirds of them that [they] will desert at first opportunity. Crew all scum of Liverpool, French, Dutch, etc. *Alabama* is very weak; in any heavy sea her upper works leak badly; she has a list to port that she may fight her starboard guns. Fires kept banked; can get full steam in twenty minutes. . . . While on board saw drill only once, and that at pivot guns, very badly done; men all ill disposed and were forced to it; lots of cursing.

A more sympathetic observer, one of the *Alabama*'s senior officers, Lieutenant Arthur Sinclair, sensed that Semmes was suffering as much as his ship. "Our captain begins to show the wear and tear of weary months of watching, thinking and anxiety," he noted in his journal.

In the weeks following the capture of the three American merchantmen near the Sunda Strait, Semmes continued to overhaul and board a large number of vessels but was distressed to find that every one of them turned out to be foreign-owned, usually British or Dutch, and he could find not one that he could burn. As Sinclair noted plaintively, "What had become of our once immense China fleet of clippers?"

It was on December 21, when he took the *Alabama* into Singapore for recoaling, that Semmes discovered the reason for the scarcity of prey. As his ship pulled up near the Peninsular and Oriental wharf, he became aware of a remarkable spectacle. There before him lay an entire fleet of American merchant ships, large Indiamen for the most part, almost all of them dismantled and laid up—their captains terrified by the threat that they might run into the *Alabama* if they as much as poked their way out beyond the marine league.

Semmes soon learned that Singapore was not the only Yankee refuge. There were two American ships laid up at Bangkok as well, one or two at Canton, two or three at Shanghai, one in the Philippines, and one or two more in Japan. "The birds had all taken to cover," he complained, "and there was no such thing as flushing them."

The governor of Singapore, who was a British army colonel, gave Semmes permission to coal. While he offered Semmes every amenity and invited him to dine at the officers mess, his welcome fell short of the enthusiastic reception the *Alabama* had received in other British ports. The lavish hospitality and warmth that had characterized her stops at Jamaica and the Cape Colony was notably more muted in Singapore. The reason became evident when the *Straits Times* published a thoughtful editorial about the *Alabama,* noting that many leaders in the shipping business—and Singapore was primarily a shipping center—had grown increasingly uneasy about the whole concept of com-

merce raiding, and while the international community might admire
the South's quest for independence, that admiration did not necessarily extend to the Confederacy's "corsair fleet."

————

Everyone on the *Alabama* seemed to be on edge. Several of the officers
decided to take an evening off and go into town, and were playing bil-
liards in a local hotel when they were invited by a number of American sea captains to join them at the bar. These were the skippers of
some of the twenty-two vessels lying in the harbor. For a while the
gathering went well enough, with old salts, North and South, swap-
ping sea stories, but then one of the Yankees proposed a toast, something to do with the war, and the Southerners took it as an insult.
There was an all-out brawl. The Southerners prevailed, but given the
cool welcome they had found in Singapore, they decided not to stay
and savor their victory. They beat a hasty retreat to the ship and just
managed to evade the local authorities.

The *Alabama*'s crew created its own problems. It was getting close
to Christmas, and the men remembered how they had spent the previous holiday in the Gulf of Mexico, preparing to disrupt the Union
Army invasion at Galveston. They were still full of hope in those days,
flush with the prospect of victory and looking forward to thousands of
dollars of prize money. Now, a year later, victory seemed increasingly
unlikely, and the only prize money that had ever materialized, the pal-
try £3,500 picked up in an illegal sale of the *Sea Bride*, had gone directly
into the ship's coffers, with nary a farthing for Jack. Homesick and re-
sentful, they sulked on board, and when the ship was warped into the
P&O wharf for coaling, some of the more determined members of the
ship's company took the opportunity to escape to the grog shops. That
night, as the ship prepared to sail, the *Alabama*'s officers spread
through the city, hunting them down. They managed to find all but ten
of the deserters and at the last minute were able to come up with four
replacements. Holding on to a crew was becoming increasingly difficult.

Semmes had originally thought to run up the China Sea as far as
Shanghai after recoaling, but the discovery of so many American ships

hiding in Singapore and elsewhere made him change his plans. With nothing left to hunt, it made more sense to return to the Western Hemisphere, where there was still some semblance of American maritime commerce.

On Christmas Eve the *Alabama* steamed out of harbor and turned northwest into the Malacca Strait. With only three captures, the Asian cruise had been a distinct disappointment. It was time to leave the Orient behind.

TWENTY

To Cherbourg

The first leg of the *Alabama*'s return to the Atlantic proved to be surprisingly productive. Semmes had assumed that his presence in the Far East had driven all American merchantmen into hiding, but in the first three weeks after leaving Singapore, he managed to capture and burn four ships and momentarily returned to the giddy kill rate of the first year of operations. But after taking the *Emma Jane,* of Bath, Maine, on January 14, 1864, he was not to find another American sail east of Cape Town.

In spite of constant recaulking, the *Alabama*'s decks continued to leak. When gales set in, late in February, water poured belowdecks, and despite constant mopping and sponging in the brief respites of calm between storms, it became impossible to dry out the ship. Damp bedding and mildewed clothing added to the misery. The seasick captain wrote disconsolately, "My ship is weary too, as well as her commander."

It took more than two months to make the westward journey across the Indian Ocean, and the *Alabama* did not reach the Cape of Good Hope until March 11, by which time the ship had exhausted most of her provisions and all of her coal. Semmes would have liked to take her into port immediately for recoaling, but he was barred from doing so under the terms of the Queen's Proclamation of Neutrality, which allowed warships of both the North and South to refuel at British ports only once every three months. Since the *Alabama* had coaled at Singapore just prior to Christmas, she would not be able to take on a new supply at Cape Town for another fortnight. To fill the time, Semmes cruised the waters south of the cape in what turned out to be a fruitless search for Yankee merchantmen, until March 20, when he finally brought the *Alabama* into Table Bay.

The triumphal return to Cape Town was a gratifying repeat of the warm welcome they had received on the occasion of their original entry six months earlier. Familiar faces greeted them, invitations poured in from "the better classes," and Semmes and his officers found themselves once again the toasts of the town.

Adding to the pleasure of the return was the fact that, for once, there was plenty of cash on hand to pay for the ship's needs. The money came from the sale of the cargo of Argentine wool and hides that Semmes had taken out of the *Conrad*, after commissioning her as the *Tuscaloosa*. The Confederacy's share of the proceeds, in gold sovereigns, was more than enough to cover all of the *Alabama*'s expenses during their stay.

Only one thing marred their return, and that also involved the *Tuscaloosa*. Before setting out for the Far East, Semmes had ordered Lieutenant Low to cruise the Brazilian coast. When his cruise was over, Low had brought the *Tuscaloosa* back to Simon's Bay for refitting, where she was peremptorily seized by British authorities and held under armed guard. The order for her seizure had come from London, where the secretary for the colonies, the duke of Newcastle, had decided that she was not a legitimate ship of war but an uncondemned prize, an illegal capture brought into a British port in violation of the Queen's Proclamation.

The thin-skinned Semmes, always ready to take offense at any imagined slight to the sovereign authority of the Confederacy, was outraged by what he saw as a scandalous breach of the law of nations. He fired off a long and closely argued legal brief to his friend Admiral Sir Baldwin Walker, the senior Royal Navy officer at the Cape, demanding restitution. Neither Semmes nor anyone else in South Africa had any way of knowing that the seizure of the *Tuscaloosa* had already created a great fuss in England. Questions had been raised in the House of Commons, and new orders, rescinding the seizure, were already on the way from London. Semmes interpreted the seizure, whether justified or not, as an indication that the British government could no longer be counted on to support the South in its fight for independence, and that Palmerston and Russell were trimming their sails and trying to find ways to appease the Yankees. The insidious snooping and hectoring complaints of a dozen U.S. consuls scattered in seaports around the world were having their effect. He vented his anger and frustration in his journal. "England is too rich to be generous. . . . All her human sympathies being thus dried up, she is ready to make friends with the stronger party."

In three hurried days, the *Alabama* was again ready for sea, and on March 25 the ship steamed out of Table Bay to the cheers and shouts of encouragement from the fleet of boats that surrounded her.

Semmes and his officers had been so busy with ship's business in port, as well as exchanging social invitations with their hosts, that there had been little time to catch up on the news. When they were once again at sea, they at last had the opportunity to read through the large supply of newspapers they had taken on board. The news from home was almost universally grim. Sherman was grinding his way through Georgia, and Grant once again threatened Richmond. Semmes's executive officer, John Kell, wrote glumly that "defeat seemed to stare our struggling people in the face, and with the failing finances and shut-in ports, ruin seemed inevitable."

Semmes remembered in his memoirs the depressing sense of foreboding:

> The news was not encouraging. Our people were being harder and harder pressed by the enemy, and post after post within our territory was being occupied by him. The signs of weakness, on our part, which I mentioned as becoming, for the first time, painfully apparent after the battle of Gettysburg, and the surrender of Vicksburg, were multiplying. The blockade of the coast, by reason of the constantly increasing fleets of the enemy, was becoming more and more stringent. Our finances were rapidly deteriorating,

and a general demoralization, in consequence, seemed to be spreading among our people. From the whole review of the "situation," I was very apprehensive that the cruises of the *Alabama* were drawing to a close.

One item in a British newspaper cheered him. It was a report of a speech by Milner Gibson, president of the British Board of Trade, detailing the enormous impact of the *Alabama* and her sisters upon the American merchant marine. Gibson confirmed that the Confederate raiders had destroyed, or driven for protection under the British flag, almost half of the United States vessels engaged in the English trade. While Semmes could—and did—take great satisfaction in this public confirmation of the devastating impact of the cruisers, he chose to ignore the main thrust of the Gibson speech.

Gibson was not celebrating the decline of the American merchant marine; he was lamenting it and warning his audience that unless Great Britain mended her ways and stopped building ships for the Confederacy, her own merchant service could easily become the next victim of an equally destructive squadron of raiders. Great Britain, with her many colonies and huge merchant marine, was extremely vulnerable to exactly the same devastating losses suffered by the United States. What would happen, he asked, if one of Britain's many colonies rose up in rebellion (the Indian Mutiny of 1857 would have come instantly to the mind of his audience), and the United States offered its shipbuilding facilities to the rebels, to build raiders such as the *Alabama* and *Florida* to prey on British merchantmen? At once the seas would be filled with rebel corsairs, American-built and American-manned, destroying British shipping wholesale, with Britain unable to protest, because she had established the precedent herself.

While Gibson's speech presented a compelling argument against the commerce raiders, it did not, by itself, directly influence government policy. Still, it forced the leaders in Whitehall to recognize that its collusion with the Confederate shipbuilding program, disguised as a "hands-off" policy, might in fact represent a serious danger to the empire. If Gibson's statistics brought comfort to Semmes, the speech itself made it a cold comfort.

———

Early in April, a fortnight out of Cape Town, Semmes noted further deterioration in the *Alabama*. "Many of the beams of the ship are splitting and giving way," he noted, "owing to greenness of the timber of which she was built." Considering the efforts of the Lairds to get properly seasoned wood for the ship, Semmes's complaint seems a trifle ungrateful. Whatever the case, the *Alabama* could still chase Yankees.

On April 22 she took her sixty-third victim, the ship *Rockingham*, from Callao, bound for Cork. After transferring such stores as she could use to the *Alabama*, Semmes decided he would use his captive for target practice before burning her. The crew fired into the hull with what Semmes described as "good effect," but other witnesses were not so favorably impressed.

The master of the *Rockingham*, standing on the bridge of the *Alabama* and watching his ship being bombarded, noted that only four of the twenty-four rounds fired into the hull took effect. Lieutenant Kell recorded that one out of three of the *Alabama*'s shells failed to explode, indicating faulty fuses. Semmes chose to ignore his crew's marksmanship and the problems with the ammunition. He did not expect to remain at sea much longer, and there would be time enough to worry about such deficiencies during the *Alabama*'s extensive refit. Eventually tiring of the sport, he ordered the *Rockingham* burned.

A few days later, on April 27, in latitude 11°16′ south and longitude 32°07′ west, the *Alabama* overhauled what was to be her sixty-fourth and last capture. She was the ship *Tycoon*, out of New York and bound for San Francisco, carrying an assorted cargo. She was a rich prize, valued at $390,000, second in value only to the *Sea Lark,* captured a year earlier in the same waters. Semmes helped himself to her cargo and then sent in his incendiaries to apply the torch. They left her burning soon after nightfall.

The *Alabama* crossed the equator for the fourth and last time on

May 2 and headed toward the Azores, the starting point of her epic cruise. Semmes, tired and ill, described her in a moving paragraph:

> The poor old *Alabama* . . . was like the wearied fox-hound, limping back after a long chase, foot sore, and longing for quiet and repose. Her commander, like herself, was well-nigh worn down. Vigils by night and by day, the storm and the drenching rain, the frequent and rapid change of climate, now freezing, now melting or broiling, and the constant excitement of the chase and capture, had laid, in the three years of war he had been afloat, a load of a dozen years on his shoulders. The shadows of a sorrowful future, too, began to rest upon his spirit. The last batch of newspapers captured were full of disasters. Might it not be, that, after all our trials and sacrifices, the cause for which we were struggling would be lost? Might not our federal system of government be destroyed, and State independence become a phrase of the past; the glorious fabric of our American liberty sinking, as so many others had done before it, under a new invasion of Brennuses and Atillas? The thought was hard to bear.

On May 12, as the *Alabama* approached European waters, Semmes ordered an inspection of all shell fuses, and when every one of them was found to be faulty for one reason or another, he ordered all shells fitted with fresh fuses. Gunpowder can be temperamental, Semmes knew, and tends to deteriorate over time, particularly at sea. But he suspected the problem with his ammunition lay with the magazines, where the powder was stored. These were often damp with excess steam from the condensers. When he ordered an inspection, he discovered that all the powder that was stored in barrels was defective and ordered it thrown over the side. The powder stored in copper canisters, however, still appeared to be in good condition. Despite these measures, two weeks later, when the *Alabama* was trying to stop a Nova Scotia schooner, her crew fired a shell across the schooner's bow, and everyone noticed that it failed to explode.

The *Alabama* reached England on Friday, June 10. After making The Lizard, she picked up a channel pilot, licensed to take her into ei-

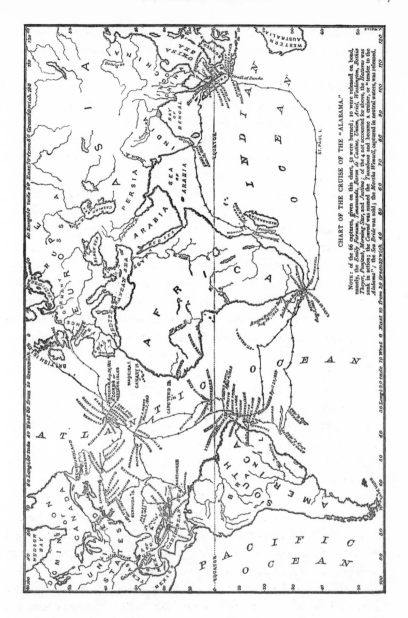

The cruise of the CSS Alabama, *as first published by the* Century Magazine, *detailing the name, sequence, and location of all her captures.*

ther an English or a French port. Which would it be? It might prove
an important decision, and Semmes pondered the question. The troubles over the *Tuscaloosa* in South Africa, along with his reading of recent newspapers, suggested to him that he might not find as warm a
welcome in England as he would in France, and he ordered the pilot
to head for Cherbourg. He noted in his journal, "I felt a great relief to
have him on board, as I was quite under the weather with cold and
fever. . . . And thus, thanks to an all-wise Providence, we have brought
the cruise of the *Alabama* to a successful termination."

The following noon, with Semmes and his officers standing on her
bridge, the most famous ship in the world steamed proudly into Cherbourg. In a little less than two years, she had overhauled 294 vessels
and captured sixty-four American merchantmen, worth an estimated
$5,163,143. In addition, her activities had caused the U.S. Navy to de-
ploy twenty-five Federal warships to search for her, drawing them away
from vital blockade duty. In all, she had cost the enemies of the Confederacy at least $7 million, about twenty-eight times the cost of her
construction, arming, and fitting out.

A final grand gesture still lay ahead, but with the end of her cruise,
she had earned her place in history.

TWENTY-ONE

Battle

A n almost gothic sense of ill omen hangs over the last days of the *Alabama*, a gloomy intimation of predestined disaster worthy of Edgar Allan Poe. Every step taken, every decision reached, seems in hindsight to foreshadow the ultimate catastrophe.

Both ship and captain were exhausted. After two years at sea, the *Alabama*'s boilers were burned out and virtually all her machinery in need of repair. She was, in the words of her executive officer, John Kell, "loose at every joint, her seams were open, and the copper on her bottom was in rolls."

Raphael Semmes was in an equally weakened state. After years of enduring the rigors of the sea and the incessant demands unique to the skipper of a man-of-war, Semmes was worn out from the unrelenting strain of command and yearned for rest and an opportunity to recoup his strength.

The morning after their arrival, a Sunday, Semmes sent his officers ashore to arrange for the landing of the prisoners from his last two captures and then sat down with Kell to make plans for the coming week. His most immediate concern was to get the *Alabama* into dry dock right away. He thought it would take about two months to make the necessary repairs, and as soon as she was in dock, he planned to pay off the crew and "give them an extended run on shore."

The next morning Semmes went into town himself, to meet with the harbor officials. On stepping ashore, he found himself an instant celebrity. News of his arrival was the talk of Cherbourg, and with his prominent mustache and distinctive gray naval uniform, he was immediately recognized everywhere and was the object of excited whispers and stares.

The naval prefect for Cherbourg, Admiral Augustin Dupouy, greeted him cordially, offering him every hospitality, but when Semmes made his request for dry-docking, Dupouy grew noticeably more reserved and apologetic. Regrettably, he explained, all the docks at Cherbourg belonged to the French navy. It might have been better had Captain Semmes brought his ship into Le Havre or some other commercial port, where docks were readily available. Before he could permit a foreign vessel, particularly a warship of a belligerent power, to enter one of the docks, he would need the personal approval of the emperor, who was unfortunately on holiday in Biarritz and temporarily unavailable. Semmes would have to await his return to Paris, which was not expected for several days.

A thoughtful Semmes returned to his ship, mindful that any delay in getting the *Alabama* into dry dock was likely to significantly alter his plans. He dictated a letter to the Confederate naval attaché in Paris, informing him of his intention to pay off his crew and pointing out that he would need fresh funds to pay for the repairs of the *Alabama*. As for himself, "my health has suffered so much from a constant and harassing service of three years, almost continuously at sea, that I shall have to ask for relief." It was time for someone else to take command.

Later that day he received word that the U.S. Navy steam frigate *Kearsarge* was on her way from Holland and could be expected to appear off the coast at Cherbourg momentarily. The news did not surprise him. The Yankees were bound to move quickly, as soon as they learned of his presence in Europe. Semmes knew the *Kearsarge* well. She had been one of the three Union Navy vessels that had successfully blockaded him at Gibraltar in 1862, when he commanded the *Sumter*. She was a close match to the *Alabama* in size, her 1,031-ton displacement almost precisely equaling the 1,040 tons of his own ship.

Semmes had a personal tie to the *Kearsarge* as well. He and her captain, John A. Winslow, had been fast friends during the Mexican War and at one point had even shared a cabin in the USS *Raritan*. While Semmes was contemptuous of almost all Northern officers, he knew Winslow's character at first hand and respected his determination and fighting spirit.

The next day, around noon, the *Kearsarge* entered the harbor at Cherbourg, as predicted. Semmes and Kell stood on the deck of the *Alabama* and trained their glasses on the new arrival.

The *Kearsarge* had been commissioned in January 1862, in Portsmouth, New Hampshire, and was thus only a few months older than their own ship. Like the *Alabama*, she carried twin engines, and while they were rated at 400 horsepower as against the *Alabama*'s 300 horsepower, the practical difference was not significant. In armament the *Alabama* could be seen to have a slight advantage. The *Kearsarge* carried seven guns: two 11-inch pivots, smoothbore; one 30-pounder rifle; and four light 32-pounders. The *Alabama* carried eight guns: the 68-pounder pivot, smoothbore; the 100-pounder pivot rifle; and six heavy 32-pounders. But whatever superiority the *Alabama* might seem to possess in terms of firepower had to be weighed against the brute power of the 11-inch Dahlgrens on board the *Kearsarge*, which could throw 180-pound projectiles into an enemy with devastating effect, particularly at close range.

Only hours after her arrival, the *Kearsarge* turned and slipped out past the long breakwater that protected Cherbourg from the open sea, having had ample time to inspect the *Alabama* at her anchorage and to transact whatever other business she might have had in the town. She took up a position in open water, where she could keep an eye on both of Cherbourg's two separate exit points, ready to pounce should Semmes attempt to escape.

That afternoon Semmes summoned John Kell to his cabin.

"I am going out to fight the *Kearsarge*," he told his executive officer calmly, "what do you think of it?" Kell looked thoughtful but said nothing, waiting for his captain to explain his reasoning, which he promptly did. It was only a matter of time, probably a few days at most, Semmes pointed out, before Cherbourg would be effectively blockaded by a squadron of Yankee cruisers. With a blockade in place, there would be no chance for the *Alabama* to get out. Right now, faced only with the *Kearsarge,* they might still be able to fight their way out and reach Le Havre or some other port where they could be sure of getting into dry dock. By the time the *Alabama* was properly repaired, the war might well have taken a turn for the better. As it was, he did not want his ship to rot in Cherbourg if there was a chance to save her. "Besides, Mr. Kell, although the Confederate States government has ordered me to avoid engagements with the enemy's cruisers, I am tired of running!"

Kell was not surprised by Semmes's decision, but he was concerned. The officers and men were weary from two years at sea with almost no shore leave. The ship required a major refit. And there was still the lingering question concerning the reliability of the *Alabama*'s gunpowder. He reminded his captain that the *Kearsarge* was built for combat, with appropriately sturdy scantlings and planking, while the *Alabama* was built for speed, with comparatively light framing, and while the Confederates outgunned the Yankees eight to seven, the *Kearsarge* threw more metal at broadside, and her 11-inch smoothbores would be devastating at point-blank range.

Semmes listened attentively to Kell's cautions, but it was obvious he had made up his mind to fight and would not back down. When Kell reminded him that only one-third of the fuses had been detonating properly, Semmes brushed him aside. "I will take the chances of one in three," he declared.

In the end it was almost certainly Semmes's romantic self-assurance and warrior spirit that decided the issue, along with his contempt for Yankees, whom he considered an inferior breed, incapable of matching the valor and élan of Southern cavaliers. At heart it was simply beneath his dignity to avoid a fight.

The irony was not lost on either man that their current circumstances owed much to the fact that the Emperor Napoléon III was on holiday with his family in Switzerland. Had he been in Paris, he would almost assuredly have allowed the *Alabama* into dry dock, and a battle would have been impossible.

Semmes immediately sent a challenge to the *Kearsarge* through the Confederacy's commercial agent in Cherbourg.

CSS Alabama, *Cherbourg, June 14th, 1864*

To A. Bonfils, Esq., Cherbourg. SIR: I desire you to say to the U.S. Consul that my intention is to fight the Kearsarge *as soon as I can make the necessary arrangements. I hope that these will not detain me more than until to-morrow evening, or after the morrow morning at furthest. I beg she will not depart before I am ready to go out.*

   I have the honor to be, very respectfully,

   Your obedient servant,

   R. Semmes, Captain.

The truculent tone of the challenge, and particularly the hint of sarcasm in the closing sentence, was vintage Semmes.

———

There was one significant difference between the *Alabama* and the *Kearsarge* that Semmes and Kell did not discuss that afternoon, presumably because they did not know about it. It was a difference that would prove of crucial importance in the coming battle. Both ships were built of wood, but at some point in 1863, Captain Winslow, following the example of Admiral David Farragut at New Orleans, had turned his ship into a sort of makeshift ironclad. He had ordered loops of spare anchor chain hung over the sides of the *Kearsarge* to form a curtain of iron that effectively protected her engines with a wall of chain mail. In all, the work had required 120 fathoms of chain, stopped up and down to eyebolts with marlines and secured by iron dogs. To keep the armor in place, he arranged to have it permanently covered by a wooden shield of pine boards, 1 inch thick, which was painted black to match the hull. It took only three days to ironclad the *Kearsarge,* at a total cost in materials that did not exceed $75. Although Captain Winslow made no attempt to keep his makeshift armor a secret, the wooden covering effectually hid it from both Semmes and Kell when they had inspected the Yankee warship from the deck of the *Alabama.*

Semmes always insisted that he did not learn of the chain mail curtain that protected the *Kearsarge's* midships until after the battle, but such a claim is difficult to accept. Even his own secretary, Breedlove

Smith, was aware of it, and the French port admiral stated that he personally warned Semmes of the *Kearsarge's* advantage in this regard. The most likely explanation is that Semmes was ignorant of the "ironcladding" at the time he offered his challenge, and when he learned the truth, it was too late to withdraw without injury to his highly sensitive code of honor. Under the circumstances he found it convenient simply to forget about it. Certainly he had other things on his mind.

———

Semmes took the precaution of transferring his entire operating funds of 4,700 gold sovereigns to Confederate agent Bonfils, along with the payroll records, the ransom bonds of vessels captured and released, and the sixty or more chronometers he had collected from his victims over the course of his cruise. The prizes that counted most with him, the American flags that he had taken off his conquests, he kept on board the *Alabama*.

Semmes was in no great hurry to meet the *Kearsarge*. Although he had specified on Tuesday that he would be ready to fight on Wednesday or Thursday at the latest, he spent three days taking on coal and drilling the crew for combat. He had the men practice boarding procedures, using pistols and cutlasses, and it occurred to some observers that the captain might be planning to lie alongside the *Kearsarge* and take her in hand-to-hand combat.

"Boatswain Mecasky has his gang busy stoppering standing rigging, sending down light spars, and disposing of all top-hamper," Sinclair noted. "Gunner Cuddy is overhauling the battery, and arranging the shot and shell rooms for rapid serving of guns, and coals are ordered for our bunkers."

It was not until Saturday afternoon, June 18, that Semmes finally decided he was ready. He notified the port admiral that the *Alabama* would be departing the following day to engage the *Kearsarge*. That night he and his officers attended a banquet given in their honor by Southern sympathizers in Cherbourg. Amid the customary toasts, the officers vowed either to sink the *Kearsarge* "or make another corsair out of her"—that is, to capture her and send her out as a new Confederate commerce raider. While the party continued, Semmes slipped away to a small Catholic church and, by prearrangement, attended Mass before returning to his ship for what would be the last time.

———————

Captain Winslow, who had welcomed the surprising challenge from Semmes, was by now wondering when the *Alabama* might come out. The challenge was dated Tuesday and delivered Wednesday. He hoped to fight her before the weekend. By Saturday night, with the *Alabama* still in Cherbourg, Winslow had given up anticipating. But he was not overly concerned and simply charged his lookouts to remain alert. There was virtually no way the *Alabama* could get out of Cherbourg without his knowing of it.

———————

At six o'clock on Sunday morning, June 19, Semmes's chief engineer, Miles Freeman, started the *Alabama*'s fires, and the men, after a leisurely breakfast, assembled for muster in fresh white shirts and blue trousers. Captain Semmes and his officers, all dressed in full uniform, inspected the eager but apprehensive crew and complimented them on their smart appearance. The crew could see excited crowds gathering on shore for what was universally recognized as the most spectacular highlight of the summer season.

Finally, sometime between nine and ten o'clock, Semmes gave the order to weigh anchor, and the *Alabama*, freshly scrubbed and followed by the cheers of well-wishers on shore, stood out of the western entrance to the harbor. She was followed closely by the French ironclad frigate *Couronne*, which was in attendance to ensure that any action would have to take place in open waters, beyond the 3-mile limit of French sovereignty. Not far behind the *Couronne* steamed an elegant and luxurious private yacht wearing the flag of the Royal Mersey Yacht Club. She was the *Deerhound*, owned by John Lancaster, a wealthy English businessman. Lancaster and his family had been on a continental holiday, and when he offered his children the choice that Sunday of either going to church or going out to watch the battle between the *Alabama* and the *Kearsarge*, they opted, not surprisingly, for the latter.

There were other observers on the water, but not nearly so many as there were on land. Wherever the men of the *Alabama* looked, there were hundreds of curiosity seekers eagerly crowding every vantage point from which they might see the battle. Some fifteen thousand people crowded onto the 2-mile-long breakwater that protected the mouth of the harbor and watched from the bluffs overlooking the channel. Others stood in the rigging of ships at anchor, gazing seaward. Excited groups of sightseers, from as far away as Paris and beyond—sporting spyglasses, parasols, and picnic baskets and looking like figures in a Renoir painting—strained to catch sight of the action. Down at the docks, one of Renoir's contemporaries, Édouard Manet, booked passage on a small boat, so that he might get close enough to the action to catch the details of the battle with his pencils and sketchbook. He would eventually translate his sketches into a classic painting of this celebrated event—two American ships fighting to the death off the coast of France.

Still another interested group were the officers and crews of the *Rockingham* and the *Tycoon,* the *Alabama*'s last captures, who had been prisoners on board the raider since April and had been landed at Cherbourg only a few days previously.

The day was bright and beautiful, with a light breeze blowing. As the *Alabama* rounded the breakwater, lookouts spotted the *Kearsarge* about 7 miles to the northeast, and Semmes immediately shaped course to intercept her. The crew was called to quarters, and orders were given to cast loose the starboard battery. Then Semmes mounted a gun carriage to speak to the men.

"Officers and seamen of the *Alabama*!" he addressed them. "You have at length another opportunity of meeting the enemy—the first that has been presented to you since you sank the *Hatteras*! In the meantime you have been all over the world, and it is not too much to say that you have destroyed, and driven for protection under neutral flags, one-half of the enemy's commerce, which at the beginning of the war covered every sea. This is an achievement of which you may well be proud, and a grateful country will not be unmindful of it. The name of your ship has become a household word wherever civilization extends! Shall that name be tarnished by defeat? The thing is impossible!"

"Never! Never!" shouted the enthralled crewmen.

"Remember that you are in the English Channel, the theatre of so much of the naval glory of our race, and that the eyes of all Europe are at this moment upon you. The flag that floats over you is that of a young republic, which bids defiance to her enemies whenever and wherever found! Show the world that you know how to uphold it! Go to your quarters!"

There was time for three cheers, and then the crew scattered to their guns.

The *Alabama* was burning Welsh coal; the *Kearsarge* was burning Newcastle coal, which produced a blacker smoke. As the distance between the two ships narrowed, sharp-eyed observers on shore claimed they could trace the movements of each ship distinctly by the color of smoke coming from the funnel of each.

When the captain of the *Couronne* judged that the ships had passed the marine league limit of French neutrality, he promptly put down her helm and steamed back into port, leaving the *Alabama* steaming forward. The steam yacht *Deerhound* continued in attendance and remained nearby.

As the two vessels approached what was to become the scene of action, Semmes ordered the magazines and shell rooms opened, filled tubs of water as a precaution against fire, and sanded the decks to keep them from getting slippery with blood. He had decided to use his starboard broadside, and to add strength to it, he ordered one of his 32-pounders shifted from the port side.

In about forty-five minutes, with the *Alabama* about a mile from the *Kearsarge* and both ships perhaps 7 miles offshore, the Union warship turned and headed directly for the raider. At about 10:57, as the two ships closed, Semmes opened fire from the starboard bow, with his 100-pounder pivot gun. The distance between the two ships, still almost a mile, was beyond the range of the *Kearsarge*'s guns, and for several minutes only the *Alabama*'s guns were active. As they closed to about 900 yards, the *Kearsarge* returned fire, and soon the action became general. John Kell noted that the guns of the two ships resounded differently and gave off a different quality of smoke. The report from the *Kearsarge's* battery was clear and sharp, the smoke a thin vapor, indicating fresh, fast-burning powder. In contrast, the guns of the *Alabama* boomed low and dull and produced a thick and heavy vapor.

Semmes urged his gunners to aim low rather than high. There was no point in damaging the enemy's masts and rigging, he told them, and even if they aimed too low, the sea was calm, and the shot would ricochet off the water and hit the target.

At least fifteen minutes passed before either ship inflicted significant damage on the other. The *Alabama* was first to draw blood. A shell from one of her guns exploded on the quarterdeck of the *Kearsarge,* wounding three members of a gun crew. A few minutes later, she landed what could have been a decisive hit. A shell from the forward pivot gun lodged in the *Kearsarge's* sternpost, near the steering mechanism. Due to a faulty fuse, the shell failed to explode and had no effect. Had it exploded, it would have disabled the *Kearsarge's* rudder, which could have decided the battle then and there and allowed the *Alabama* to make good her escape.

Soon after, a well-directed shot from the *Kearsarge* destroyed the *Alabama's* steering apparatus. Throughout the rest of the engagement, she had to be steered by jury-rigged tackle. The tide of battle was becoming evident.

By now the ships were about 500 yards apart, each presenting her starboard broadside to the other. They were facing in opposite directions, each using a strong port helm to prevent the other from passing. As a result, they were both moving in a clockwise circle, proceeding at top speed around a common center.

As the two ships settled into their circular course, the gunners in the *Alabama* switched to explosive shells rather than the solid shot they had used at the longer range. Semmes, standing on the horse block, where he could get an unobstructed view of the enemy ship through his glass, observed the effect of his gunner's work. "Mr. Kell, use solid shot," he called to his executive officer. "Our shells strike the enemy's

The battle between the Alabama *(foreground) and* Kearsarge, *as shown in a contemporary engraving.*

side and fall into the water." The chain mail on the *Kearsarge* was having its effect.

By that time the *Kearsarge*'s two 11-inch Dahlgrens had found their range and were pummeling the *Alabama*'s quarterdeck section. Semmes's reaction was one of minor irritation. "Confound them, they've been fighting 20 minutes, and they're cool as posts!" At one point the *Alabama*'s flag was cut down by enemy fire, but it was quickly restored. Soon after, three shells in succession passed through the port of the *Alabama*'s 8-inch pivot gun. The first swept off the forward part of the gun's crew, the second killed one man and wounded several others, and the third struck the breast of the gun carriage but failed to explode. It spun around on the deck, threatening the entire section, until one of the men picked it up and threw it overboard. Once again a shot from the *Kearsarge* took down the *Alabama*'s colors, but they were quickly restored on the mizzenmast. The decks of the *Alabama* were soon covered with the dead and wounded, and the ship began careening heavily toward starboard, pulled over by the weight of the guns and taking on water from the shot holes on the waterline. A shell fragment tore into Semmes's right arm, but the wound was hastily dressed, and he continued to command the action.

Both ships had gone into battle using steam power alone, with their sails furled and tucked out of the way, in part as a precaution against fire. But the *Alabama*'s worn-out engines were not providing the necessary speed, and the *Kearsarge* had proved far more nimble than Semmes had anticipated. The *Alabama* was getting the worst of it, and Semmes saw that his only chance of survival was to make it back to the safety of the French waters. He ordered Kell to wait until the clockwise path of the *Alabama* brought her toward land and then make all sail possible. He planned to pivot the ship to port and make toward shore, hoping to continue the action with the port battery while they limped toward the French coast.

The difficult maneuver was accomplished without a hitch, and the *Alabama* was able to settle smoothly into her new course, her guns operating throughout. For a long moment the *Alabama* had to expose her vulnerable bow to raking fire from the enemy's deadly broadside, but to the surprise of the Confederates, the *Kearsarge* held her fire and did not take advantage of the opportunity.

By now the port side of the quarterdeck had taken on the aspect of a slaughterhouse, and Kell had to order the mangled trunks of the dead thrown overboard, in order to fight the after pivot gun. The chief engineer stumbled onto the deck and reported that the fires were out below and he could no longer work the engines. Semmes turned grimly to Kell and said, "Go below, sir, and see how long the ship can float."

The sight that greeted the executive officer was appalling. Assistant Surgeon David Llewellyn stood at his post in the wardroom, but his operating table, and the wounded man on it, had been swept away by another 11-inch shell, which had opened a gaping hole in the side of the ship. The *Alabama* was fast taking on water. Kell hurried back on deck and reported that the ship could not last another ten minutes.

Semmes took the news calmly. "Then, sir, cease firing, shorten sail and haul down the colors," he said with resignation. "It will never do in this nineteenth century for us to go down, and the decks covered with our gallant wounded."

The last moments of the Alabama, *as she sank stern first into the English Channel. In the background, just to the left of the victorious* Kearsarge, *is the English yacht* Deerhound.

The lowering of the flag in surrender should have signaled the *Kearsarge* to cease firing, but the Federal ship continued to shell the fast-sinking *Alabama*. Semmes was predictably outraged at this breach of battlefield honor, and for years after the war was over, it remained a matter of bitter contention. Apparently Captain Winslow was not sure whether the Confederate colors had been deliberately lowered or, as earlier in the action, shot away. He also suspected a trick from the wily Semmes. In any case, he did not give the order to hold fire until sometime after the *Alabama* displayed a white flag across her stern.

When at last the guns stopped, Semmes ordered a boat dispatched to the *Kearsarge* to tell the Yankees that his ship was sinking and beg them to save the wounded, as the *Alabama*'s boats were disabled. Kell sent Master's Mate Fullam in the little dinghy, which had not been damaged. When the *Kearsarge* showed no sign of lowering boats, Kell ordered that one of the *Alabama*'s quarter boats, which had been only slightly damaged, be launched and the wounded placed in her. The crew managed to shove off just before the *Alabama* began to go down by the stern.

In those last moments, every man was ordered to grab a spar or other floating object and to jump for his life. Kell hurried back to the stern-port, now almost underwater, where he helped the wounded Semmes strip down to underwear and get into a life jacket. Both men threw their sabers in the sea rather than have them end up as Yankee trophies and then fell into the cold waters of the channel. The *Alabama*, mortally stricken, launched her bows high into the air. Kell described the last moments with feeling: "Graceful even in her death struggle, she in a moment disappeared from the face of the waters."

On board the *Kearsarge*, the crew watched the death throes of the *Alabama* in stunned silence. Many of the sailors were trying to free or repair the boats needed for rescue work, but among those awed men at the rails, there were no cheers or other shouts of triumph. Even with the *Alabama* still afloat, there were heads bobbing in the water. Some of the nonswimmers had already gone under, and others, clinging to flotsam in the choppy water, could not be expected to last much longer.

Captain Winslow, anxious to save as many as possible, signaled the yacht *Deerhound*, which had hovered about a mile to windward throughout the action, and as she passed, begged her, "For God's sake, do what you can to save them!"

The *Deerhound* immediately steamed toward the *Alabama*, which was by now on the verge of her final plunge, and lowered her two boats to pick up survivors. About twenty minutes later, Lieutenant Kell was fished out of the water by one of the *Deerhound*'s boats and found Semmes stretched out in the stern sheets, pale as death but still very much alive. Soon after, both of them were on board the *Deerhound* and being introduced to her owner, John Lancaster.

By this time the *Kearsarge* had finally managed to lower a couple of boats and was actively picking up survivors, as were two French pilot boats. Fullam, who had been sent back to the *Alabama* by Captain Winslow to collect more wounded, delivered them and himself to the *Deerhound*.

The unexploded shell from the Alabama *that lodged in the sternpost of the* Kearsarge. *The section was removed intact and sent to Washington, where it remains on display at the Navy Yard.*

On board the yacht, Kell was watching the last of the survivors being picked up when he saw one of the *Kearsarge*'s boats approaching. An American officer asked if anyone had seen Semmes. Kell answered, "Captain Semmes is drowned," and the boat moved off.

Later, in a stateroom, John Lancaster approached the exhausted Semmes. "I think every man has been picked up," he reported with satisfaction, and then, "Where shall I land you?"

Semmes, ever the lawyer, considered the issue. "I am now under English colors," he replied, "and the sooner you put me with my officers and men on English soil, the better."

TWENTY-TWO

The *Shenandoah*

On the evening of June 19, only hours after seeing his ship go down, an exhausted Raphael Semmes, swathed in blankets and suffering from his aching wound, huddled on the deck of the *Deerhound* and watched as the welcome coast of England materialized magically over the horizon. The *Deerhound* had rescued a total of forty-one officers and men, including eight wounded. At ten o'clock that evening, the yacht steamed up the river Test and docked in Southampton. Despite the late hour, well-wishers crowded the shore, eager to catch a glimpse of the famous corsair. Shepherded by the faithful Kell, the weary Semmes, after repeating his heartfelt gratitude to John Lancaster, the owner of the *Deerhound*, checked into Kelway's Hotel. The wounded were taken to the Sailors' Home on Canute Road, while the other officers and men rescued from the *Alabama* found accommodations elsewhere in the city.

The following morning the story of the battle between the *Alabama* and the *Kearsarge* dominated the European press, as it would eventually in North America when the news made it across the Atlantic. After a leisurely breakfast, Semmes and Kell visited a tailor's shop to purchase some much-needed clothing but were forced to cut short their shopping when an excited crowd, eager for a glimpse of Semmes, grew so large it blocked the street.

That afternoon, James Bulloch and James Mason, the Confederate commissioner in London, arrived on the four o'clock train to evaluate the situation and provide all necessary help.

Days later, after reports filtered in from France, it became possible to assess the statistical results of the battle. In addition to the forty-one men, including twelve officers, picked up by the *Deerhound*'s two boats, the *Kearsarge* had recovered seventy men in all, but only five officers. Two French pilot boats pulled in fifteen survivors, some of whom were delivered to the *Kearsarge,* while others were taken into Cherbourg. Nine of the *Alabama*'s crew had been killed in the action and twenty-one wounded. Twelve men were missing and presumed drowned, including Semmes's personal servant, Bartelli; along with the wardroom orderly, David White, the only black man on board; and the British Dr. Llewellyn, the ship's surgeon. All three might well have survived had they known how to swim.

Total casualties on the *Kearsarge* came to three men wounded, one of whom later died.

Over the course of time, other statistics would emerge that would indicate just how lopsided the battle had been, almost a mirror image of that between the *Alabama* and the *Hatteras* in the Gulf of Mexico. The *Alabama* had fired more than twice as many rounds as the *Kearsarge*—370 as against 173—but the Union gunnery had been far more accurate and effective.

Several naval officers who watched the fight from the Cherbourg heights corroborated Kell's observation about the relative quality of gunpowder in the battle and later told Bulloch they were struck by the difference in the appearance of the flame and smoke produced by the explosions of the shells from the two ships. Those from the *Kearsarge* emitted a quick, bright flash, and the smoke went quickly away in a fine blue vapor, while those from the *Alabama* produced a dull flame and a mass of sluggish gray smoke.

Semmes spent a week in Southampton recuperating and winding up the affairs of his lost command. He arranged for the chronometers that he had entrusted to his Cherbourg agent, Bonfils, to be shipped to a British bank. Their eventual sale would produce the only prize money the *Alabama* ever distributed. When Semmes and Kell had completed their work, they left Southampton to spend some time in seclusion with English friends.

When a group of Royal Navy officers learned that Semmes's sword had gone down with his ship, they raised funds for a replacement, which, with suitable ceremony, was duly presented to him. The inscription read:

> PRESENTED TO CAPTAIN RAPHAEL SEMMES, C.S.N.,
> BY OFFICERS OF THE ROYAL NAVY AND OTHER FRIENDS
> IN ENGLAND, AS A TESTIMONIAL OF THEIR ADMIRATION
> OF THE GALLANTRY WITH WHICH HE MAINTAINED THE HONOUR
> OF HIS COUNTRY'S FLAG AND THE FAME OF THE ALABAMA
> IN THE ENGAGEMENT OFF CHERBOURG, WITH A CHAIN-PLATED SHIP
> OF SUPERIOR POWER, ARMAMENT AND CREW, JUNE 19TH, 1864.

Most of the details connected with the loss of the *Alabama* were handled by James Bulloch. Crew members were paid off in full, either in Cherbourg or in Southampton; wages for those lost went to families or legal representatives. It was only by chance that Bulloch happened to be in England at the time and available to take care of such matters. For weeks he had been busy elsewhere, immersed in a tangled scheme to get another four ironclads out of France and into the hands of the Confederate Navy.

Bulloch was convinced that ironclads held the key to victory in the war, and after the fiasco over the Laird rams, he had transferred his shipbuilding efforts to the Continent and was trying to build them in France. He had long since given up any interest in commerce raiders, and certainly the last thing on his mind was the likelihood of arranging to send another one to sea. So it came as a considerable surprise to him to receive urgent orders from Secretary Mallory to find a replacement for the *Alabama* as soon as possible. "The loss of the *Alabama* was announced in the Federal papers with all the manifestations of joy which usually usher in the news of great national victories," Mallory argued, "showing that the calculating enemy fully understood and appreciated the importance of her destruction." It was a matter of "paramount importance" for Bulloch to fit out a replacement for the *Al-abama* as soon as possible.

Clearly there was no time to build such a ship. Bulloch would have to buy something off the shelf. Within two weeks he did just that and was able to write Mallory, "I have the satisfaction to inform you of the purchase of a fine composite ship, built for the Bombay trade, and just returned to London from her first voyage." Her name was the *Sea King*. She was about the same size as the *Alabama* and was planked from keel to gunwale with East India teak, which meant she would require little in the way of structural reinforcement to carry guns. "You will be gratified to learn of this good fortune in finding a ship so admirably suited to our purpose," he wrote with obvious satisfaction, "and I will only now assure you that no effort will be spared, and no precaution neglected, which may help to get her under our flag."

As soon as his newest raider picked up her guns at Madeira, she would be rechristened the CSS *Shenandoah,* and during her hurried refitting, Bulloch made it a point never to set foot on her himself, lest he be observed by one of Dudley's spies. The imperative to get her into action intensified when, almost simultaneously with her secret departure from England, news arrived that the *Florida,* the ship Bulloch had sent out so long before as the *Oreto,* had been captured by the Federal Navy in Brazil. With both the *Alabama* and the *Florida* out of action, the *Shenandoah* alone was left to complete the work of Bulloch's commerce raiders. She would more than live up to the task.

In Washington the noisy celebration over the sinking of the *Alabama* was quickly drowned out by the bellows of outrage over the escape of Raphael Semmes and his subsequent lionizing by the British press and public. Gideon Welles, the secretary of the navy, was particularly incensed. For years Semmes had been his bête noir, the elusive and infuriating "pirate" who had caused him so much trouble, and Welles was determined to bring him up on charges to answer for his mischief.

Charles Francis Adams, acting on instructions from William Seward, vigorously denounced the actions of the *Deerhound* in bringing the rescued men to England rather than turning them over to the

Kearsarge. Lord Russell dismissed the complaint out of hand. Standing for once on the moral high ground, in a sharply worded response to the American note, he wrote that in his judgment the owner of the *Deerhound* "performed only a common duty of humanity" in saving Semmes and the others and, as a British subject, was under no obligation to turn over the rescued men.

The principal figure in all this diplomatic squabbling, the redoubtable Raphael Semmes, was by now fully rested and restored after a leisurely tour of the Continent in the company of agreeable friends, and around the time that Bulloch sent the *Sea King* off to become the *Shenandoah*, he left England for home. Yankee agents, who had been tracking his every move, rushed the news to Washington, where Gideon Welles made plans to capture him. He alerted the blockading squadrons off Charleston and Wilmington, the two ports Semmes would most likely try to enter, and scheduled extra patrols.

But once again Raphael Semmes outthought the United States Navy, by avoiding the east coast altogether and landing at Matamoros, Mexico, where he quietly crossed the Rio Grande into the Confederacy aboard an unarmed skiff.

In February 1865, after picking his way mournfully across his broken and beloved South, Semmes was promoted to rear admiral and placed in command of the James River squadron, in Virginia, guarding the water route to Richmond. In April, when Grant's army took the capital, Semmes scuttled his ships and retreated overland with Jefferson Davis and the rest of the government to Danville, Virginia. Here he received the unique honor of being commissioned a brigadier general, in which rank he helped organize the last desperate attempts to stave off the inevitable. After Lee's surrender at Appomattox and the collapse of the Confederacy, Semmes was finally captured at Greensboro, North Carolina, and subsequently released.

———————

The war at last was over. Or so it might have been, had it not been for James Bulloch's last contribution to it. On August 2, 1865, months after Appomattox and far out in the Pacific, the CSS *Shenandoah*, under Captain James Waddell, stopped the British bark *Barracouta*, in hopes of learning the most recent news of the war. The *Shenandoah* had just come south from the Bering Sea, where she had effectively destroyed the last major element of the American merchant marine that had heretofore escaped the fury of the Confederate raiders—the Pacific whaling fleet.

When the boat returned from the *Barracouta* with the San Francisco newspapers, Waddell and his crew learned for the first time the doleful details of the final collapse of the South. The *Shenandoah* had been operating for almost four months after the end of the war and in that time had illegally captured, and destroyed or bonded, twenty-five victims. It was time to go home. But where was home?

Waddell was too proud to bring his ship into an enemy harbor. He decided to ignore California entirely and, in his determination to find a more welcome port of call, turned south toward Cape Horn. Early in September, having doubled the horn and regained the Atlantic, he turned north, toward England. Finally, on November 5, 1865, seven months after the end of the war, the *Shenandoah* entered the Mersey, her Confederate flag snapping proudly at her peak, and steamed up-river, to the surprise and wonder of astonished onlookers lining both the Liverpool and Birkenhead banks. Dropping anchor, Waddell retired to his cabin and dictated a long letter to Lord Russell at the Foreign Office, surrendering his ship to the British government.

For Russell the sudden and unexpected reappearance of the *Shenandoah* at Britain's doorstep could not have come at a more awkward moment. Ever since the end of the war, Charles Francis Adams had been vigorously pressing the British government for reparations for the millions of dollars of damages inflicted by the *Alabama* and the other English-built raiders. The Foreign Office had disdainfully rejected the American demands, disclaiming any responsibility in the matter, when the *Shenandoah* appeared out of nowhere, an unwelcome reminder of the ultimately disastrous British policy of meddling in another country's war. The diplomatic battle over the *Alabama* claims was only just beginning.

Charles Francis Adams, American minister to England throughout the war. His detailed complaints about Confederate shipbuilding activities were the cornerstone of the Alabama *claims.*

III

Adams

TWENTY-THREE

The Claims

In the early months of 1865, Charles Francis Adams suddenly and unexpectedly found his social standing in London markedly improved. For many years the American minister had been little better than a social pariah. The ruling classes of Britain saw him as the representative of a pretentious and generally offensive republican government on the other side of the Atlantic whose very existence deeply offended them. Now, in the closing months of the Civil War, he discovered a new openness, a new warmth and friendliness on the part of the people who ran England. Adams, always correct, always restrained, always something of a cold fish, looked upon his new popularity with sardonic amusement.

For years the British aristocracy had anticipated a Confederate victory in the war. The London press had fed that expectation with biased reports that pumped up every Northern defeat and smoothed away the pain of every Southern failing. In the pages of the *Times,* the most influential paper, Mr. Lincoln and his people were presented as little more than barbarians. That Americans had elected—and then reelected—such an unpromising bumpkin was seen as proof of the inherent instability of the democratic experiment and evidence of its ultimate failure. But by the early spring of 1865, the fact that the South was on its last legs could no longer be hidden, and it was dawning on the leaders of Britain, including those in the Palmerston government, that they had bet on the wrong horse. The egregious Yankees were going to win.

Adams knew that behind the new and unaccustomed cordiality he now encountered in London society lay the cold stink of fear. The aristocrats, worried about their vast fortunes, so much of which were tied up in various overseas enterprises, were afraid of him. There was widespread apprehension that the Union victory that now appeared inevitable was likely to be followed by a war of revenge against Britain. The United States now had the largest and most modern navy and the largest, best-trained, and best-equipped army in the world, and the talk in the clubs was that the government in Washington was bound to use its almost irresistible strength to attack those powers, primarily Britain, that had tried to influence the outcome of the war for their own advantage. Such grim thoughts were not limited to a hysterical minority. The directors of England's greatest banking house, Baring's, wrestled seriously with the problem of how to protect their interests in America should it come to war.

Adams watched the shifting emotional scene with amusement and cautioned the State Department in Washington that the United States was going to have to raise the question of reparations with extreme delicacy, or else it might frighten the British too much.

If Charles Francis Adams lacked a certain sense of humor, he more than made up for it in his appreciation of history's ironies. Throughout the long and anxious years in London, he never lost sight of the absurd fact that the Foreign Enlistment Act—the single most troublesome piece of legislation on Britain's books, the set of regulations that had been at the heart of Lord Russell's duplicitous game—was based on an American law.

In 1793, when Britain was at war with revolutionary France, the ministers of the Crown were worried that the United States government might allow French warships cruising in the western Atlantic to use American ports, which would make the Royal Navy's job considerably more difficult. To ease British anxieties, Congress enacted a law prohibiting such activities on the part of any belligerent power. While the law was designed primarily to protect American neutrality, it had the effect of severely restricting French naval activity in American waters while in no way impeding the activities of the Royal Navy, which maintained well-appointed naval stations in Canada, Bermuda, and the West Indies.

The British were suitably grateful to the Americans, and Parliament, at the instigation of George Canning, eventually passed its own neutrality law, the Foreign Enlistment Act of 1819, specifically modeling it on the original American law.

Why had the American law worked in Britain's favor while the British version of the same law worked against the Americans? To Adams the answer was simple and straightforward. In 1794 America was a weak country, very much intimidated by the might of Great Britain and anxious to accommodate her, but in 1861 Great Britain was the most powerful nation on earth and openly contemptuous of the interests of other nations, including those of the United States. It was British arrogance, plain and simple, that Adams saw as the principal reason for the antagonistic relations between Britain and the United States throughout the war.

Adams came by his distrust of British intentions as a matter of heritage. He was the third generation of Adamses to serve as American ambassador to Britain. Both his father and grandfather had held the same office, and neither they nor he had ever found reason to trust Britain. His son Henry would one day make the point that, for more than a hundred years, "the only public occupation of all Adamses . . . has been to quarrel with Downing Street."

Importantly this mistrust was not an expression of personal animosity. It accurately reflected a prejudice widely held throughout America in the eighteenth and nineteenth centuries. There was a great deal of transatlantic bad feeling that has since faded away, but at the time it was very real. Alexis de Tocqueville, the most prescient of all European observers of the American experiment, wrote after his visit in 1831, "Nothing can be more virulent than the hatred which exists between the United States and the English."

Lord John Russell, British foreign secretary, who long maintained that the British government would not consider the Alabama *claims under any circumstances.*

Now that the war was over, Adams planned to bring up the *Alabama* claims with Lord Russell one last time and hoped to dispose of the problem for good and all. With the return of peace, he thought it was just possible that the British government might bring itself to bend a little and to reconsider the very serious losses suffered by American shipping interests as a result of the Mersey-built commerce raiders. It even seemed possible, given America's overwhelming military superiority, that the British might come to some sort of reasonable accommodation on the matter. But when Adams raised the question in

May, carefully couching his petition in the most diplomatic language, he found Lord Russell more intransigent than ever. He saw the American proposal as an accusation that he and his government had been guilty of deliberately misinterpreting their own laws and took immediate umbrage. "Her Majesty's Government are the sole guardians of their own honour," he responded frostily. The idea that a foreign government might presume to judge whether the British had been right or wrong in their behavior was an insult to national dignity and character. The Crown law officers were better interpreters of British statutes than any Yankee. There would be, Russell made clear, no further consideration of the *Alabama* claims.

When Lord Palmerston died in October 1865, Russell succeeded him as prime minister, and Adams realized that there could be no question of reopening negotiations. The British government would not consider the *Alabama* claims under any circumstances. The door that Russell had slammed was now bolted shut. But Adams knew that Russell led a shaky coalition and would not remain in power forever. He put the issue aside in hopes of finding a more propitious moment to bring it up again.

In the meantime the best he could do was to make it clear to the British aristocracy that the *Alabama* claims were not about to go away and that Americans felt deeply that the creation of the commerce raiders represented an outrage that must somehow, sometime, be paid for. The country was united on that score, and American politicians of every stripe found it convenient to demonstrate their patriotic fervor by damning British perfidy and demanding recompense. It was a wound that would not heal, and its unresolved presence would continue to influence every aspect of Anglo-American relations for years to come.

In July 1866 Russell and his Liberal party fell out of power and were replaced by a Tory government headed by Lord Derby, with his son, Lord Stanley, as foreign secretary. Adams considered the possibility of reopening negotiations on the *Alabama* claims, and the American navy provided a little indirect encouragement. The USS *Miantonomoh,* a double-turreted, oceangoing ironclad monitor, stopped in England on its way to Russia on a goodwill tour. Royal Navy experts were invited to tour the warship and readily agreed that Britain had nothing to match her. A nervous *Times* described the powerful American cruiser anchored amid the pride of the Royal Navy and warned, "There is not one [British warship] that the foreigner could not have sent to the bottom in five minutes. . . . In fact, the wolf was in the fold, and the whole flock was at its mercy."

Coincidence or not, soon after the *Miantonomoh* resumed her passage to St. Petersburg, the new Tory government, with no prompting from Mr. Adams, proposed that Britain and America reconsider the *Alabama* claims. Adams responded enthusiastically, but Lord Stanley immediately imposed so many restrictions on the nature of the talks that when Adams alerted William Seward in Washington, the secretary of state rejected the proposal out of hand, and once again the question was left hanging.

———

And then, quite unexpectedly, something happened in a totally unrelated quarter that gave the question of the *Alabama* claims a new urgency and provided a fresh impetus for resolving the issue. It involved a dissident Irish-American secret society that called itself the Fenian Brotherhood.

The brotherhood, an organization of Irish-American immigrants that would years later change its name to the Irish Republican Army, had been founded in New York in 1858, as part of a worldwide league of Irish patriots dedicated to overthrowing British rule in Ireland. By 1866 the Fenians had gained considerable strength in America, and their numbers included a large contingent of veterans of the Civil War. In June a group of some fifteen hundred armed Fenians, under the command of "General" John O'Neill, attempted an invasion of Canada across the Niagara River, and while they were quickly repulsed by a battalion of Canadian volunteers, their efforts caught the attention of the world and exposed the fragile nature of Canada's security.

That same summer British police began cracking down on Fenian activities in England and Ireland. Many of those arrested claimed American citizenship and produced naturalization papers in proof, demanding to see the nearest U.S. consul. British authorities refused to recognize such naturalization, pointing out that according to their law, it was impossible for anyone born under British rule to change his nationality. This provoked an angry reaction in America and built up sympathy for the Fenians and their cause.

It was at that point that Congressman Nathaniel P. Banks of Massachusetts—a clever, if unscrupulous politico who was quick to spot an opportunity—found a way to tie the troubles of the Fenians directly to America's smoldering resentment over the *Alabama* claims. He introduced a bill in the House of Representatives that would replace the stringent American neutrality laws with weaker legislation, *based specifically on the British Foreign Enlistment Act.* Under such ambiguous laws, he pointed out, the Fenian Brotherhood would be allowed to launch their own commerce raiders from American ports and fill the oceans with dozens of *Alabama*s, possibly manned by Yankee crews, built to cruise against the British merchant marine.

It was a clever move and immediately caught Great Britain's attention. But before Congress could act, Secretary Seward had already decided to take a different tack. Rather than seeking revenge or monetary compensation, he proposed to settle the *Alabama* claims in exchange for real estate. Early in 1867, using the newly installed Atlantic cable, he wired Adams, suggesting a plan whereby the United States would formally absolve Britain of all responsibility for the *Alabama* claims. A grateful Britain would, in return, allow the United States to purchase the Bahamas.

When his idea failed to spark interest in Whitehall, Seward turned around and purchased Alaska from the Russians and then publicly announced that his purpose in doing so was to increase American influence in British Columbia (which at the time was not part of Canada) with the ultimate intention of annexing it to the United States. A correspondent in Washington wrote to Charles Francis Adams and described Seward as boasting that "the Alabama Claims would soon be settled, but now they could only be settled in one way, by such acquisition from England as to enable us to round off our North-Western territory."

When Seward sent the proposal to London for formal presentation to the Foreign Office, Adams warned him that the British were too proud to accept such a swap. "In my belief, the maintenance of the connection with Canada is a matter of pride with the British nation," he wrote, "which will only be made the more stubborn in resistance to change by the smallest indication on our part of a disposition to impair it."

Unfazed, Seward upped the ante and offered to throw into the mix the unresolved Anglo-American dispute as to which country owned San Juan Island, in Puget Sound. Years before, in settling the Oregon question, Britain and America had agreed that the national boundary would lie in the middle of the San Juan Channel, but the question later arose as to whether the channel was to the west of San Juan Island or to the east of it. The Americans claimed it was to the west; the British claimed it was to the east. The issue came to a head in 1859, when an American on the island shot a pig belonging to the Hudson's Bay Company, at which point both countries established armed encampments and prepared to arbitrate. Before that could happen, the Civil War broke out and the matter was shelved.

Seward now suggested that all the contentious issues—including the San Juan Straits, the legal status of naturalizations, treatment of the Fenians, and, of course, the *Alabama* claims—be packaged together and considered as a whole.

By this time Charles Francis Adams had long since tired of the game. He had spent seven years in London and was worn out. He yearned for home, referring to his years in England as his "exile." He had done his job. He had not accomplished everything he might have wanted to, but he had kept Great Britain out of the war. That was enough. With the advent of the Atlantic cable, which gave the government in Washington virtually instantaneous communication with London, he felt free to turn the job of administering American activities in Britain over to others.

As to the *Alabama* claims, they were almost certainly a dead letter. Between the ill-conceived opportunism of Mr. Seward's State Department and the obdurate foot-dragging of the Foreign Office, he doubted they would ever be resolved. Or so he believed in December 1867, when he submitted his resignation.

TWENTY-FOUR

Sumner's Speech

Despite Adams's misgivings, Seward was determined to pursue the *Alabama* claims aggressively. He sent an amiable but naive lawyer named Reverdy Johnson to London to replace Adams and urged him to make the claims his chief priority. Johnson was eager to comply. The result, unveiled in January 1869, was the Johnson-Clarendon convention, a stunningly lopsided agreement hammered out by the combined efforts of the American minister and Lord Clarendon, foreign secretary in the new Gladstone government. Clarendon was a subtle and well-seasoned diplomat who knew precisely how to handle the unsophisticated American. Together this oddest of couples managed to cobble together a treaty that left out anything that might offend British sensibilities while shoehorning a number of innocent-looking subparagraphs and codicils into the text designed to line British pockets at the expense of the American treasury. If anyone was going to pay for the *Alabama* claims, apparently it was going to be the United States.

It was not simply an inadequate treaty, it was a dog's breakfast, and William Seward knew it. At first he tried to lay the blame on Reverdy Johnson, whose total lack of negotiating abilities undoubtedly contributed to the document's inadequacies. But in truth, the chief culprit was Seward himself, whose disastrous attempts at long-distance tinkering and micromanagement via the Atlantic cable had allowed the

English negotiators to cut and trim the final convention precisely to Whitehall's fashion. In the light of hindsight, one can only wonder if the Foreign Office ever believed the Yankees would be foolish enough to ratify it. More likely they did not care.

The agreement was too sloppily drawn to be saved by amendments, and by the time it was ready to be signed, it was too late for Seward to start over again. He would soon be out of a job. The new administration of General Ulysses S. Grant was about to take office, and Grant would be bringing his own secretary of state, Hamilton Fish, with him. Ever the optimist, Seward reverted to his old hobbyhorse: somehow everything could be settled by an exchange of real estate. "Great Britain owes the United States for injuries committed," he wrote to Johnson, adding that "the injury is of a nature that cannot be estimated in pecuniary damages; atonement ought therefore be demanded in the form of an acknowledgement of that wrong with a concession of territory." That the Johnson-Clarendon convention offered no machinery for either an apology or a land swap was to be lamented.

By the time the document came to the Senate for consideration, Grant had assumed the presidency and Seward was no longer a factor. Whether the treaty would be ratified depended first and foremost on the opinion of the chairman of the Senate Committee on Foreign Relations, Charles Sumner, senior senator from Massachusetts.

Sumner was one of the most powerful men in Washington politics. He was a man of great influence and commanded national attention. When, on April 13, 1869, he rose to address the Senate on the subject of the Johnson-Clarendon convention, there was a general expectation that he would not recommend ratification. But no one in his audience could have guessed how dramatically he was about to change the argument over the *Alabama* claims or the degree to which he would heighten the emotional level of the dispute, which had by now been overshadowing Anglo-American relations for eight years.

Sumner was a statesman of the old school, a spellbinding orator on the order of Daniel Webster and John C. Calhoun, famous for his thundering pronunciamentos and dramatic declamations, which had earned him an international reputation. He was a man in his late fifties, of prepossessing size and authority, standing 6 feet, 4 inches tall, with broad shoulders and a massive frame, and still possessed of Byronic good looks and a voice of great clarity and power. He was a consummate performer, and his use of gesture was, by one admiring account, "unconventional . . . but vigorous and impressive."

Sumner had made his name as a leader of the abolitionist movement, and in the tumultuous years leading up to the war, his passionate attacks on "that harlot, Slavery," had earned him the bitter enmity of virtually every Southern leader. In 1856 the mutual animosity between Sumner and the slave owners reached a crisis when the senator, after delivering himself of a bitter diatribe against the proslavery guerrillas in Kansas, was brutally attacked at his desk by a congressman from South Carolina who stormed into the chamber and beat him senseless with a brass-headed cane, leaving him so disabled that it was four years before he recovered enough to return to the Senate. After the caning Sumner was never quite right in his head, and even his most ardent supporters suspected that the beating had permanently clouded his judgment and left him with a tendency to overreact and to become arrogant and extreme in his opinions.

Another factor that may have influenced his argument that day was his personal anguish over a private matter, the details of which were well known to everyone in his audience. A year previously, after a lifetime of bachelorhood, Sumner had married a young and pretty widow, Alice Mason Hooper, who had subsequently left him under scandalous circumstances, having discovered, as one contemporary account put it, "that he was not gifted with 'full powers.' " Humiliated, lonely, personally unpopular, and suffering still from the caning that may have forever affected his reasoning, Charles Sumner arose to give the Senate his opinion of the Johnson-Clarendon convention and to address its principal object, the resolution of the *Alabama* claims.

———

Sumner's speech, addressed to the Senate in executive session, managed to encapsulate, for the first time, all the anger, the outrage, the bitter sense of betrayal that many Americans felt toward Britain in

Charles Sumner, senior senator from Massachusetts, whose fiery address to the Senate on the issue of the Alabama *claims encapsulated, for the first time, the anger and outrage that many Americans felt toward Britain in the years after the Civil War.*

connection with the *Alabama* claims. In the tradition of the great rhetoricians, he opened his remarks with a quiet, reflective exposition of the subject and made it clear that he was going to recommend that the Senate reject the treaty before it "in the interests of peace" between the United States and Great Britain. In reasoned tones he pointed out that while the treaty might seem to provide a means of finally settling the *Alabama* claims, such was not the case. "It does not," he said flatly, and then, his voice rising for the first time, "It is nothing but a snare."

With the first hint of anger in his tone, he continued, "The massive grievance under which our country suffered for years is left untouched; the painful sense of wrong planted in the national heart is allowed to remain. For all this," he said, indicating the draft treaty with a contemptuous wave of his hand, "there is not one word of regret or even of recognition; nor is there any sense of compensation."

Warming to his subject, he continued, "Whatever may have been the disposition of the negotiators, the real root of evil remains untouched in all its original strength."

As his voice began to take on the heat of his argument, he defined the *Alabama* claims as "a national grievance of transcendent importance in the relations of two countries." The key word of his definition was *national*. He went on to express the heart of the argument he planned to make. In the draft treaty under discussion, "the national cause is handled as nothing more than a bundle of individual claims," he explained. There were no allowances for national grievances, no acknowledgment that such grievances might exist. The entire nation had been injured by the actions of the British government, but the Johnson-Clarendon convention addressed only the injuries to individuals.

And who were the individuals? Not just Americans. Not just those whose ships had been captured and burned, whose cargoes had been destroyed, whose fortunes had been lost forever. Such unfortunates would indeed be dealt with by the convention, but they would not be alone. There were British injured parties, too, individuals who had suffered loss as a result of the American Civil War, and they were to be treated in precisely the same way as the Americans. Think of it. English blockade-runners would be eligible for compensation! And they were not alone. With rising anger he added to the list of those whose claims would be covered by the treaty. "Already it is announced in England that even those of 'Confederate bondholders' are included," he charged. English negotiators had so twisted the wording of the treaty that London speculators holding worthless cotton bonds that had been floated to finance the Confederate war effort were to be recompensed by the United States! He paused to let the enormity of the outrage sink in. "I learn that these bondholders are very sanguine of success under

the treaty as it is worded, and certain it is that the loan went up from
o to 10 as soon as it was ascertained that the treaty was signed." Another pause. "I doubt if the American people are ready just now to provide for any such claims," he noted dryly, adding that the simple fact
that those worthless bonds had risen in the market was reason enough
to vote against the treaty.

And then Sumner launched into the main thrust of his argument,
addressing the perfidy of an England that had deliberately set out,
from the very opening of the war, to work against American interests
and to do everything within its power to aid the Confederacy, short of
actually declaring war on the United States. The first and most important hostile act, as he defined it, was the Queen's Proclamation of Neutrality, issued in May 1861.

"Close upon the outbreak of our troubles, just one month after the
bombardment of Fort Sumter, when the rebellion was still undevel-
oped, when the national Government was beginning those gigantic efforts which ended so triumphantly, the country was startled by the
news that the British Government had intervened by a proclamation,
which accorded belligerent rights to the rebels."

And what was so pernicious about the proclamation? Principally
that it recognized the Confederacy as a *naval power* as well as a military power on land. "At the early date when this was done the rebels
were, as they remained to the close, without ships on the ocean, without Prize Courts or other tribunals for the administration of justice on
the ocean, without any of those conditions which are the essential pre-
requisites to such a concession, and yet the concession was general, being applicable to the ocean and the land, so that by British fiat they
became ocean belligerents as well as land belligerents."

Taking on the tones of an Old Testament prophet, he called upon
his colleagues to consider the profound ramifications of such a concession on England's part. "From the beginning, when God called the dry
land earth, and the gathering of the waters called He seas, the two have
been separate and the power over one has not necessarily implied
power over the other. There is a dominion of the land and a dominion
of the ocean. But whatever power the rebels possessed on the land,
they were always without power on the ocean."

So apparently innocent, the Queen's Proclamation was, he charged, the key to Britain's duplicity. "The direct consequence of this concession was to place the rebels on an equality with ourselves in all British markets, whether of ships or munitions of war." By this simple device, "the asserted neutrality between the two began by this tremendous concession when rebels, in one stroke, were transformed not only into belligerents, but into customers."

The most reprehensible aspect of the proclamation was that it assumed an entirely false equality between the United States government and that of the Confederates. "It was a proclamation of equality between the National Government on the one side and rebels on the other, and no plausible word can obscure this distinction of character." And with that he turned to specifics. "Then came the building of the pirate ships, one after another. While the *Alabama* was still in the shipyard it became apparent that she was intended for the rebels. Our Minister at London and our Consul at Liverpool exerted themselves for her arrest and detention."

Then in quick order Sumner outlined the familiar details of Dudley's spies, Adams's impassioned demands, the legal support for the American case given by high British authorities, the determined stonewalling of Lord Russell, and the *Alabama*'s eventual escape.

But, Sumner pointed out meaningfully, the British government eventually relented and sent orders to stop the *Alabama*, orders that arrived too late. But when the *Alabama* left Liverpool, he reminded his listeners, she did not leave Britain. "The pirate ship found refuge in an obscure harbor in Wales," where she remained another day and a half, while the *Hercules* was able to deliver her crew. "These thirty-six hours were allowed to elapse without any attempt to stop her," he emphasized.

Then he used the foreign secretary's own words to further his argument. "Lord Russell . . . more than once admitted that the escape of the *Alabama* was a 'scandal and reproach,' which, to my mind, is very like a confession."

He discussed the nationality of the crew. "The *Alabama*, whose building was in defiance of law . . . whose escape was 'a scandal and reproach,' and whose enlistment of her crew was a fit sequel to the rest, after being supplied with an armament and with a rebel commander, entered upon her career of piracy."

Sumner was a street fighter. Throughout his speech, which was now entering its second hour and had become more like a tirade, he constantly referred to the *Alabama* and her sisters as pirates rather than raiders. "Mark now a new stage of complicity. Constantly the pirate ship was within reach of British cruisers, and from time to time within the shelter of British ports." He described Semmes's triumphant reception in the British port of Jamaica after sinking the USS *Hatteras*. "For six days unmolested she enjoyed the pleasant hospitality . . . obtaining freely the coal and other supplies so necessary to her vocation. But no British cruiser, no British magistrate ever arrested the offending ship, whose voyage was a continuing 'scandal and reproach' to the British Government," he noted dryly. "No British cruiser could allow her to proceed, no British port could give her shelter without renewing the complicity of England."

With lawyerly exactitude, he nailed down British responsibility. "Thus, at three different stages, the British Government is compromised, first, in the concession of ocean belligerency, on which all depended; secondly, in the negligence which allowed the evasion of the ship in order to enter upon the hostile expedition for which she was built, manned, armed and equipped; and thirdly, in the open complicity which, after this evasion, gave her welcome hospitality and supplies in British ports. Thus her depredations and burnings, making the oceans blaze, all proceeded from England, which, by three different acts, lighted the torch. To England must be traced also all the widespread consequences which ensued."

The Confederate raiders, he charged, "were British in every respect except their commanders, who were rebel, and one of these," he added, in a reference to Semmes's rescue by the *Deerhound*, "as his ship was sinking, owed his safety to a British yacht, symbolizing the omnipresent support of England."

Now Sumner had another score to settle. He was, he claimed, a lifelong Anglophile, with a strong emotional attachment to England. For years he had maintained a voluminous correspondence with many of the best and most liberal minds in Great Britain. But his admiration for Britain, which stemmed in part from his high regard for that country's efforts to eradicate the world slave trade, had turned to fury and suspicion at what he saw as her active support of the Confederacy. Now he would at last address the issue.

He complained about the "flagrant, unnatural departure from that anti-slavery rule, which by manifold declarations, legislative, political, and diplomatic, was the avowed creed of England. Often was this rule proclaimed, but . . . now, when the slaveholders, in the madness of barbarism, broke away from the National Government and attempted to found a new empire with slavery as its declared corner-stone, anti-slavery England, without a day's delay . . . made haste to decree that this shameful and impossible pretension should enjoy equal rights with the National Government in her ship-yards, foundries and manufactories, and equal rights on the ocean."

He quoted with approval John Bright's 1863 speech in Parliament, where he had announced, "I regret, more than I have words to express, this painful fact, that of all the countries in Europe this country is the only one which has men in it who are willing to take steps in favor of this intended slave Government. We supply the ships; we supply the arms, the munitions of war; we give aid and comfort to the foulest of crimes."

Having made his case for Albion's perfidy, Sumner now turned to the enumeration of America's losses brought about by it. "At last the rebellion succumbed. British ships and British supplies had done their work, but they failed. And now the day of reckoning has come, but with little apparent sense of what is due on the part of England."

Sumner began with the simplest costs, those suffered by American victims of the *Alabama* and her sisters. "Individual losses may be represented with reasonable accuracy. Ships burned or sunk with their cargoes may be counted and their value determined." His audience was familiar with such figures. They had been discussed for years and ranged anywhere from 8 to 15 millions of dollars, depending on how the damages were assessed. Sumner dealt only briefly with such individual claims. They represented just the tip of the iceberg, he asserted, and did not take into account the permanent damage to commerce driven from the ocean, which he listed as "national" losses.

The Confederate raiders had devastated the entire American merchant marine, and he would prove it. "How to authenticate the extent of national loss with reasonable certainty is not without difficulty," Sumner admitted, "but it cannot be doubted that such a loss occurred. It is folly to question it. The loss may be seen in various circumstances, as in the rise of insurance on all American vessels; the fate of the carrying trade, which was one of the great resources of our country; the diminution of our tonnage; the falling off of our exports and imports, with due allowance for our abnormal currency and the diversion of war."

He began to throw statistics at his audience. "American shipping had been transferred to English capitalists as follows: in 1850, 33 vessels, 13,638 tons; 1859, 49 vessels, 21,673 tons; 1860, 41 vessels, 13,638 tons; 1861, 126 vessels, 71,673 tons; 1862, 135 vessels, 64,573 tons; and 1863, 348 vessels, 255,579 tons . . . during the decade from 1852 to 1862, sixty-seven per cent of the total tonnage entered from foreign countries was in American vessels, and during the five years from 1863 to 1868, only thirty-nine percent of the aggregate tonnage entered from foreign countries was in American vessels, a relative falling off of nearly one half."

Even those of his listeners who could not follow the numbers could see the trend. America, once a leading maritime power, had seen its merchant fleet shrink drastically while Britain's had grown. "It is not easy to say how much of this change, which has become chronic, may be referred to British pirates; but it cannot be doubted that they contributed largely to produce it."

Sumner had presented his statistics in a deliberately logical, dispassionate style. When at last it came time to add the numbers up, he announced, almost casually, that the national loss incident on the ravages of the Confederate commerce raiders was somewhere in the neighborhood of $110 million.

There was a stunned moment of shock, followed by mutters of anger and disbelief. A hundred and ten million dollars! It was a colossal sum. Could he seriously picture Great Britain's paying anything so enormous? But Sumner was not through. Far from it.

"This is what I have to say for the present on national losses through the destruction of commerce. These are large enough; but there is another chapter, where they are larger far. I refer of course to the national losses caused by the prolongation of the war and traceable directly to England." He spoke slowly now. He had reached the heart of his argument, and he wanted his listeners to understand each and every word.

"No candid person who studies this eventful period, can doubt that the rebellion was originally encouraged by hope of support from England; that it was strengthened at once by the concession of belligerent rights on the ocean; that it was fed to the end by British supplies; that it was quickened into renewed life by every report from the British pirates, flaming anew with every burning ship; nor can it be doubted that without British intervention the rebellion would have soon succumbed under the well-directed efforts of the National Government. . . ."

This was an argument familiar to his audience, that Britain might not have encouraged the South to start the war, but once war came, she had done everything in her power to support the rebel government.

How much longer did the war drag on as a result of British efforts? Sumner asked. "Not weeks or months, but years were added in this way to our war, so full of the most costly sacrifice. . . . The United States paid for a war waged by England upon the national unity. The sacrifice of precious life is beyond human compensation; but there may be an approximate estimate of the national loss in money."

The senators, still trying to adjust their thinking to the huge, hundred-million-plus figure Sumner had already charged against Britain, fell into awed silence as they began to grasp the dimension of the costs he was now to delineate. "The rebellion was suppressed at a cost of more than four thousand million dollars. . . . If, through British intervention, the war was doubled in duration, or in any way extended, as cannot be doubted, then is England justly responsible for the additional expenditure to which our country was doomed; and whatever may be the final settlement of these great accounts, such must be the judgment in any chancery which consults the simple equity of the case. This plain statement, without one word of exaggeration or aggravation, is enough to exhibit the magnitude of the national losses, whether from the destruction of our commerce or the prolongation of the war."

Another stunned silence, this one considerably longer than the first. Sumner was suggesting that Britain owed America half of the four thousand million dollars it cost to win the war! Two billion dollars! The figure was beyond fantasy, beyond imagining. Half the cost of the most expensive war in human history! "It will be for a wise statesmanship to determine how this fearful accumulation, like Pelion upon Ossa, shall be removed out of sight, so that it shall no longer overshadow the two countries," Sumner said quietly.

"If the case against England is strong, and if our claims are unprecedented in magnitude, it is only because the conduct of this power at a trying period was most unfriendly, and the injurious consequences of this conduct were on a scale corresponding to the theatre of action. Life and property were both swallowed up, leaving behind a deepseated sense of enormous wrong, as yet unatoned and even unacknowledged, which is one of the chief factors in the problem now presented to the statesmen of both countries. The attempt to close this great international debate without a complete settlement is little short of puerile."

How was this unimaginably huge debt to be negotiated? Sumner gave no clue. It was enough that he define the price. Let others work out the terms of payment. But payment there must be, he implied. Nowhere in his speech had he threatened reprisals, but now that he was reaching the end, he pointed out that while England might find it painful to pay, it might prove even more painful not to. He warned that "it is not difficult to imagine one of our countrymen saying, with Shakespeare's Jew, 'The villainy you teach me I will execute, and it shall go hard, but I will better the instruction.'" It was not lost on anyone in the chamber that he was conjuring up the image of a fleet of *Alabamas*, scourging the sea of British merchantmen. Others had made the same threat in the past, but now it was coming from one of the most important politicians in Washington.

In the end he held out an olive branch, of sorts.

"Again I say, this debate is not of my seeking. It is not tempting, for it compels criticism of a foreign Power with which I would have more than peace, more even than concord. But it cannot be avoided. The truth must be told, not in anger, but in sadness. England has done to the United States an injury most difficult to measure. Considering when it was done, and in what complicity, it is most unaccountable. At a great epoch of history . . . when civilization was fighting a last battle with slavery, England gave her name, her influence, her material resources to the wicked cause, and flung a sword into the scale with slavery. Here was a portentous mistake. . . . And yet down to this day there is no acknowledgement of this wrong; not a single word. Such a generous expression would be the beginning of a just settlement, and the best assurance of that harmony between two great and kindred nations which all must desire."

Amid resounding applause, Sumner gathered up his papers and sat down.

Predictably the speech caused a sensation. Clearly it had tapped a deep root in the American conscience. "I had always felt that I was wronged as an American citizen by England," ran one letter to Sumner, "but never set down seriously to inquire wherein that wrong consisted. . . . Your speech has just shown me my heart—or rather, enabled me to analyse my own feelings." In London the American consul general reported that many in Britain believed that a war with America was now "next to certainty." In a letter to Sumner, Charles Nordhoff, managing editor of the New York *Evening Post,* said his speech had given the British the worst fright since the Indian mutiny.

In Massachusetts Charles Francis Adams read the speech in his newspaper, where it was reprinted in its entirety, and noted in his diary, "The practical effect of this proceeding is to raise the scale of our demands of reparation so very high that there is no chance of negotiation left, unless the English have lost all their spirit and character."

TWENTY-FIVE

Geneva

President Ulysses S. Grant was a pragmatist. He did not really care whether the *Alabama* claims represented an outrageous breach of international law or even a grievous affront to American honor. He saw only that the claims represented a huge stumbling block to getting on with the nation's business, and he wanted them out of the way. Postwar America was expanding rapidly. There were railroads to build, cities to develop, and markets to exploit, all of which was going to require large infusions of capital, much of which was sitting idle in the City of London, because English financiers were reluctant to commit unlimited sums of money to America while the political tensions relating to the *Alabama* claims remained unresolved.

Grant would probably have been happy to write off the *Alabama* claims completely, but Sumner's speech had made that impossible. The senator's eloquence had so stimulated public anger against Great Britain, and raised the demand for damages to such impossible heights, that no one in the new administration dared suggest anything that might be interpreted as backing down from Sumner's demands.

There was a similar impasse in England. Both the Liberals and the Conservatives had expressed a desire to settle the claims—albeit on terms highly favorable to Britain—but Sumner's speech had so stunned the leaders of both parties that they no longer dared bring up the question and simply buried the issue. But Prime Minister Gladstone soon discovered he could not afford to ignore the *Alabama* claims completely. Like Grant, he kept bumping into them. They were poisoning whatever goodwill remained between the two countries and making it increasingly difficult to deal with all sorts of pressing issues, from Fenian mischief to Canadian fishing rights.

The diplomatic tension engendered by the *Alabama* claims persisted throughout the remaining months of 1869 and well into 1870, with a sullen and angry America on one side of the Atlantic and a worried but defensive Britain on the other, the two governments separated by an international dispute that refused to go away. In fact, the tension seemed to grow ever more insoluble. Neither side was willing to bend, and it seemed more and more likely that a permanent state of suspicion and ill will was to be the final legacy of the *Alabama* claims.

What finally broke the logjam was a startling and unexpected event that had nothing directly to do with either of the two feuding antagonists but that heralded an important international power shift. In September 1870, Britain awoke to discover that the Prussian army, after a brilliant six-week campaign, was standing at the gates of Paris. Almost without warning, a major new player had emerged upon the Continent, one that Great Britain could ignore only at her peril. The sudden emergence of Bismarck's new German Confederation carried with it important global ramifications that went far beyond continental rivalries. Veteran statesmen pondered the situation. If this powerful new Germany ever found common cause with that other emerging power, the United States, such an alignment would not bode well for the sprawling British Empire. All of a sudden, it was very much in Britain's interest to mend its fences with America and to patch up whatever differences may have strained relations in the past. Obviously that meant resolving the inconvenient dispute over those Confederate raiders.

And so, for the first time, thanks largely to the military and diplomatic genius of Otto von Bismarck, settlement of the *Alabama* claims became a matter of first importance to the British Foreign Office. When, shortly thereafter, President Grant called upon Congress to find a resolution to the claims, things moved quickly. Sir John Rose was hurriedly sent to Washington for secret meetings with Secretary of State Hamilton Fish. The two men, working clandestinely and in great haste to avoid alerting Sumner and his allies, quickly produced a plan for negotiating the diplomatic differences between the two countries. Out of their initial six-hour meeting came the Treaty of Washington, a catchall agreement that set up specific mechanisms for disposing of each one of the outstanding Anglo-American disputes. It was signed in May 1871 and immediately ratified by the Senate. By far the most important issue covered by the treaty, of course, was the question of the *Alabama* claims, which was to be judged by a specially created tribunal of five arbitrators, to be made up of one American, one Englishman, and three others to be appointed by the emperor of Brazil, the king of Italy, and the president of the Swiss Confederation. The panel was to meet in Geneva the following December.

From the beginning the tribunal was hailed by the international community as a daring and imaginative concept, a potential landmark in the history of the law of nations. It was to be the world's first great tribunal of arbitration, the first time that two proud nations had allowed a dispute of such significance to be put before an international panel of jurists. By the terms of the Treaty of Washington, Great Britain, the single most powerful nation on earth, was to be placed on trial for all the world to see, to answer charges brought by the United States.

Given the potential hazards inherent in such a step, the British government was understandably sensitive about the details of the treaty, and its emissaries took what they thought were great pains to establish precise limits on what could and could not be brought to the tribunal for consideration. With an eye to the threats contained in Sumner's speech, they insisted that the tribunal was to consider only the so-called direct claims against the Confederate raiders—those related to the costs incurred in the loss of ships and their cargoes; it was not to consider the "indirect claims"—the huge, undefined ancillary expenses that Sumner had thrown together in his laundry list, ranging from the damages resulting from the increase in insurance rates all the way to the cost of the war itself.

The British were distressed when President Grant selected Charles Francis Adams to serve as the American arbitrator. The Gladstone government complained that Adams had been one of the leading actors in the drama and therefore could not possibly have an open mind or be trusted to pass judgment with any degree of objectivity. But the White House was adamant, and eventually the British withdrew their objection.

Throughout the summer and autumn of 1871, teams of lawyers in both London and Washington feverishly prepared their cases, before sending them to the printer to be bound into books, as required by the treaty. Finally, on December 15, 1871, the officials gathered in Switzerland, and the tribunal convened in a large room in Geneva's Hotel de Ville. Adams led the American delegation. The other four arbitrators were Sir Alexander Cockburn, chief justice of Great Britain, a ruddy, highly excitable jurist of great intellect, who made no attempt to hide his sense of his own superiority; the swarthy, stolid Jacob Stämpfli, ex-president of Switzerland; the courteous and dignified Count Frederic de Sclopis, of Italy; and the diminutive and epicene Baron d'Itajuba, of Brazil.

Things got off to an uneven start. Count Sclopis was chosen to act as presiding officer, and in recognition of his status, his chair was placed in a central position on the dais, elevated slightly above those of the other four. Stämpfli, the Swiss arbitrator who sat to the immediate right of Sclopis, objected and suggested that, as he represented the host nation, his chair be elevated to the same height. The idea was eventually dropped but only after some heated discussion.

Count Sclopis then raised the important question of language. He could understand English, he explained, but he admitted he could not speak it with sufficient fluency, and since neither the Swiss nor the Brazilian arbitrator was proficient enough to follow arguments in English, he moved that all proceedings be carried out in French. The proposal was quickly adopted. Chief Justice Cockburn recognized the basic absurdity of conducting a critically important legal action between two English-speaking parties in French, particularly since the arguments on both the American and British sides would turn to a large extent on the meaning and interpretation of specific English words. At the first convenient moment, Cockburn pulled Adams aside, explained his misgivings, and suggested that the two of them get the other three arbitrators to resign. Adams admitted the logic of Cockburn's objection but declined to go along with the Englishman. Such a move was bound to fail, he pointed out. There were questions of national honor at stake, and the other arbitrators were not likely to willingly forgo the prestige of serving on such an important panel.

The first session had been deliberately designed to be brief, to last only long enough to establish procedural matters and allow the two sides to present their cases to the court. The following day, as scheduled, the tribunal adjourned after arranging to reconvene six months later in June to hear the countercases from each side, after which it would finally get down to the business of arbitrating the claims.

———————

The British legal team received copies of the American case at Geneva, and a few days later in London, the American minister dropped off a number of additional copies at the Foreign Office, but it was Christmastime, and it was not until almost New Year's Day that anyone in England thought to read the five-hundred-page document. When someone finally got around to it, there were immediate bellows of outrage and indignation. The Yankees had betrayed them! The American case presented at Geneva revived all the angry charges of Britain's "insincere neutrality" and "veiled hostility" that everyone had hoped had long since been forgotten. The Yankees were not limiting their case to the "direct claims" of loss of ships and cargoes, as promised, but were demanding all the "indirect claims" as well, the ones for which Sumner had called in his infamous speech! Those British statesmen who had convinced themselves that they had successfully finessed the worrisome question of the indirect claims in the Washington negotiations were appalled to see them all again: the cost of pursuing the Confederate cruisers, the increase in insurance rates, the losses sustained as a result of transferring American merchant ships to the British flag, and, most onerous of all, the vaguely defined and prohibitively expensive costs relating to the alleged prolongation of the war. The Americans were claiming that Britain owed them the entire cost of the war subsequent to the Battle of Gettysburg, computed from July 1, 1863, the first day of the battle, plus 7 percent interest! There it all was, spelled out in black and white and much of it couched in inflammatory language lifted directly from Sumner's speech!

Accusations of calculated deception on the part of the American leaders echoed through Parliament and Fleet Street. The distress of England's statesmen was not improved when a close reading of the Treaty of Washington revealed that, in spite of all their efforts, considerable ambiguity remained on the question of what could and could not be claimed. The American signatories, affecting dewy-eyed innocence, returned bluster for bluster across the ocean, and the question was hotly debated throughout the winter and spring of 1872.

Charles Francis Adams, with his usual dispassion, observed the transatlantic brouhaha from his home in Quincy, Massachusetts. He was not overly surprised by all the fuss. Of course the British were not going to allow themselves to be put in such an untenable position. He had predicted as much three years earlier, when he first read Sumner's totally unrealistic demands. It was just as obvious to him that the Americans had inserted the indirect claims into their case not because they expected to squeeze billions out of Britain but simply out of fear that, if they did not include them, they would be accused of cowardice by Sumner and his allies. Now, with all the publicity, they were afraid to abandon the indirect claims voluntarily, and someone was going to have to do it for them.

———

When the tribunal reconvened in June, the British immediately petitioned for an eight-month recess to prepare their response to the indirect claims. The British called it a postponement, but everyone understood that if it were granted, it was highly unlikely the tribunal would ever reconvene. Adams saw that the opportunity for resolution of the *Alabama* claims was about to be lost forever. For ten years he had been trying to get some satisfaction out of Britain. Now, at last, the opportunity for an honorable resolution to the question was at hand. If he wanted to settle the issue, he was going to have to get rid of the British objections, and that was likely to require diplomatic surgery.

Adams contacted Count Sclopis and arranged for the five arbitrators to reject the indirect claims out of hand. This act, so apparently simple in execution yet so complicated in its hurried negotiation, turned out to be a masterpiece of backdoor diplomacy. It satisfied the British objection and at the same time protected President Grant's people from the wrath of Senator Sumner, since the decision had been made by the tribunal rather than by the Americans. With their problem resolved, the British withdrew their request for postponement, and finally, on July 15, the tribunal sat down again to consider the counter-cases of the two disputing parties.

The five arbitrators, who sat at a raised dais on one side of the room, listened to the arguments presented by the lawyers below them and occasionally asked questions. They were acting as judges, not advocates, but Cockburn made little or no attempt to maintain even the semblance of impartiality. As often as not, he appeared to be pleading his country's case, and as a result, there were times that summer when the chamber took on aspects of a Gilbert and Sullivan courtroom. Cockburn would sometimes attack the American lawyers with such obvious bias that even the British lawyers were embarrassed and worried privately that his brusqueness might be damaging their case. Fortunately for Cockburn, newspaper reporters had been barred from the conference hall from the start, and word of his outbursts did not reach the public.

Not all of Cockburn's complaints were unfounded. His earlier prediction that the use of the French language might impede attempts to examine the meaning of English words proved to be the case when the court came to consider the meaning of the term *due diligence*. The question lying at the heart of the *Alabama* claims was whether the British had practiced due diligence when they failed to seize the ship *290* and allowed her to leave Liverpool, after the Americans had warned them she was a Confederate cruiser. Had they properly investigated the American claims and acted in such a way as to protect America's interests, or had they deliberately acted in such a manner as was likely to harm those interests? Had they, in a word, practiced due diligence? The British lawyers argued that British officials had behaved properly, because due diligence should be defined as the way a neutral nation normally conducted its own affairs, but the Americans charged that such a definition was wholly inadequate and no better than "business as usual." They argued that due diligence should be defined as "adequate to the occasion" and that Britain's behavior in regard to the Confederate raiders had not met that standard. The court decided to accept the American definition, and the British were judged not to have exercised sufficient zeal in their defense of American interests. In an extension of that finding, the arbitrators also held that Britain had subsequently violated the law of nations by not detaining the Confederate cruisers on later occasions when they entered British ports.

After one such decision against Britain, Cockburn exploded and, turning to his four peers, suggested bluntly that they were not sufficiently knowledgeable to deal competently with questions of the law. He seemed surprised when they took offense and hastily assured them that he meant nothing personal.

With terms defined and other questions of semantics out of the way, the tribunal voted to examine the case of each Confederate ship individually. At one time or another, the Confederate government had commissioned twelve different commerce raiders, but most of them had either been ineffective or had little or no connection to Great Britain, and the court threw out the cases against them. Eventually the arbitrators narrowed their interest to the claims against just three ships—the *Alabama*, the *Florida*, and the *Shenandoah*—along with the four tenders, including the *Tuscaloosa*, that had been commissioned by the three raiders and "must necessarily follow the lot of their principals."

The case against the *Alabama* was so clear that even Cockburn found himself grudgingly voting against Great Britain. In the case of the *Florida*, which closely paralleled that of the *Alabama*, the court also found for the United States. But the question of the *Shenandoah* was seen as a different matter altogether. The ship had not been built as a cruiser but as a merchant steamer and was only later purchased by

James Bulloch and quickly dispatched from England, to be fitted out as a Confederate raider. It would have been almost impossible for customs officials to guess that the merchant vessel that left England under the name *Sea King* would soon become the armed raider *Shenandoah,* so the tribunal found that Great Britain had practiced due diligence in reference to her departure. However, the court took note of the fact that the *Shenandoah,* by then an armed vessel of the Confederate Navy, had illegally augmented her crew before departing from Melbourne and therefore decided in favor of the United States for all of her extensive depredations after leaving Australia.

Once Britain's responsibility for the cruisers had been established by the tribunal, all that remained was to determine how much money she should pay the United States in recompense. Here the British lawyers brought up a truly imaginative defense. They suggested that their country should pay nothing, because Britain was not responsible for any of the costs involved. All of the acts of destruction on the high seas were perpetrated by Confederate officers on behalf of the Confederate States. These same states were, by 1872, once more part of the United States. "They send their members to the Senate and the House of Representatives," the lawyers argued, "they take part in the election of the President; they would share in any benefit which the public revenue of the United States might derive from whatever might be awarded by the Arbitrators to be paid by Great Britain." The parties responsible for commerce raiding were therefore acting on behalf of certain United States against certain other United States, and Britain was just an innocent onlooker and therefore not liable. Cockburn found the argument trenchant but had little success convincing his fellow jurists to take it seriously.

To help the arbitrators define the scale of the award, the tribunal examined the claims of individual shipowners who had lost their vessels to Confederate action as well as the claims of those insurance companies that had already paid off the losses of policyholders. Once again Cockburn found fault with the evidence and angrily accused the American counsel of deliberately padding the accounts. This was too much for Adams, who shot to his feet and, glaring at the chief justice, said in a voice quivering with emotion, "I will not sit here, on this Tribunal, and hear my country traduced!" He turned, as if to leave the room, and there was a moment of shocked silence. What was the court to make of this? Even the steadiest, coolest, most objective member of the panel was flying into a rage. Had Cockburn's bullying tactics finally triggered an international incident? And to what unforeseeable ramifications might they lead? Was the whole fragile diplomatic construction of the tribunal, so laboriously pieced together after years of dangerous acrimony and saber-rattling, about to fall in upon itself like a house of cards?

Sir Alexander was nonplussed by Adams's fury. It was clear he had not meant to arouse such a reaction from the dour New Englander. Adams was, after all, the only other arbitrator he respected. He mumbled an apology of sorts, and Count Sclopis rose and with a few calming words brought peace to the chamber. Adams resumed his seat. It was all over in an instant, and the tribunal went back to work.

In the end Adams and Stämpfli each suggested an award of $18 million as an appropriate sum for Great Britain to pay in satisfaction of all the *Alabama* claims. Sclopis wanted to make the figure $16 million, d'Itajuba came in for $15 million, and Cockburn, predictably, thought $4 million was about right. Eventually they settled on $15.5 million, payable in gold within a year. It was not a large enough sum to seriously distress the world's richest nation, but it was enough to hurt, and as naval historian Chester G. Hearn observed, from a British point of view, "it was a cheap price to pay to recover commercial dominance of the seas."

———

On September 14, 1872, the tribunal met for the last time. It was a beautiful late-summer day, and to mark the significance of the occasion, the conference room was open for the first time to outsiders. With an assembly of dignitaries in attendance, the hall was in a festive mood. Cockburn alone seemed unhappy. One observer recalled the scene years later: "Cockburn was a handsome man, stately, a haughty, clear-limned face, character deeply written. He was very angry. . . . I stood beside his chair, and remember the magnificent scowl as he glared over the assemblage."

With all five arbitrators in their seats, the secretary of the tribunal rose to announce to the world the final decision on the *Alabama* claims. Amid the profound silence of the audience, he read the entire decision in English but dispensed with the French text. Then all the arbitrators, with the exception of Cockburn, signed it in turn, and moments later a dignified but beaming Count Sclopis closed the session with some appropriate remarks. Across the city, bells rang out in celebration, and the steady boom of an artillery salute echoed across the square below.

The furious Cockburn could suffer no more and, snatching up his hat, bolted for the door and was gone, without a word of farewell to his colleagues.

l'Envoi

The total award, calculated at the official exchange rate of $4.80 to the pound sterling, came to £3,229,166 in gold. After the money was transferred from Her Majesty's Exchequer to the United States Treasury, only one last detail remained: how to distribute it. The American government set up a special court to sort through the individual claims, and eventually $9,416,120.25 was paid out to the various injured parties. For a while no one was quite sure what to do with the remaining $6 million, which was left sitting in the Treasury gathering interest, but eventually it was decided to share it out on a pro rata basis to those shipowners whose claims had been rejected by the tribunal.

Raphael Semmes, who had followed the news from Geneva in the papers, was incensed by the international uproar over the *Alabama* claims and outraged that Britain should be forced to pay anything, although he was probably secretly pleased that the largest portion of the award went to the victims of his *Alabama*, confirming her record as the most successful commerce raider in history.

After the war Semmes had returned to civilian life in Alabama, where he scratched out a living as a lawyer in Mobile. He was greatly revered throughout the state and region and might have aspired to high office but for the harsh Reconstruction laws ordained by vengeful Radical Republicans in Washington, which barred him from politics.

For several years after Appomattox, Semmes was bedeviled by a bitter legal campaign of persecution that can be described only as a vendetta engineered by Gideon Welles, the secretary of the navy. At one point Welles ordered Semmes arrested and held prisoner in the Washington Navy Yard, where he was to be tried on trumped-up charges of violating the usages of war by leaving the scene of his surrender in the *Deerhound,* but the government's case fell apart, and Welles was forced to release him, although he continued to plot against him. Throughout the ordeal Semmes maintained an attitude of amused defiance, and refused to be intimidated.

In 1868 Semmes published his account of his experiences in *Memoirs of Service Afloat During the War Between the States,* a generally accurate but predictably disputative and argumentative justification for his actions, filled with bellicose rage, withering attacks upon his enemies, and contempt for Yankees in general.

Long after the war, an English friend wrote to ask whether the admiral still disliked the North, and Semmes assured his correspondent that he did. "I believe the Yankee, puritanical race of New England to be, taken all in all, the most unamiable and corrupt race that the sun shines upon—cowards . . . treacherous and fanatical." He remained fiercely unrepentant and defiant to the day he died. The old warrior breathed his last at 7:30 in the morning of August 30, 1877. On the day of his funeral, the city of Mobile declared a full day of mourning for its most distinguished citizen. All businesses were closed, and guns fired salutes from dawn until sunset.

After his death his reputation continued to grow, particularly in Germany. In 1894 Kaiser Wilhelm II told an American visitor, "I reverence the name of Semmes. In my opinion he was the greatest admiral of the nineteenth century. At every conference with my admirals, I counsel them to read and study Semmes's Memoirs of Service Afloat." The kaiser was impressed with Semmes's brilliant use of subterfuge and his ability to extend his range of operations by his skillful deployment of tenders. It is perhaps a dubious legacy that Semmes's example would inspire the U-boat wolf packs that roamed the Atlantic, spreading death and destruction, in the two great wars of the twentieth century.

James Dunwoody Bulloch, who had also closely followed the news of the Geneva tribunal, was equally angered by the award. He insisted that he had broken no laws in sending his three raiders out to sea, and therefore Great Britain could not be found liable for their actions.

Bulloch never returned home after the war but remained in Liverpool, where he had established many friendships and commercial interests. He prospered in the shipping business, specializing in the cotton trade, and was for many years a commission merchant in the firm of Bulloch and Robertson. He became a naturalized British subject and a pillar of the Conservative party.

In 1884, many years after the great events covered in these pages, he published his account of his work during the war in *The Secret Service of the Confederate States in Europe*, a riveting memoir, notable for its modesty and discretion. While the book barely touches on his personal life, the accounts of his remarkable achievements, often attained in the face of great obstacles, say much about the man and his uncommon good sense, drive, and imagination. His efforts on behalf of the highly successful commerce raiders and the abortive Laird rams represent only a portion of his activities during the war, which also included the construction of a squadron of ironclads in France and the purchase and deployment of a number of high-speed blockade-runners. One of these, the *Bat*, was captured in 1864 and became the flagship of Admiral David Porter. Abraham Lincoln slept on board several times during the closing weeks of the war.

Bulloch traveled widely on business, and on at least one occasion, in the winter of 1871, returned to America, where he stayed in New York with his much-loved sister Martha and her husband, Theodore Roosevelt Sr. Martha's charming but sickly little boy, "Teedy" Roosevelt, worshiped his uncle Jim. Years later, after he was graduated from Harvard and was writing his *Naval History of the War of 1812*, young Theodore made a trip to Liverpool to enlist his uncle's help on the manuscript. In his preface to the published work, the author acknowledged the importance of Bulloch's contribution, describing him simply as "formerly of the United States Navy" and making no reference to his uncle's work for the Confederacy. It is quite possible that Bulloch, in light of his nephew's political ambitions, thought it prudent to ignore his role in the Great Rebellion.

Theodore Roosevelt took great pride in his connection to the Bulloch family and, as president, made a pilgrimage to the old Bulloch estate in Roswell, Georgia. By that time his uncle had long since died. James Dunwoody Bulloch passed away on January 7, 1901, having lived long enough to see his nephew elected vice president.

———————

After his return from Geneva, Charles Francis Adams retired and devoted his remaining years to editing the diaries of his father, John Quincy Adams. During the first few years of his retirement, there was occasional talk of a return to public life, of a senatorial appointment (to succeed Charles Sumner), and even of a possible presidential nomination (after Grant's second administration), but nothing came of it, nor was it likely to. Adams's brilliant mind—he was generally acknowledged to have been a greater intellect than either his father or his grandfather—slowly but inexorably gave way in his later years, and he ended his days a sad and helpless shadow of his former self.

He died in Boston on November 26, 1886. James Russell Lowell, president of Harvard, summed up the contribution of this cold but passionate patriot: "None of our generals in the field, not Grant himself, did us better or more trying service than he, in his forlorn outpost of London."

———————

Lord John Russell, whose carefully calibrated disinterest in Bulloch's Merseyside shipbuilding activities can be said to have created the crisis that grew into the *Alabama* claims, and whose willful determination after the war to block any attempt by the United States government to obtain redress, even at a time when a simple apology might have been sufficient to secure amity between the two powers, was already seventy years old when the *Alabama* escaped. He would remain active in politics for another decade and more, and was still trying to quash the *Alabama* claims as late as June 1872, in defiance of a personal appeal from Queen Victoria to allow the Geneva tribunal to reconvene. His very long public life, which included any number of cabinet appointments and two stints as prime minister, was so eventful and crowded with achievements that his closely worded ten-page entry in the *Dictionary of National Biography* barely mentions the *Alabama,* although it finds space to make the curious assertion that "during the American civil war Russell maintained a strict neutrality between the belligerents."

Russell died in 1878. As his life was ebbing away, he is reported to have said to his wife, "I have made mistakes, but in all I did my object was the public good." Even those skeptics who might question his motives in regard to the *Alabama* claims would be hard put to gainsay that assertion.

In November 1984 the French minesweeper *Circe* was knifing through the choppy seas of the English Channel on a routine training exercise off the coast of Cherbourg when the sonar operator noted something unusual on his screen. Moments later the ship's captain, Lieutenant Commander Bruno Duclos, was standing hunched over the operator's shoulder, peering intently at the cryptic image flickering in front of them. Clearly whatever Duclos and the sonar operator were looking at was a wreck of some kind, but the floor of the English Channel is filled with wrecks. It would require direct inspection by navy divers to confirm just what the object was, but the longer the captain studied the sonar image, the more confident he became that he and his crew had come across something of historic importance. With a growing sense of excitement, he radioed the news to shore: pending confirmation, the *Circe* had discovered the remains of the *Alabama.*

Soon after the *Circe*'s 1984 discovery, French navy divers were able to confirm—at first tentatively, and later positively—that the wreck off Cherbourg was indeed the remains of the *Alabama.* In 1988 any lingering doubts as to the wreck's identity were erased when divers triumphantly brought up the bronze plate from the ship's helm, bearing the Alabama's famed motto, AIDE-TOI ET DIEU T'AIDERA.

Work on the site continues every summer. The recovery operation is extremely difficult. The *Alabama* lies in nearly 200 feet of water, and dives on the wreck are limited to brief, fifteen-minute periods, and only during the slack neap tides. The currents, which run at more than 4 knots, are a constant challenge, but despite the difficulties inherent in their work, the divers have been able to recover a number of highly important artifacts from the wreck, the most spectacular of which is the 3.5-ton rifled Blakely that once served as the *Alabama*'s forward pivot gun. (On examination it was discovered to be loaded.)

Meanwhile, what remains of the ship rests at a 30-degree starboard list, on a sandy bottom, littered with mussel shells and other sediment. Both bow and stern are severely damaged, and a large hole in the port side is open to the shifting vagaries of the current. Every day the tide changes four times, and with every change the sediment is swept back and forth over the wreck, alternately hiding and disclosing what remains of the once-feared, and still contentious, *Alabama*.

The recovery program, sponsored by a joint French and American consortium, is under the direction of Captain Max Guerout, a senior officer of the French navy and an internationally recognized marine archaeologist. The United States, as legal successor to the Confederacy, claims ownership of the wreck, but since it lies well within 12 miles of the coast (the present offshore territorial limits), it is clearly in French waters. By the terms of a special pact signed in 1989, the two nations have agreed that the United States owns the ship but the French retain custody.

In Geneva, in the city's old sixteenth-century Hotel de Ville, the conference room where the tribunal sat in judgment in 1872 is still known as Alabama Hall. A plaque defines the landmark event that took place there:

LE XIV SEPTEMBRE MDCCCLXXII
LE TRIBUNAL D'ARBITRAGE CONSTITUE

PAR LE TRAITE DE WASHINGTON
RENDIT DANS CETTE SALLE
SA DECISION SUR LES RECLAMATIONS
DE L'ALABAMA
AINSI FUT REGLE D'UNE MANIERE PACIFIQUE
LE DIFFEREND SURVENU ENTRE
LES ETATS UNIS
ET LE ROYAUME DE LA GRANDE BRETAGNE

The Swiss take their memorials seriously, particularly those related to the search for world peace, and attorneys who practice in the still vaguely defined puzzle palace of international law point out that the settlement of the *Alabama* claims established a unique precedent that was formally recognized at the Second International Peace Conference at The Hague in 1907 and is now embodied in the law codes of virtually every member nation of the United Nations. In time, they say, the *Alabama* claims decision, and the body of law that has grown up around it, will be recognized for what it is, the indispensable keystone of global peace and the equivalent in international law of the Magna Carta.

The *Alabama*, a celebrated instrument of war, has been transformed into a building block of peace. A surprising legacy, perhaps, but then surprise was always her stock-in-trade.

Acknowledgments

Researching the story of the CSS *Alabama* has led me down all sorts of unfamiliar paths and into a number of arcane corners not usually associated with the American Civil War, such as the trade routes of the Indian Ocean, rates of exchange for pounds sterling, and the differences between manifests and bills of lading. Any number of people helped and encouraged me along the way, and I owe all of them my gratitude and thanks. I am indebted first off to my editors at Ballantine, Peter Borland and Tracy Brown, and to my agent, Al Zuckerman, all of whom were supportive throughout, and extraordinarily patient when the work went long over deadline. Mark Tavani, also at Ballantine, deserves special thanks. In matters of research, there were a number of librarians who provided essential help, particularly Paul O'Pecko, at the G. W. Blunt White Library of the Mystic Seaport Museum, Mystic, Connecticut; Eilean Edwards, of the Liverpool Maritime Museum in England; and the staffs at Connecticut College Library, New London, Connecticut; the Stonington (Connecticut) Free Library; the Westerly (Rhode Island) Public Library; and the Hoole Library at the University of Alabama. I owe a particular debt to naval historian Kevin Foster, whom I met more or less by accident at a conference and who turned out to know everything there is to know about the *Alabama* claims, and who went out of his way to guide me to some of the most valuable sources. I need to thank Dr. William

Dudley, of the Naval Historical Center in Washington, who has been helpful in more ways than I can enumerate. Another important contributor to this book was Donald Petrie, who was able to offer valuable legal expertise (from start to finish, this has been a story about lawyers) and was generous enough to give me his personal copy of the American Case, which I treasure. J. Revell Carr, who until recently presided over the Mystic Seaport Museum, alerted me to the special characteristics of Merseyside docking, and Mike Stammers, of the Liverpool Maritime Museum, put me in touch with Adrian Jarvis, curator of port history, who was able to explain what Revell was talking about. My sister-in-law, Rachel Parkhouse, was able to give me directions to Moelfra Bay, and my neighbors, Jock and Kathie Shirley, both veterans of the United States Foreign Service, steered me through the intricacies of "plenipotentiary" rights and privileges.

The contributions of my wife, Belinda, have been crucial and too diverse to enumerate.

Sources

Although this book is designed for a general audience, academic readers may want to know something about my sources. I relied in large part on the personal accounts of the three main figures in the narrative, namely: *The Secret Service of the Confederate States in Europe*, by James Dunwoody Bulloch, with an introduction by Philip Van Doren Stern (New York: Thomas Yoseloff, reprint 1959); *Memoirs of Service Afloat During the War Between the States*, by Raphael Semmes, with introduction and notes by John M. Taylor (Baton Rouge: Louisiana State University Press, reprint 1996); and the *Diaries of Charles Francis Adams*, in the Adams Family Papers, available on microfilm through the Massachusetts Historical Society, Boston. Other primary sources included the accounts of three of Semmes's officers: *The Journal of George Townley Fullam*, edited by Charles G. Summersell (University, Ala.: University of Alabama Press, 1973); *Two Years on the Alabama*, by Arthur Sinclair (New York: Konecky and Konecky, reprint, no date); and "Cruise and Combats of the Alabama," by John McIntosh Kell, in *Battles and Leaders of the Civil War* (Harrisburg, Pa.: Archive Society, reprinted 1991). Another invaluable source was the thirty-volume *Official Records of the Union and Confederate Navies in the War of the Rebellion* (ORN), recently reissued (1999) on compact disc by the Guild Press of Indiana, Carmel, Ind. Other primary sources include *CSS Shenandoah: The Memoirs of Lieutenant Commanding James I. Waddell*,

James D. Horan, editor (Annapolis: Naval Institute Press, 1996); *The Case of the United States* (Washington: Government Printing Office, 1871); *Reminiscences of the Geneva Tribunal*, by Frank Warren Hackett (Boston: Houghton Mifflin, 1911); and portions of *CSS Alabama: Builder, Captain, and Plans*, by Charles Grayson Summersell (University, Ala.: University of Alabama Press, 1985).

Secondary sources include, but are not limited to:

Adams, Charles Francis, *Charles Francis Adams* (Boston: Houghton, Mifflin, 1900).

Adams, E. D., *Great Britain and the American Civil War* (New York: Russell & Russell, reprint, no date).

Adams, Henry, *The Education of Henry Adams* (New York: Modern Library, 1931).

Balch, Thomas Willing, *The Alabama Arbitration* (Philadelphia: Allen, Lane & Scott, 1900).

Bowen, Charles S. C., *The Alabama Claims and Arbitration Considered from a Legal Point of View* (London, 1868).

Commager, Henry Steele, editor, *The Blue and the Gray* (Indianapolis: Bobbs-Merrill, 1950).

Cook, Adrian, *The Alabama Claims* (Ithaca, N.Y.: Cornell University Press, 1975).

Current, Richard N., editor in chief, *The Encyclopedia of the Confederacy* (New York: Simon & Schuster, 1993).

Davis, J. C. Bancroft, *Mr. Sumner and the Alabama Claims and Their Settlement* (New York: 1878).

Duberman, Martin B., *Charles Francis Adams* (Boston: Houghton, Mifflin, 1961).

Hearn, Chester G., *Gray Raiders of the Sea: How Eight Confederate Warships Destroyed the Union's High Seas Commerce* (Baton Rouge: Louisiana State University Press, 1996).

Jones, Howard, *Union in Peril* (Chapel Hill: University of North Carolina Press, 1992).

Luraghi, Raimondo, *A History of the Confederate Navy* (Annapolis: Naval Institute Press, 1996).

Mahin, Dean B., *One War at a Time* (Washington: Brassey's, 1999).

Marvel, William, *The Alabama & the Kearsarge* (Chapel Hill, N.C., 1996).

Merli, Frank J., *Great Britain and the Confederate Navy* (Bloomington, Ind.: Indiana University Press, 1970).

Musicant, Ivan, *Divided Waters: The Naval History of the Civil War* (New York: HarperCollins, 1995).

New York Times, 1861–1872 (Microfilm).

Owsley, Frank Lawrence, Jr., *The CSS Florida* (Philadelphia: University of Pennsylvania Press, 1965).

Owsley, Frank Lawrence, Jr., *King Cotton Diplomacy* (Chicago: University of Chicago Press, 1959).

Porter, David D., *Naval History of the Civil War* (Mineola, N.Y.: Dover reprint 1998).

Robinson, Charles M., III, *Shark of the Confederacy* (Annapolis: Naval Institute Press, 1995).

Shingleton, Royce, *High Seas Confederate: John Newland Maffitt* (Columbia, S.C.: University of South Carolina Press, 1994).

Sideman, Belle Becker, and Lillian Friedman, editors, *Europe Looks at the Civil War* (New York: Orion Press, 1960).

Soley, James Russell, *The Blockade and the Cruisers* (Harrisburg, Pa.: Archive Society, reprint 1992).

Spenser, Warren F., *The Confederate Navy in Europe* (Tuscaloosa: University of Alabama Press, 1997).

Stern, Philip Van Doren, *The Confederate Navy* (Garden City, N.Y.: Doubleday, 1962).

Still, William N. Jr., editor, *The Confederate Navy: The Ships, Men and Organization, 1861–65* (Annapolis: Naval Institute Press, 1997).

Still, William N., Jr., John M. Taylor, and Norman C. Delaney, *Raiders and Blockaders* (Washington: Brassey's, 1998).

Taylor, John M., *Confederate Raider: Raphael Semmes of the Alabama* (Washington: Brassey's, 1994).

The Times (London) 1861–1873 (Microfilm).